Fighting for Fallujah

Fighting for Fallujah

A New Dawn for Iraq

JOHN R. BALLARD

PRAEGER SECURITY INTERNATIONAL
Westport, Connecticut • London

Library of Congress Cataloging-in-Publication data

Ballard, John R., 1957–
Fighting for Fallujah : a new dawn for Iraq / John R. Ballard.
p. cm.
Includes index.
ISBN 0-275-99055-9 (alk. paper)
1. Iraq War, 2003—Campaigns–Iraq–Fallujah. I. Title.
DS79.76.B355 2006
956.7044′342–dc22 2006001235

British Library Cataloguing in Publication Data is available.

Library of Congress Catalog Card Number: 2006001235
ISBN: 0-275-99055-9

First published in 2006

Praeger Security International, 88 Post Road West, Westport, CT 06881
An imprint of Greenwood Publishing Group, Inc.
www.praeger.com

Printed in the United States of America

The paper used in this book complies with the Permanent Paper Standard issued by the National Information Standards Organization (Z39.48–1984).

10 9 8 7 6 5 4 3 2 1

In honor of the Marines, Soldiers, Sailors, and Airmen
who fought and died in Iraq.
Military service is the ultimate form of patriotism.

Contents

List of Maps

Preface

On March 31, 2004, four American civilians drove into the Iraqi city of Fallujah and unknowingly opened a new chapter in America's decade-long involvement with Iraq. They had only just departed from their base camp and had traveled less than 5 miles when their small convoy was halted at a traffic intersection in the center of the city in Iraq's Sunni triangle. Without warning, two gunmen attacked and killed all four of them. Then, as the gunmen withdrew, everyday workers and passersby pulled the bodies from the vehicles and began hacking them apart with picks and shovels in full view of dozens of other residents of the city of mosques. The murders occurred less than 100 meters from the main city police station. Later, the bodies were burned, hauled around for several city blocks, and eventually hung to rot from the green steel girders of the old bridge leading to the west across the Euphrates River.

These civilian contract employees of the security firm called Blackwater, USA were well experienced in the security business, but they had clearly underestimated the danger present in Fallujah that day. Similarly, the newly arrived Marines of the 1st Marine Expeditionary Force, also based in nearby Camp Fallujah, did not yet understand the key elements of the insurgency they were to encounter in Iraq or the unique character of their neighboring city. Fallujah had stymied no less harsh a man than Saddam Hussein and for centuries had been well known as a fiercely independent and largely ungovernable town.

Less than a year later, many of these Marines, reinforced by other U.S. Army and Marine units and units of the new Iraqi army, would assault into Fallujah and destroy what had over the intervening months become a key node of the insurgency that had nourished the anti-Iraqi movement in the country. The destruction of the terrorist sanctuary that was Fallujah changed the future of the war in Iraq as much as the defeat of Saddam Hussein and his army in 2003. It did not destroy the insurgency, but it fundamentally altered the way insurgent forces would attack the coalition from that point forward. It ended any thought that insurgent forces could beat coalition units in conventional combat.

Most importantly, the fight for Fallujah showed the resolve of the new Iraqi government to defeat the insurgency in cooperation with its multinational partners. Largely because of the insurgent defeat in Fallujah and the suppression of the insurgency in several other cities, Iraqis willingly turned out in huge numbers to vote in their first free national election on January 31, 2004. The insurgency in Iraq would not be the same after that winter.

This book tells the story of the fight for Fallujah so that future combat operations can benefit from the important lessons learned there. It also illustrates the innovations that characterized combat in Iraq and the heroism demonstrated by countless Marines, Soldiers, Sailors, and Airmen in the face of a determined and skilled enemy. The lessons from combat in Fallujah are germane not only for other operations in the war on terror, but also for future combat in general, as urban warfare and similar technology will certainly dominate most battlefields in the future.

Finally, this story also shows the American people another side of the war in Iraq. It reveals the civic improvements made from coalition initiatives and the great efforts of the coalition to shield and assist the Iraqi people from the consequences of the war. It makes the important relationships between the U.S. and Iraqi leaders more clear, and it tells much about the everyday lives of people in the Sunni triangle. It should make everyone involved more proud of the work done in Iraq.

Acknowledgments

My service in Iraq, from August of 2004 to March of 2005, provided both first-hand experience with the operations in and around Fallujah and a working relationship with most of the key personnel who directed operations during that time. I also benefited from access to many of the first-hand accounts and the official military records of the period immediately prior to my tour of duty – from March to July 2004. Many members of the 1st Marine Expeditionary Force and 1st Marine Division also contributed to my understanding of operations in Al Anbar province. My thanks and deep appreciation go to each member of these proud professional organizations.

I thought it was important to record the names of many of the servicemen and women who lost their lives in Iraq as this story is being told. I do this to honor those who died, although I understand well that the circumstances surrounding the deaths of each of these men and women are unique. I have not listed all those who died in support of the war on terror, and I sincerely regret any omissions or inaccuracies among these names listed. We Americans should honor everyone who has sacrificed for our freedom.

Beyond anyone else, this book has been supported by the diligent and kind encouragement of my beloved wife, Rosaline. She has been friend, advisor, researcher, critic, and sounding board; her uniquely valuable insight and her genuine love and devotion have made every part of this book and everything in my life better. She supported me during my time in Iraq and during every day that this book has been in our minds. It is also for our girls.

Although it has benefited from a great deal of government information, this book does not reflect the views or opinions of the U.S. government or the U.S. Marine Corps; nor does it reflect their policies or those of any of the Marine organizations listed above. The views expressed in this book are mine alone, as are any errors or omissions.

John R. Ballard
Washington, D.C.

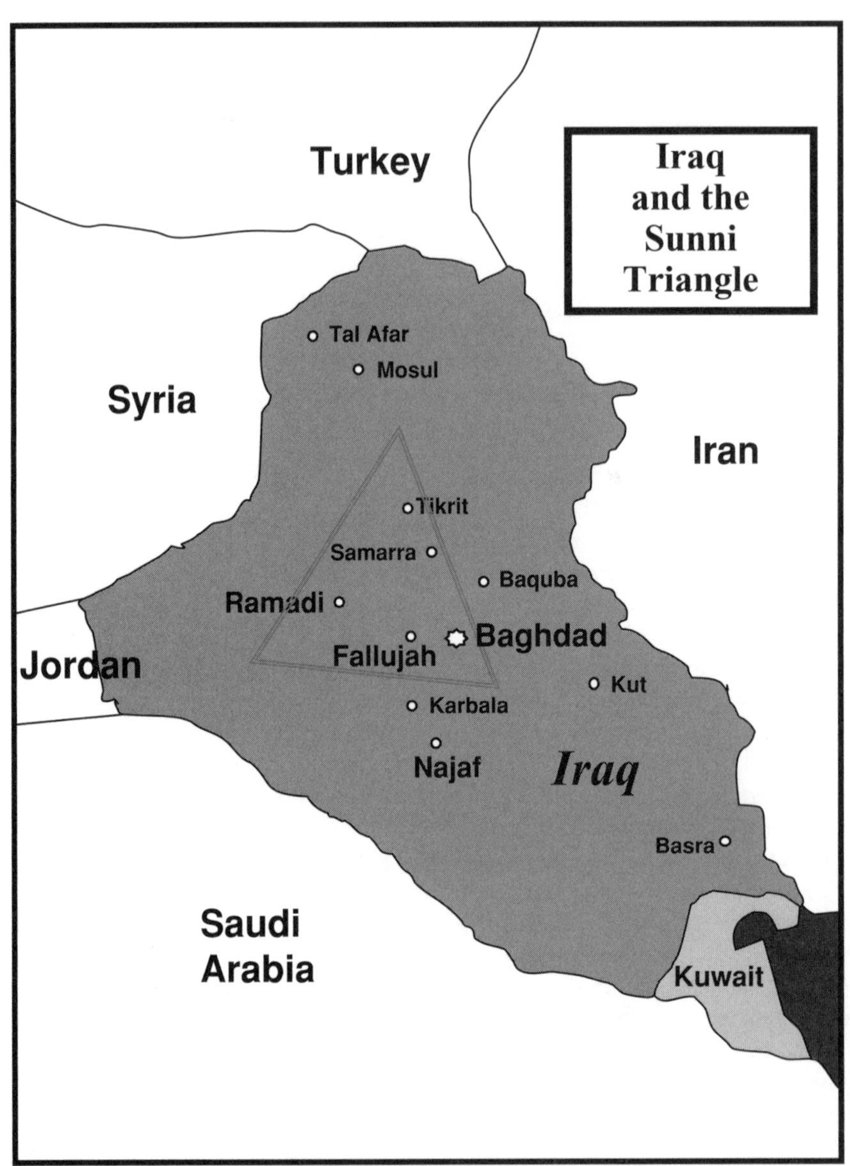

Map 1. Iraq and the Sunni Triangle

Chapter One

The Old Bridge

For the four contract employees of Blackwater, USA, awakening with the rising desert sun made the last day of March 2004 like so many days that had passed before in Iraq.[1] Although it was already quite hot when they packed their gear, they wanted to get an early start driving through the nearby Iraqi city of Fallujah. Iraqis do not do much early in the day, so the traffic was not expected to be heavy. As American defense contractors, they did not work for the U.S. military and did not feel it necessary to coordinate all of their activities with the newly arrived Marine command at Camp Fallujah, where they lived. Plus, three were former members of the elite Army Green Berets[2] and the fourth, Scott Helvenston, was a former Navy SEAL (Sea-Air-Land),[3] so they knew many people in the camp well and felt confident of their own abilities in country.

They also understood very well that their security rested in part on their anonymity, so they sought simply to blend in as they drove west in two Mitsubishi Pajeros, four-wheel-drive sport utility vehicles, off the camp and down the divided highway, mixing with the ever more numerous cars on the road. Everything seemed normal as they drove under the overpass and straight down Highway 10 through the very center of the city in the two SUVs. Ignoring the longer, but less congested, route on the interstate highway that skirted the northern edge of Fallujah, they passed the beautiful new blue mosque and minaret next to the fire station and continued west toward the Euphrates River only to find more traffic congestion than usual near the city center.[4]

They eventually crossed the main intersection of the city (just past the mayor's complex and police headquarters) and then veered left on the main street, heading for the "new bridge" crossing the river. Only two blocks further, however, as they slowed at another major intersection, a lone attacker armed with a rocket-propelled grenade launcher walked confidently up to the lead SUV and fired at point-blank range into its chassis. Other Iraqis sprayed the vehicles with bullets from their

AK-47 assault rifles. "When an American with bullet wounds in his chest staggered out and fell to the ground, he was kicked, stomped, stabbed, and butchered."[5] As the first vehicle was engulfed in flames, the driver of the second SUV quickly attempted to drive over the highway median and escape back out of the city. But before it could even leave the intersection, that vehicle was also hit by numerous AK-47 bullets and both of its passengers were killed.

In 2004, such a vicious attack on foreigners was not new to Fallujah or to Iraq; what followed, however, gave evidence of the extreme emotions that were building inside the city. As word of the attack spread, crowds of local residents, whipped into a frenzy of anger, assaulted the destroyed vehicles and pulled the bloody bodies of the Americans from them. They were celebrating the horrible deaths of four men whom they did not even know but who they felt represented the influence of America in Iraq. Armed only with work tools, the huge crowd of jubilant locals, including many children, beat and dragged the bodies block by block through the streets of their city. Two of the four bodies were eventually paraded through five or six city blocks and hung "like slaughtered sheep"[6] with wire from the green painted ironwork of the old Euphrates River bridge. All the while, local Iraqis openly chanted and cheered before cameras.

The old green bridge over the Euphrates was a cultural icon in Iraq, but once those charred bodies were hung there, it became a new sort of symbol and brought a completely different type of attention to the city of Fallujah. Perhaps the people of Fallujah did not understand the implications of this attack, but on that date decision makers in the United States and the international media took notice of the city in a way they never had before. Less than 1 year later, the fortunes of Fallujah would turn full circle as multinational forces and units of the Iraqi Army assaulted and significantly damaged the city, at least in part because of the violence and enmity shown on March 31, 2004.

FALLUJAH: THE CITY OF MOSQUES

The city of Fallujah sits on the east bank of the Euphrates River only 35 miles west of Baghdad. Although population figures for Iraqi cities are imprecise at best, most analysts accept that over 200,000 Fallujahns lived in the city prior to the start of the war in Iraq in March 2003. The city has no real natural resources but does lie across the traditionally important lines of communication that link the Iraqi capital with Syria to the west and Jordan to the north. One of the first roads leading west from Baghdad to Jordan was built through Fallujah in 1914. It is located in the province of Al Anbar midway between Baghdad and the provincial capital, the similarly restive Sunni city of Ramadi. Even under the British occupation of Iraq after the collapse of the Ottoman Empire, the city was a trouble spot. In the spring of 1920, Lieutenant Colonel Gerald Leachman, a renowned explorer and a senior colonial officer, was sent to quell a rebellion in the city, but he was killed just south of Fallujah in a fight with local leader Shaykh Dhari. In response, the British sent an

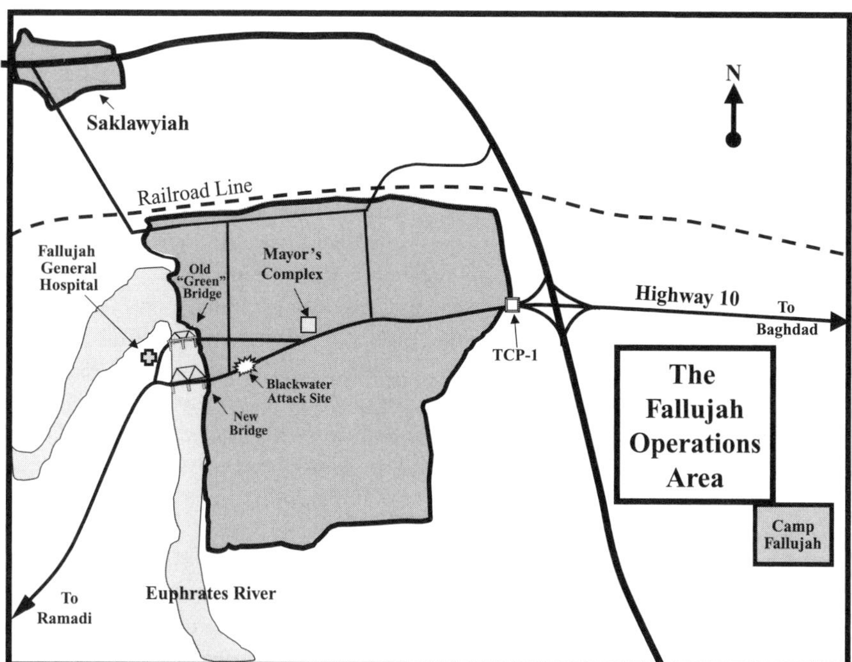

Map 2. The Fallujah Operations Area

army to crush the uprising, an action that took the lives of more than 10,000 Iraqis and 1,000 British soldiers.[7] By most accounts even Saddam Hussein had trouble dealing with Fallujah and bought the city's loyalty with passive acceptance of the smuggling trade, which included automobiles and other western luxury items and brought it much of its prosperity.

War has touched Fallujah several times throughout history. The Romans battled near the city in the third century. Xenophon had also fought there 600 years earlier. Its location astride the Euphrates and at the western doorway to Baghdad has always made it valuable territory. Today, however, its value rests more on high-value smuggling than any other commodity outside of providing material support for terrorism. It has been said that "Fallujah is where the deals go down in western Iraq. It's where the sheiks and imams take their cut from international smugglers and issue their threats, promises, and praise."[8] Stolen cars are reworked for sale in Iraq, and other illicit materials are often transferred to Baghdad markets. Thus, it has traditionally been and remains a city beyond the law.

Fallujah has a very ugly history with coalition forces, and much of this history is linked to its now-famous bridges. During the first Gulf War, one errant laser-guided bomb from a British jet intended to destroy the bridges over the Euphrates failed to guide and landed in the city market area, killing approximately 100 local residents. This was only the first of several bad incidents that only heightened the natural distrust between the residents of Fallujah and the coalition forces in Iraq.

In 2003, after many portions of the Al Anbar province were taken under the control of special operations forces during the early weeks of operation Iraqi Freedom, elements of the 82nd Airborne Division, centered on the 325th Airborne Infantry Regiment, arrived in the city briefly starting on Saddam's birthday, April 28. Yet even this first visit was marred by error, as several residents of Fallujah were killed after U.S. soldiers fired on residents during a demonstration the initial night the Americans were in the city. According to press reports, the local Fallujahns claimed to be unarmed, although the American soldiers did confiscate several weapons.[9] The locals were certainly chanting anti-American slogans and massing in a way that threatened the soldiers. What is certain is that several Iraqis were killed in the confrontation and that it spawned a second demonstration the following night, which also received fire from the American forces. One soldier was quoted as saying, "a couple of hundred people gathered out in the streets; they threw rocks, so we shot back, and they all ran down that way."[10]

The Iraqi version of these events included between 6 and 12 dead and over 50 wounded, but there were conflicting reports given to members of the press.[11] One of the people interviewed by Cable News Network reporter Karl Penhaul was a doctor at Fallujah General Hospital. The staff at that hospital would later become infamous through their regular support of the insurgency using exaggerated media claims. Later in the same week, a third incident occurred in Fallujah that resulted in injuries to seven soldiers. The U.S. Army V Corps chief of staff, Brigadier General Daniel Hahn, stated, "We have information that former Ba'ath Party members remain in Fallujah and are organizing small groups to demonstrate against coalition forces. These outside agitators then use the demonstrating crowds as cover as they fire on coalition forces."[12]

Still, regardless of the truth of these incidents, the injuries suffered by the locals inflamed the preexisting perception that the American forces were anti-Iraqi. And the actions of the 82nd Airborne clearly set an extremely negative precedent for multinational forces operating in the city, as they eventually withdrew from the company-size fighting position they had established downtown.[13] The local demonstrators played into the hands of those in the city who wanted to confront the American military and the 82nd Airborne were not fully prepared to deal with a hostile population, given the assumption during planning that liberated Iraqis would welcome the American army following the end of Saddam Hussein's regime.

By early June 2003, senior coalition commanders realized they had a real problem in Fallujah. In response, they dispatched a brigade from the 3rd Infantry Division (3rdID), which became the first American force to really control the area around the city.[14] The 3rdID was directed to reinforce the coalition presence in the region and support the efforts of the 3rd Armored Cavalry Regiment (3rdACR) operating in northwestern Iraq.[15] At the time it moved on Fallujah it was a tired unit, spent after the long historic run on Baghdad from Kuwait in the opening attack of the war. Fallujah, meanwhile, had profited from the gap in military coverage during

April and May to attack numerous anticoalition elements and begin to develop itself into a zone of defiance. The 3rdID had planned a full-scale attack to shut Fallujah down but ended up executing a quasi-peacekeeping mission in the city instead. The city quickly took advantage of the lenient approach and began to fight back. The first improvised explosive device (IED) employed against coalition forces was used in the western outskirts of Fallujah on July 18, 2003.

One of the key lessons learned by all units that served in Fallujah is that the city understood power better than it understood negotiations. The criminal-backed leadership of the city was used to dealing forcefully with one of the most repressive governments in the world and after Saddam's fall any occupier who used less forceful approaches became easy prey for manipulation. The involvement of the 3rdID in Fallujah ended quickly and rather unsuccessfully in the late summer of 2003. Unfortunately, its less than forceful actions continued a trend of multiple transitions executed by U.S. military units who permitted the city leaders to slowly gain a powerful position in opposition to the coalition. After their short time in Fallujah, the soldiers of the 3rdID were shifted back to Baghdad and the area around Fallujah became the responsibility of the overextended 3rdACR.

The 2nd Battalion of the 3rdACR from Fort Carson, Colorado, assumed the mission in Fallujah in early August and became the first American unit to work effectively, albeit temporarily, with the residents of the city.[16] The 3rdACR made some inroads with the local residents by giving up their mechanized vehicles to run patrols in Humvees, thus reducing damage to the city infrastructure, but even after such a positive start the 3rdACR failed to establish real control in the city. Its forces were just far too spread out to be effective in such a challenging city.

The 3rdACR was replaced again, in mid-September, by the 505th Parachute Infantry Regiment (the 3rd Brigade) of the 82nd Airborne Division, commanded by Colonel Jeffrey Smith, which was encamped just outside the city.[17] The 82nd took a much more aggressive approach with the insurgency than had its predecessor, with some initial negative consequences. During the handover of responsibility between the two units, members of the 82nd fired on and killed eight local Fallujah policemen and a guard for the nearby Jordanian hospital on September 12, 2003. Five days later the paratroopers from same unit opened fire at a wedding, killing a 14-year-old boy and wounding six other people after mistaking celebratory gunfire for an attack.[18] Such actions did not endear the residents to the 82nd, but the All American Division did not relent in its aggressive approach.

In October and November, in response to numerous incidents in Fallujah, that Division began a series of cordon-and-search raids throughout the city targeting known insurgents and Former Regime Element (FRE) supporters of the insurgency. On October 13 the local Iraqi police fired on soldiers inside Fallujah, and on October 31 another big firefight occurred near the fire station downtown. On November 2, insurgents based in Fallujah shot down a U.S. CH-47 helicopter, killing 16 soldiers.[19] As the insurgency increased its opposition, the paratroopers of the 82nd matched it with ever-greater aggressiveness and firepower. Later the same month, a bomb destroyed the office of Mayor Taha Bedawi, who had been appointed in April 2003 by tribal sheiks. Bedawi, who was subsequently forced to leave his post, was known to cooperate with U.S. forces.[20]

From December 2003 to March 2004, the 82nd continued to conduct operations in Fallujah, all the while working to build the confidence and capability of the Iraqi Civil Defense Corps (ICDC) and police forces in the city. The leaders of the 82nd knew that saturating the streets with soldiers was the only way to control the environment and establish real security. Every mission was accompanied by psychological and information operations to help the people understand the role of the coalition forces and the options they had for future progress in the new Iraq. Lieutenant Colonel Brian Drinkwine, the commander of the 1st Battalion, 505th Infantry, explained, "with the increased street operations and interaction among the local populace, more Fallujahns may view us not as just Americans, but as people with a sense of purpose – to rebuild Iraq into a free, democratic nation."[21] The American and Iraqi soldiers were even conducting limited joint patrols in January 2004 to include a hugely successful mission to confiscate weapons from the city conducted on January 6. The 82nd Airborne integrated a strong civil affairs program with their operations to improve schools and other facilities in the area, but they could never shake the opposition of the "behind the scenes" city leaders.

These early forces had very few troops with which to control a huge, yet sparsely populated, area along the strategically valuable Euphrates River. Some of the residents of Fallujah had been circumventing the rules of even Saddam Hussein's oppressive regime for years and were well adept at finding ways around any restrictions on their activities. With a large amount of space to cover, no recognized "enemy" formations in the field to focus on, and no way of distinguishing neutral Iraqis from potential insurgents, the military units of the coalition had a very difficult task to accomplish. As late as May 2005, after 2 years of living in the area, coalition forces discovered a very sophisticated underground bunker complex filled with a huge amount of weapons and ammunition in a location within 5 miles of the main Multinational Force (MNF) base camp outside of the city of Fallujah.[22] This complex had most likely been in use since the very first days of U.S. activity in the area, yet it was not discovered for 3 years. The enemy threat posed to the MNF in the area was well organized and well employed, presenting a significant challenge for counterinsurgency operations.

THE NATURE OF THE INSURGENCY IN IRAQ

The insurgency facing the coalition forces in Iraq was multifaceted and complex in motivation. Most simply, it was a conglomeration of three separate but loosely cooperating groups with different but complimentary agendas. The most distinct of these groups was the FRE,[23] who had previously been members of Saddam Hussein's Ba'ath Party. These people were fairly well known from their previous government positions and were clearly opposed to the coalition and the new Iraq because, as Sunni members of Saddam's government and army, they had been disenfranchised by the de-Ba'athification policy of the Coalition Provisional Authority (CPA). In some cases these Iraqis had previously been powerful government officials who had committed acts of injustice. Some members of the FRE had simply been lower-level functionaries working to put food on their tables, but all of the Iraqis who were actively employed by the former regime lost their jobs and honest livelihoods when Ambassador Paul Bremer decided on de-Ba'athification, so among members of all these Ba'athist groups, there was no love for the new Iraq. FRE insurgents were more practical than idealistic, they were all Iraqis, and they were well networked in Al Anbar province. They were not necessarily well trained, unless they had been members of the Iraqi armed forces or security services under Saddam, but in 2003 there were very few alternatives open to them and they were extremely committed to their cause.

The second category of insurgents consisted of the hardened terrorists, members of a terrorist group, or employees of a terrorist group. The most famous of these groups was the Al Qaeda-linked terrorist organization led by Abu Musab al-Zarqawi, known as Al Qaeda in Iraq. Zarqawi deserves special mention because he came to be the major terrorist actor and primary terrorist coordinator in Iraq during this period. He is Jordanian by birth and met Osama bin Laden in Afghanistan as have so many of the Al Qaeda converts of his generation. Unlike many of his fellow terrorists, however, Zarqawi's motivation was much less religious and much more criminal in nature. He was a thug and personally participated in some of the most vile acts committed by his group of terrorist-insurgents.

Terrorists came to Iraq from a host of nations to join in the war as idealistic supporters of any group who attacked the United States, Israel, or even "western institutions" more generally. Terrorists were ideological in their motivation and normally well trained and well financed. Their training gave them flexibility and their financial support gave them mobility, so they rarely stood to fight in Iraq, preferring to strike quickly and run from major engagements.

An important aspect of the terrorist motivation in Iraq was inspiration from jihadist Muslim ideologues. Although rarely was a direct connection obvious, many of the terrorists who came to fight in Iraq did so because they were motivated by the writings and media issued by bin Laden or conservative Muslim religious leaders. This brought a sense of holy war to the fighting on the part of the terrorists and certainly created a climate where acts like suicide bombings, which would otherwise be extremely rare, came to be commonly employed. The jihadists did not limit their attacks to Americans, but felt perfectly justified in killing other Muslims anytime they came in proximity to American or Iraqi national targets.

The third opposition group in Iraq was much more ill defined and was largely composed of criminals and malcontents who saw the war as a way to profit from instability and lack of governmental control. Saddam had opened the Iraqi prisons prior to his fall, and western Iraq was full of people who would prey on any soft target or take advantage of opportunities for theft and profiteering. Most of these people were Iraqi and very few were well trained or financed, but they were extremely difficult to identify and had a completely opportunistic approach to the war.

The FRE and their cause were a magnet to the terrorists, and although they both sought to attack both the coalition and the new Iraqi government, they frequently had different longer-term goals, so any linkage between members of the FRE and the true terrorists was normally short term. Criminals might join either group and frequently operated on the fringes of both groups, seeking simply to fan the flames of instability and get paid for their actions. Any alliance of these three groups was weak and normally temporary, but from the coalition perspective, because they often acted similarly, it was very difficult to sort out with any certainty individual members or attribute responsibility for an act to any specific group. In 2004, Fallujah came to be inhabited by numerous members of all three groups. Unless someone was captured or killed, or a group claimed responsibility for a given attack, it was frequently impossible to tell who made an attack or for what reason, so wargaming, or outthinking these groups, as was traditional with an enemy in conventional conflict, was always a very difficult challenge fraught with risk.

This inability to categorize and analyze the enemy in Iraq made the fighting there much more difficult for professional Soldiers and Marines. Convoys were frequently attacked by different groups on the same day, and those enemy actions may or may not have been coordinated. The process of identifying and targeting key leaders, normally an important tool for western military forces, was extremely complex in Iraq. Even if an enemy leader or cell could be identified, the loose nature of the opposition made understanding where it might fit into the overall enemy organization very problematic. This was one of the most frustrating aspects of the conflict in Iraq.

THE MARINE EXPEDITIONARY FORCE TAKES CONTROL

One of the key lessons of any insurgency is the absolute requirement to remain engaged with the local population – to prevent the insurgents from freely swimming in the ocean of local support. Without regular access (and, to be frank, the 82nd Airborne was far too overextended to be present in all of the tense areas of the province), the influence of the coalition slowly but precipitously dropped in the early months of 2004. When the 1st Marine Expeditionary Force (MEF)[24] assumed control of the region from the 82nd Division in late March 2004, relations with Fallujah were limited and constrained at best. Still, the MEF arrived with great new energy and a much more deliberate and aggressive approach to operations.[25] Typified by the catchphrase of the 1st Marine Division, "No Better Friend, No Worse Enemy," the Marines had specifically designed a new training plan and even changed their uniform policy to signal that "a new sheriff was in town."[26]

The MEF and all of its major subordinate commands had participated in the initial assault in Iraq during the first phase of operation Iraqi Freedom. Moving on the right flank of the coalition's two-pronged attack up the Euphrates River valley, it had taken Basra and Nasiriyah and then crossed the river to enter Baghdad on April 8. Following the effort to secure the Iraqi capital, one of the MEF's subordinate units, Task Force Tarawa, pressed on northward to take Saddam Hussein's hometown of Tikrit before major combat operations became less vigorous and the coalition command repostured its forces to assert control over the entire country.[27] In the late spring of 2003, the MEF was finally assigned to control the majority of southern Iraq, between the British sector, Multinational Division-South (MND-South), and Baghdad, including the cities of Hillah, Kut, Diwaniyah, Karbala, and Najaf. This period allowed the MEF to focus on stability operations in a relatively quiet sector of Iraq dominated by Shia interests prior to its redeployment to the United States in October 2003. Very quickly following their return home, however, the Marines of the MEF learned that they would be returning to Iraq for phase two of the war – the stabilization of Iraq and operation Iraqi Freedom II.

Understanding well that stability operations require different approaches and indeed different skills than do conventional combat operations, the subordinate commands of the MEF began a very aggressive training program to reorient on different tasks and a different mind-set in December 2003. The 1st Marine Division training program was based on long-standing Marine doctrine and lessons learned from previous low-intensity combat operations, reaching as far back as the Banana Wars of the 1920s. The Marines had pioneered a *Small Wars Manual*[28] and had a large stock of reading material designed to frame a different attitude among the troops to better deal with the complexities of counterinsurgency operations.[29] The Division also had a different strategy for stability and support operations, which required each individual Marine to understand Iraqi culture and traditions and interact openly with the Iraqi people. These programs would go a long way toward preparing the forces for the very different type of war they would encounter in Iraq during 2004.

Still, changing from a conventional more "kinetic" mind-set to a more engaged stabilization approach required aggressive leadership and daily example from the senior leaders of the MEF. The drive, commitment, and style of the MEF leadership would be a critical factor in the ability of the force to transition to counter the evolving threat in Iraq while gaining and developing the trust of the Iraqi people. The key leaders of the MEF included its veteran commander, Lieutenant General Jim Conway,[30] who had led the MEF in the assault into Iraq the previous year, and his aggressive, no-nonsense chief of staff, Colonel John Coleman. Other key players included the gruff commander of the 1st Marine Division, Major General Jim Mattis,[31] who had commanded the Marines in Afghanistan as well as in Iraq, and his savvy assistant division commander, Colonel Joe Dunford.[32] These men rounded out a long roster of leaders who had already served in Iraq but who would have to meet very different challenges during their second tour in country.

Unfortunately, very soon after taking over responsibility from the 82nd Airborne Division, the newly arrived Marines were confronted with the charred bodies of their countrymen hanging from the old green bridge less than 5 miles away in Fallujah.[33] The incident not only horrified the world, but it also directly affected the pace and style of counterinsurgency operations conducted by the coalition forces in Iraq. At first, there was little the Marines could do, but they were soon directed to execute an operation named Vigilant Resolve,[34] the destruction of the insurgency in Fallujah in response to the Blackwater attack.[35] After March 31, 2003, Fallujah took on a worldwide significance far greater than its physical size. For the next year, the name *Fallujah* resonated in media outlets across the globe on a daily basis. During that year, the city would rise to even greater prominence before being pummeled and then rebuilt by the Marines and their coalition partners. For that year the old bridge leading west pointed to a very different future dominated by jihadist-inspired sharia courts.

Chapter Two

Showing Resolve

The coalition response to the killings of the Blackwater contractors in Fallujah was sadly ironic. Without a directed military response, generated by the horrific nature of the incident, a new relationship between the coalition forces and the residents of Fallujah might have been forged. Because the Marines of MEF had arrived with a very different, more Iraqi-centric, and more integrated approach to the stability operations mission than had been used previously by the U.S. Army forces in the area, the Fallujahns could have been weaned away from the insurgency. A crucial part of the Marine approach called for engagement with the Iraqi people in a way reminiscent of the Civic Action Program (CAP) pioneered by the Marine Corps during the Vietnam conflict.[1] The Marines expected that by demonstrating they could be good friends with the Iraqi people they could soften Sunni perceptions of an occupation and develop better communications and unity of effort against the insurgents. Eventually, of course, the Marine goal was to minimize support for the insurgency among the local Iraqis and reduce the need for combat operations.

But, by the time the Marines arrived, the 82nd Airborne had effectively ceased active patrolling inside Fallujah, after repeated acts of violence indicated security was better left to the local police and ICDC soldiers within the city.[2] Notwithstanding the lack of coalition activity in the city, before the Blackwater incident, the Marines still wanted to engage with the people of Fallujah to show the benefits of their unique approach, and they quickly resumed active engagement with the population. Yet, almost immediately after their arrival the Marines began to sense that the situation in Fallujah was not as calm as they had been led to believe.[3] First, a rocket was fired from the city into the coalition force base at Camp Fallujah,[4] killing a doctor assigned to the 82nd Airborne on March 20. Later, on March 26, an attack on a logistics convoy nearby resulted in the death of a Marine, Private First Class Leroy Sandoval, Jr., and about 18 Iraqis.[5]

Thinking these attacks were isolated incidents in a dangerous country, Colonel John Toolan, the commander of the 1st Marine Regiment, charged with security in the area, and other Marine leaders entered Fallujah the next day to discuss the new Marine way of interacting with local residents in the mayor's complex of the city. During that meeting, seven Marines were wounded by mortar fire.[6] The next day yet another Marine was wounded near the highway intersection on the east side of the city, and a Special Forces soldier was killed by a command-detonated IED while leaving Fallujah.[7] It was then clear to the Marines that something unanticipated was going on in the city. On the same day of the Blackwater murders, five U.S. Army soldiers died in an IED attack in nearby Habbaniyah, Iraq.[8]

So it was a rising level of violence that was already in evidence, combined with the deaths of the five soldiers outside Fallujah on March 31, not just the chilling Blackwater murders that drove the MEF toward a traditional assault on the enemy in Fallujah in late March. In fact, the initial forays of this assault actually began as early as March 29, even as Colonel Toolan and his 1st Marines were accepting tactical responsibility for the city from the 82nd Airborne. On that date the 2nd Battalion, 1st Marines had begun a limited objective raid into the northeastern corner of the city to discover the source of the recent attacks on March 27.

Although the main assault did not begin in earnest until Monday, April 5, the Marines had immediately begun conducting tactical operations to identify and deal with the threats in Fallujah because it was obvious to them that insurgent activity was a significant threat.[9] Of course, there was no doubt that an even greater response was needed after the incidents of March 31, but it appears in retrospect that the insurgents in the city were actually taking advantage of the turnover between the 82nd Airborne and the Marines to attack the coalition during a period of weakness. This ability to identify and exploit a potential gap in coverage caused by the turnover between the two units shows that the insurgency in Fallujah was being directed by a commander or commanders capable of observing and analyzing coalition activities for opportunities and then taking action to gain tactical advantage. It was a much more sophisticated and capable enemy than many people in Washington, D.C., and elsewhere in America realized.

VIGILANT RESOLVE, NO WORSE ENEMY . . .

The April attack by the coalition forces into Fallujah changed the insurgency in Iraq in several ways. Most critical among these changes was the fact that for months afterward, the insurgents believed they could both defeat coalition forces in urban combat and manipulate influential Sunnis in Baghdad to negotiate on their behalf against coalition forces. The April fighting in Fallujah also established some important precedents for operations to follow, in both Najaf and in other areas of Al Anbar province, including the second attack in the city, which would follow in November. For these reasons an overview of the April operation is important to a full understanding of what followed.

Although the U.S. military can respond very quickly to a host of situations in crisis, attacking into a city the size of Fallujah remains an extremely complex task. Such complexity requires time for detailed planning and positioning forces. A few additional days of breathing room before the assault would have elicited a different Marine response in Fallujah, but war all too frequently forces commanders to react under less than optimal circumstances. Within hours of the March 31 incidents, the MEF began to shift additional units toward Fallujah and to posture supplies for offensive operations. In less than a week, the MEF, in coordination with its subordinate tactical commands, the 1st Marine Division, and Colonel Toolan's 1st Marine Regiment (assigned to provide security in the area), had produced an assault plan focused around employing two Marine battalions and parts of two Iraqi battalions inside Fallujah to root out the insurgents in the city. The operation was named Vigilant Resolve.

The plan called for Regimental Combat Team 1 (RCT-1),[10] under the command of Colonel Toolan, to surround the city and then penetrate it from two angles immediately before launching a series of raids to capture the key individuals linked to the most extreme violence in the city. The main physical objectives identified in the plan were to establish control over the mayor's complex at the city's center and the Iraqi military compound to its west.[11] Through the first 3 days of April, units were moved from nearby areas of the province and the key access points into Fallujah were occupied by coalition forces, with Golf Company 2nd Battalion, 1st Marines taking control of the western approaches into the city, including the old green bridge where the contractor bodies had been hung.

The 2nd Battalion, 1st Marines (commanded by Lieutenant Colonel Greg Olsen) in the northwest and 1st Battalion, 5th Marines (commanded by Lieutenant Colonel Brennan Byrne) in the southeast were the key maneuver forces working for Toolan.[12] The two local ICDC battalions deemed combat capable by the MEF were intended to support the Marine penetrations in the city. All of these units were to be supported by AC-130 Specter gunships at night and F-15 Eagle fighters and AH-1 Cobra helicopters during the daylight hours.

This plan appeared to be an effective approach to the problem, fully integrating the Iraqi forces and employing a focused effort to isolate the insurgents while conducting operations with an eye to protecting the local residents. Unfortunately, the Iraqi units involved in the operation got off to a very bad start, with one battalion encountering an IED as it began movement from Baghdad. That was all it took to convince the unit's soldiers that they did not want to fight in Fallujah. The second battalion arrived in time to provide a company to each of the two Marine assault battalions, but even it lost a great deal of its effectiveness after suffering three fatalities in the first few days of the fighting. In the early spring of 2004, the ICDC units simply did not have sufficient unit cohesion and training to successfully fight the insurgents.

After access to the city had been controlled by coalition units occupying the major entry routes, the initial combat patrols entered Fallujah early on Monday morning April 5, broadcasting warnings for the residents to stay indoors for their

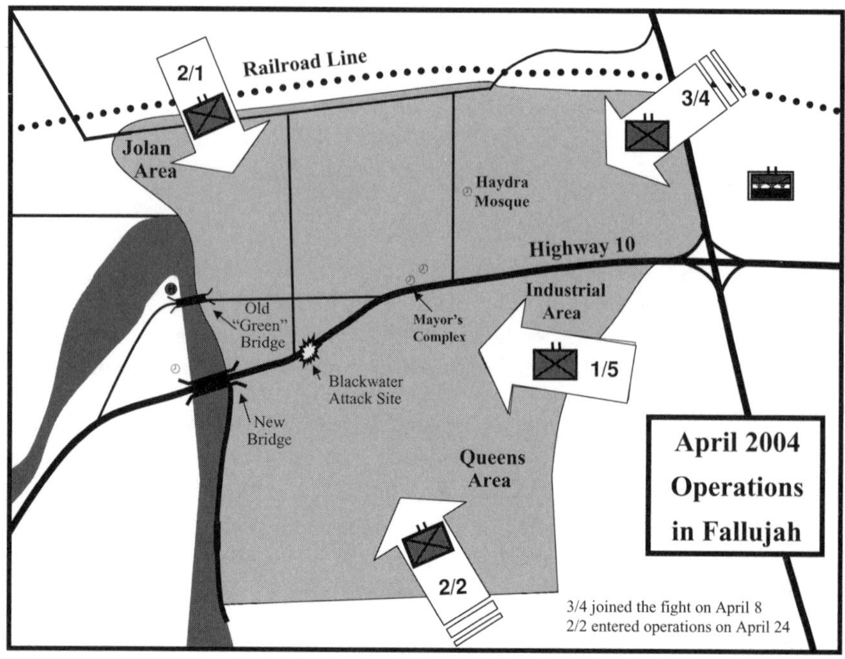

Map 3. April 2004 Operations in Fallujah

own safety.[13] Many of the financiers, recruiters, and weapons suppliers for the insurgent movement were rounded up in early raids.[14] "Iraqi police dropped off U.S. leaflets at city mosques, announcing a daily 7 P.M. to 6 A.M. curfew and ordering residents not to carry weapons."[15] The prohibitions on weapons and free movement were to help differentiate between the insurgents and the locals. The Marines even developed and broadcasted techniques for residents to stay sheltered in their homes and ways to safely approach coalition forces.

Unfortunately, the Marines' reception in the city was anything but safe. Troops came under fire almost immediately from insurgents, who used rifles, automatic weapons, rocket-propelled grenades (RPGs), and mortars, firing from homes, vehicles, and even mosques. Insurgent snipers fired from rooftops and the windows of homes and businesses. The Marines returned fire and quickly brought helicopter gunships to bear against the enemy positions, but four Marines were killed on the first day of combat operations in the city.[16] It was very clear that many of the local residents were aiding the enemy fighters, who wore black clothing and scarves wrapped around their faces.[17]

Lieutenant Colonel Brennan Byrne's 1st Battalion, 5th Marines (commonly known by the abbreviation 1/5) attacked from the east into the heavy industrial area of the city and bore the brunt of the initial casualties. One Marine commented, "As soon as we pulled up, they started shooting at us. There were mortars, rockets and bullets flying everywhere. . . . It seemed like everyone in the city who had a gun was out there."[18] Still, the Marines tried to avoid civilian casualties by limiting the use of indirect fires in the city. At this early stage in the second year of the war, the employment of artillery and close air support inside cities was still considered risky. Even with the intensity of the Iraqi response, Byrne commented that the action was "about making the city livable so people don't have to live in fear of the thugs who have taken over the city."[19]

Still, by Tuesday, April 6, 1/5 had consolidated among several strong positions in the industrial area of the city's east side.[20] In 2004, that part of the city was primarily filled with small factories, auto shops, and warehouses, and covered with junk machinery and car parts. So it was particularly rough urban terrain for combat operations, but, at least it then had many fewer residents than the other sections of the city – certainly many fewer people lived there than lived in the densely packed northwestern sector of Fallujah known as the Jolan. Using cannon from AC-130 gunships and aircraft-delivered rockets, Byrne's battalion was able to carve out control of a fairly large section of the city and reinforce its positions around an old soda factory, used as a strong point.

Elsewhere in Fallujah, things were not going smoothly at all. Small, scattered groups of insurgent fighters were waging hit-and-run attacks and running street battles against the Marines in both the northwestern and the northeastern sectors of the city. "For hours into the night, the sides traded fire, while teams of Marines moved in and out of the neighborhood, seizing buildings to use as posts and battling gunmen. Helicopters weaved overhead, firing at guerilla hide-outs."[21] Four homes were destroyed in the initial fighting and between 20 and 50 Iraqis were killed or wounded. Perhaps just as troubling, after suffering their initial casualties, the supporting Iraqi units began to fail and never again performed as expected in the operation. For the fight in Fallujah, it was really only the newly arrived Marine battalions that counted – and they were set against a much better situated and stronger enemy force than was anticipated.

The residents remaining in the city figured out quickly that the ongoing attack in Fallujah was something very different than anything they had experienced before. Consequently, on the third day of the operation, the city erupted with a flow of residents fleeing from the combat. The Marines had thought to provide food and water for a needy population but were amazed to observe over 80,000 Iraqis flow through the exit points in a matter of only 20 hours.[22] Everyone understood that this operation indicated a big change in the way the coalition was waging the second year of war in Iraq.

NOT JUST FALLUJAH

Unfortunately for the Marines, Fallujah was not the only challenge the coalition was facing in early April. At the same time they began operations in the city of mosques, the 1st Marine Division also began increased operations elsewhere in the province so as to put additional pressure on the insurgents and limit any reinforcements to those enemy fighters already in Fallujah. Unexpectedly, the enemy in Ramadi and other Sunni cities mounted surprisingly strong counterattacks in response to the Division's efforts and, to make things worse, a Shia holy man named Muqtada al-Sadr began a parallel campaign focused against the coalition in general and the CPA in particular in the southern Iraqi city of Najaf.

In Ramadi, the fighting was particularly intense, requiring augmentation of the front line fighting troops by the support sections and division headquarters units to deal with the severe insurgent response. Fox News reported, "Dozens of Iraqis attacked a Marine position near the governor's palace" in Ramadi and quoted military sources saying, "This is unlike any other firefight we've seen so far."[23] The insurgent response was so strong that all American officials in Iraq were directed to remain inside their compounds for security reasons. Fighting also broke out in Nasiriyah, Kut, and Karbala and in the Sadr City section of Baghdad. Ominously, eight fuel trucks intended for Camp Fallujah were attacked and burned by insurgents between Baghdad and Fallujah, leaving a huge plume of black smoke in the sky over the epicenter of the conflict.

In a moment of terrible timing, the U.S. Administrator in Iraq, Paul Bremer, had chosen April 5 to declare al-Sadr an "outlaw."[24] This declaration inflamed many among the Shia majority in Iraq and started a Shia confrontation in central Iraq at the same time that the coalition was dealing with the Sunnis in Fallujah and throughout the rest of Al Anbar province. Soon, the world, and particularly the White House, was concerned about the stability of Iraq, with two of its major religious groups in open conflict with the U.S. civil administration, only weeks before the transfer to full Iraqi sovereignty was scheduled to occur. Al-Sadr called for open revolt against the coalition forces and Ambassador Bremer cancelled a return to Washington to brief congressional leaders on the situation in Iraq.

Fortunately, these various outbreaks were only loosely related. It is certain that al-Sadr's decision to overtly attack the coalition had been brewing for months, and the attacks in Ramadi were a response to coalition posturing. But the overall effect was to make it appear that both Sunni and Shia insurgents were working together against the coalition – which had never been expected. Early April was a period of great tension. One year had passed since the fall of Saddam and few of the American promises for prosperity had materialized. Additionally, Zarqawi and his Al Qaeda-linked movement began a much more aggressive campaign of terror in the country as well. All of these factors cast an ominous cloud over the activities of the coalition in Iraq during early April and made maintaining the political support needed for any tactical success in Fallujah much more difficult to achieve.

In Baghdad and other Sunni areas of Iraq, residents were shocked at the intensity of the fighting and dismayed at reports that many Fallujahn civilians were being killed and injured in the city. Few people understood the facts behind the attack or the real conditions inside Fallujah, but most suspected the worst about the coalition because the news coverage, by both western and Arab journalists, was very critical. In response to this concern, nearly 5,000 Iraqis drove toward Fallujah on April 6 to deliver food and other forms of aid to their neighbors.

MAINTAINING VIGILANCE

On Wednesday, April 7, the Marines continued their push toward the center of Fallujah, "darting across roads and crouching on corners as the echo of mortars and rifles mingled with the wail of prayers and warnings from minarets."[25] Although the MEF claimed that a quarter of the city was under coalition control, the level of fighting was clearly still escalating, as were casualties.[26] As they drove deeper into the city, the Marines were forced to use more weapons systems against a broader range of targets.

In one case, in response to rifle and grenade fire from inside the building, 1/5 employed fixed-wing and helicopter fires against the Abdelaziz Samarri Mosque, reportedly injuring a group of Iraqi residents and seriously damaging the building. General Mattis, the hard-bitten commanding general of the 1st Marine Division, who was on site at the time, along with the Commandant of the Marine Corps, General Michael Hagee, concurred with the attack on the mosque, noting that the insurgents had "profaned" the site by first using it to attack the Marines.[27] This would become the first of many examples of insurgents ignoring the commonly held laws of armed conflict in Fallujah.

The issue of employing weapons in and around mosques was an extremely difficult challenge at the time. The Marines were well aware of the Iraqi sensitivities concerning their holy sites and used due caution; however, they found that their Muslim enemy had no compunction against employing mosques as bases and firing positions. This put the Marines in a no-win situation, forcing them to attack the holy sites with as much precision as possible, yet still accepting that some inevitable damage – both physical and cultural – would occur. Robert Kaplan, who accompanied Bravo Company 1/5 into the city, noted, "By the standards of most wars, some mosques in Fallujah deserved to be leveled. But only after repeated aggressions was any mosque targeted, and then sometimes for hits so small in scope that they often had little effect. The news photos of the holes in mosque domes did not indicate the callousness of the American military; rather the reverse."[28]

Through the afternoon and early evening the fighting raged block by block and house to house. Chants from minarets called on God to protect Fallujah and, some thought, urged holy war against the American invaders. After dark, enemy mortar rounds fell all around 1/5's headquarters, killing an 11-year-old girl and wounding her sister. Some Marines were already saying that the urban combat in Fallujah was more dangerous and unpredictable than what they had experienced in Baghdad the year before. Navy Corpsman Percy Davila said, "It is urban and scary. There are windows everywhere, bullets and grenades whizzing over your head. When you cross the street, you just put your head down and pray."[29] Colonel Toolan was already maneuvering two additional Marine battalions into Fallujah because of the intensity of the fight.[30]

More intense fighting continued in the city on April 8.[31] An F/A-18 Hornet fighter, from the nuclear-powered aircraft carrier *USS George Washington* (CVN 73) in the Arabian Gulf, conducted a 20-millimeter strafing run against an enemy position, and the Marines were able to push deeper into the city and shore up their defensive positions throughout the area.[32] The same day, General Sanchez provided a briefing to reporters in Baghdad, noting that the ICDC forces continued to work with the Marines in the city, making "tremendous progress in restoring legitimate authority to Fallujah."[33] He also promised that once the security situation is stabilized, the quality of life of the residents of Fallujah would be improved through the substantial resources available to the MEF.

In fact, the MEF had made plans to assist Fallujahns, but the fighting during the night and into the next day largely prohibited much assistance from being delivered into the city. Another F/A-18 dropped two 500-pound, GBU-12 laser-guided bombs on another enemy position in Fallujah the following morning, April 9. But, at noon that same day, the Marines unilaterally suspended combat in Fallujah on the direction of Ambassador Bremer, to hold meetings between members of the local governing council and the leadership of the anti-coalition forces in the city and to permit the delivery of supplies provided by the relevant departments of the Iraqi government.[34] Unfortunately, the insurgents wanted no part of a ceasefire and combat operations resumed in less than 2 hours.[35]

Muslim views on the fighting grew exceedingly critical as the days of combat passed, and by April 9 anti-coalition sentiment was very strong all around the Middle East. An *Al-Jazeera* correspondent in Fallujah, quoted by the *Palestine Chronicle*, noted, "People are scared. They are angry," and then he described corpse-littered streets and hundreds of dead and wounded civilians.[36] In nearby Baghdad, Sunnis were openly rallying support for the insurgents in Fallujah, donating blood, money, and medical supplies.[37] Those on the scene knew better; Kaplan wrote, "The overwhelming percentage of the small arms fire – not to mention mortars, rockets, and RPGs – represented indiscriminate automatic bursts by the insurgents. Marines responded with far fewer, more precise shots."[38]

As with any combat operation in urban terrain, the toll on the civilian population was nearly unavoidable and its effects had a profoundly negative impact on the international media and the CPA – the national authority in Iraq at the time. After April 8, with the bombs being dropped so visibly in the city and a great deal of sympathetic reporting by the Arab press, senior officials were questioning some of the tactics used in the fight.[39] Very quickly, the Iraqis near the seat of government in Baghdad not only urged restraint, but also began negations with the insurgents.

The "temporary halt to offensive operations" was intended to support real negotiations and to reduce civilian suffering. But because the insurgent leadership had little faith in negotiations and little concern for civilian welfare, such politically motivated halts in the combat did little except give the insurgents time to rearm and augment their forces. Every day saw continued fighting. Hundreds of the enemy fighters were combining to conduct well-coordinated attacks on Marines by midmonth.[40]

In one such action, some 300 insurgents launched multiple RPGs against a platoon of Marine amphibious assault vehicles, resulting in the complete destruction of one vehicle, the death of one Marine, and multiple Marine injuries in the platoon. The firefight continued in adjacent houses in the city, with insurgents repeatedly attacking the wounded Marines with rifle and RPG fire and hurling grenades. After 6 hours of heavy combat, the dead and injured Marines were evacuated, leaving dozens of insurgent bodies in and around the site of the original ambush.[41]

By April 13, high-level negotiations had started to gain some traction and the combat operation to destroy the insurgents in Fallujah was effectively on hold.[42] Unfortunately, although the Marines consistently pursued a number of basic demands with the insurgents (represented by token city leaders in the negotiation process), the enemy failed to make good on any of their promises, even after the Marines began withdrawing tanks and forces from the city as they had agreed.[43] Some older, largely unserviceable, weapons were turned in, but the insurgents never made a significant commitment to fulfilling the agreements made during the negotiations. Bringing about an end to the contest through negotiations was at an impasse.

The idea of a "Fallujah Brigade" to clean up the city under the command of an Iraqi general was first discussed on April 16 during negotiations at Camp Fallujah between the locals and the MEF.[44] An Iraqi army general from Fallujah, Jasim Mohamed Saleh, was named to help solve the security situation in the city. As the former commander of the Iraqi 39th Division, he was respected by the Sunnis and seemed agreeable to a new relationship where he would serve under MEF command. But even as these new more innovative negotiations continued, rounds and rockets were still being exchanged every day in the winding streets of the city. In fact, April 17 saw some of the toughest fighting of the operation. With no real progress in the one-sided "dialog" with the insurgents, the Fallujah Brigade seemed to offer the only viable option.

On April 19, in discussions with the Iraqis, another former general, Mohammed Latif, offered that a Fallujah Brigade could restore order inside the city, and General Conway agreed to give the idea 2 weeks to prove itself. The Fallujah Brigade was to operate under MEF command and control, and General Saleh seemed, at least at the time, to be the right leader to put the idea into action. By April 22, a more general cease-fire was proposed yet again in the city, but fierce fighting continued in smaller pockets throughout Fallujah. The insurgents simply had no desire to stop fighting after midmonth, for they believed they had turned the tide of public opinion against the coalition and that every additional day of combat in Fallujah was to their strategic benefit. In part, they were exactly right.

By that time, a post-combat concept of operations had been developed (April 21) to provide immediate humanitarian aid to the city in the wake of the fighting. This included a Civil Military Operations Center (CMOC) to work with Nongovernmental Organizations (NGOs) to provide relief supplies. Over the course of the battle, many among the civilian population had been caught inside their homes and as many as 150,000 people were trapped in the isolated city, without regular supplies of food and fuel. The humanitarian plan was envisioned to be put into action preceding any renewed combat operations in the city. It addressed aid, as well as construction and cleanup projects, for the residents of Fallujah and some road and building repair.

Also of note, by the end of April, the MEF's lack of robust Public Affairs (PA) and Information Operations (IO) activities had become obvious in relation to the effective efforts of the insurgents. So the MEF placed new emphasis on those techniques, and they began to figure much more prominently in the scheme of maneuver than they had in the initial operations order. This showed the MEF to be a learning organization, even in combat. PA and IO were areas that the MEF consistently worked hard to improve, under difficult constraints imposed by higher headquarters, and that would contribute much to the future success in Fallujah, once the improved techniques were brought to bear.

Still, after April 22, the situation in Fallujah was very uncertain. The enemy fighters inside the city were reinforcing their positions and growing in power. They were using mosques and hospitals as defensive positions and some analysts believed they would use the local residents as human shields when combat resumed. The insurgents clearly understood that civilian casualties and coalition attacks on mosques and other normally restricted targets played very well in their favor in the international media. Combat continued intermittently in the city as the Marine units shifted positions to avoid being targeted by the insurgents while trying to maintain a climate conducive to negotiations.

Then on Monday April 26, 3 weeks after the offensive started, several new major engagements between groups of insurgents and Marines rang throughout the city. The insurgents counterattacked on that date because they believed the Marines were readying for a renewed assault. Indicative of the valor and sacrifice of those days, in a small corner of the tightly packed city, Lance Corporal Aaron C. Austin gave his life to protect his fellow Marines during a vicious massing attack by some 300 insurgents against his platoon from Echo Company, 2/1. The insurgents had moved in from three directions, all along the alleyways amid the houses where the Marines were positioned; both sides fired rifles and hurled grenades. One grenade blast started a fire, igniting several other explosives and wounding several Marines. As the enemy prepared yet another assault, Austin exposed himself to enemy fire to throw a grenade and halt their attack. For his heroic actions, Lance Corporal Austin was later awarded the Silver Star.[45] During the same action, Master Sergeant Donald Hollenbaugh, U.S. Army, won the Distinguished Service Medal for his bravery while helping the Marines to hold off the insurgent assault during evacuation of casualties from the house the Marine unit was occupying.

From actions like these and the continued stress on the city's population, great political pressure began to be applied to cease any further combat and seek a negotiated settlement. As a result of this pressure, and the continued lack of progress on the ground and in the negotiating room, a Fallujah Brigade, constructed from former Iraqi army soldiers with the sole purpose of restoring order to the city in the Marine's stead, seemed to be the best option. Because the idea was presented by a group of former Iraqi military officers, it also seemed to have the advantage of obtaining some level of Sunni reintegration under the CPA – it appeared to be the only practical Iraqi solution to an Iraqi problem.[46]

THE FALLUJAH BRIGADE

The Fallujah Brigade was a unique and always tenuous construct. Its conceptual leader, Major General Salah, arrived in the city in his Iraqi army uniform to great cheers from the residents. But no sooner was he acknowledged by the locals than his past human rights violations against Iraqi Kurds made him politically untenable as a coalition partner. So the Fallujah Brigade was eventually commanded in the field by Brigadier General Latif (and still later by a General Abdullah, who claimed to be Latif's successor but did little or nothing in the city). Initially formed during the last week of April, it began operations with an initial compliment of nearly 600 members after May 1.

The concept behind the Fallujah Brigade was for it to act as a buffer between the insurgents and the coalition, to isolate the foreign fighter element of the insurgency in Fallujah, and to destroy that group while protecting the local population and restoring order in the city. It was supposed to collect weapons from the insurgents and initiate investigations into the murders of the Blackwater contractors. Unfortunately, the leadership of the Fallujah Brigade – both Saleh (who was an insurgent sympathizer) and Latif (who was reluctant to act against Iraqis) – was heavily influenced by the city's insurgent-supporting tribal leaders. Both Iraqi generals played to both sides of the confrontation, telling the Marines what they wanted to hear and acting as expediently as possible with the insurgents inside the city of Fallujah. Not only was the leadership of the Fallujah Brigade ineffective, the unit itself was also severely infiltrated by insurgents, so it was never fully capable of accomplishing what it was intended to do.

The test of the Fallujah Brigade began on May 4, when, after another Marine withdrawal, General Latif agreed to take over the remaining Marine positions around the city and to reassert control over the city center the following day. By the following week, the Marines had begun providing limited humanitarian assistance to the residents of Fallujah and had even developed a claims process for battle damage in the city. The cease-fire was holding and the coalition was planning to conduct a major convoy into the heart of the city on May 10, but the city had yet to give up any crew-served weapons systems – one of the essential preconditions of any continued cease-fire from the coalition perspective. Although the convoy was conducted as scheduled (bringing General Mattis and 10 Marine vehicles to the mayor's compound for a meeting with city leaders), clear signs were already evident that the Fallujah Brigade leadership was not going to make good on its claims to rid Fallujah of foreign fighters and provide security in the city.

The interposition of the Fallujah Brigade, which effectively ended operation Vigilant Resolve, proved in the end to disappoint everyone. Although well equipped by the coalition to do its job, the Fallujah Brigade quickly showed itself unable to oppose the Sunni anti-Iraqi Forces (AIF) in the town, and over the summer it slowly dissolved as an effective military force. At the very least the Fallujah Brigade was a first attempt at an Iraqi solution to Fallujah's troubles, and when it failed to maintain the peace, the blame could no longer be pinned on coalition forces exclusively.[47] Iraqis began to see that they too were at least partially responsible for the problems confronting the city.

At the same time the Fallujah Brigade was failing, the police in Fallujah, which were never very supportive of the coalition, began to side more with the insurgent and AIF that gathered in the city. One of the conditions of the Fallujah Brigade's existence was that the city of Fallujah became solely the Brigade's responsibility, meaning that Marine forces were not to enter Fallujah with out prior coordination. This understanding established a slow deterioration of security in Fallujah with various insurgent groups vying for control in the city.

By June it was clear that the city was no longer open to the coalition and its patrols. Insurgents increasing controlled the daily life of the residents of Fallujah. The city police were intimidated into turning a blind eye to insurgent activity. Finally, regular military communications between the Fallujah Brigade and the coalition became strained and then increasingly infrequent. Although Colonel Toolan met daily with representatives of the Fallujah Brigade, General Latif and the other leaders of the Brigade were clearly coming under insurgent control and only rarely acting to accomplish their stated mission. The Fallujah Liaison Team (FLT) site was opened outside Traffic Control Point 1 (TCP-1) to facilitate dialog between the city and the MEF leadership, but in doing so TCP-1 itself became one of the most dangerous locations in the world, taking daily indirect fire and small arms attacks. Life in Fallujah became more dominated by the insurgents and Taliban-like, conservative religious practices.

STRATEGIC CHANGES

On June 28, the CPA turned over full sovereignty to the Interim Iraqi Government (IIG) in a surprise move 2 days prior to the announced date of turnover of sovereignty. In part this shift was enabled by the cooperation in evidence during the negotiations and termination of the April fight in Fallujah. Unfortunately, although the new Iraqi government was an effective compromise politically and culturally, no one knew if it would become a true, effective government.

Through July and August, insurgent forces had an increasingly free run of the city, and over time Fallujah became an area restricted from coalition ground and air movement, effectively blocking military transportation from using Highway 10 from Baghdad to the provincial capital of Ramadi. Over time the insurgency in the city expanded its influence to surrounding areas and troop movement anywhere near Fallujah became risky. In August, anti-Mahdi Militia[48] fighting in nearby Najaf took the attention of the world off of Fallujah for a few weeks, but the influence of the insurgency that "turned back the Marine assault" only grew.

The transition from the CPA to the IIG and the shifting of the military command and control organization in Iraq at the same time permitted a general atrophy of the national focus on Fallujah at the very time the Fallujah Brigade was slowly but clearly decomposing. At the same time, the insurgents were only increasing their powerbase in the city of Fallujah. The summer months saw a steady rise in insurgent control and a similar decrease in coalition force freedom of maneuver around Fallujah. For the residents of the city, the summer also brought an ever more restrictive, fundamentalist regimen to activities in Fallujah.

LESSONS FROM FIRST CONTACT

For the coalition in general and the Marines in particular, operation Vigilant Resolve was very instructive. The enemy proved to be extremely smart and adaptable and demonstrated the capacity to fight under extreme conditions. Combat against the insurgents in Iraq would be vicious, close, and unbounded by traditional laws of armed conflict. Marines proved to be extremely effective in small unit actions with close air support. Snipers, tanks, grenades, and the Advanced Combat Optical Gunsite (ACOG) proved invaluable. Marine urban tactics and fire control measures also proved themselves in counterinsurgency combat where the civilian population remained close to combat actions.

Unfortunately, the Marine's Iraqi counterparts did not serve well overall and remained suspect as coalition partners. In part this was because of inadequate training, but it was also a symptom of the fact that the new Iraq had no professional military after de-Ba'athification. Some individual Iraqi soldiers performed well, but as units above the company level they were too weak to be employed in combat without very close control.

Worse for the coalition, in the face of such an enemy, the Iraqi leaders of the Iraqi Governing Council were uncertain in their commitment to fight insurgents in Iraqi cities. The CPA had too limited support from the people, and the prospect of civil war was too likely in the early months of 2004 for many Iraqis, particularly Sunnis, to back coalition combat of any duration beyond a few days.

The MEF saw quickly that such a tenacious enemy would fight hard in urban terrain and had to be separated from its base of support in the local population if it was to be decisively engaged and defeated. Unfortunately, Fallujah was one city where the residents at least tacitly supported the insurgency, a place where traditional counterinsurgency operations might not work. The temperament of the locals was clearly anti-coalition and new approaches were needed to effectively combat the threat.

In 2004, the Marine leadership learned quickly that some aspects of combat operations were going to be very different from the way they were the year before. Operations were much more politically constrained and tactics were much less fluid in the urban terrain. Even more importantly, the coalition realized that the public affairs fight was just as important as the tactical battle. The objectives and benefits of any future operation had to be clear to all concerned, and all civil–military activities had to be planned and integrated from the outset with an aggressive information plan. As Robert Kaplan wrote, "none of the above matters if it is not completely explained to the American public – for the home front is more critical in a counterinsurgency than in any other kind of war."[49]

Finally, a fully integrated command structure and capable Iraqi forces were required for any future operation. The ICDC forces in the area were worthless, many members of the initial Iraqi forces sent from Baghdad to participate in the battle were timid, and the Fallujah Brigade was ineffective against fellow Sunnis. Better strategic coordination with the new Iraqi government was needed, and much better trained and integrated Iraqi forces had to be developed for any long-term solution to be viable in Al Anbar province in general and Fallujah in particular. Even with such improvements, however, Fallujah would remain a very tough nut to crack.

Chapter Three

The Lion of Najaf

Because the ICDC was completely ineffective against terrorists, during the summer months of June, July, and August 2004 insurgent forces had an increasingly free run of the city of Fallujah. Over the same period, insurgent capability grew and grew as the city became known as an enemy sanctuary. Because of the fact that the city was supposedly under the control of the ICDC and was not the responsibility of the coalition, as the enemy grew in strength, Fallujah increasingly became restricted from American ground and air movement for force protection reasons. It was simply too dangerous to enter the city, given the limited role the MEF was allowed to play there.

Political constraints aimed at reaching out to Sunnis and strategic force protection considerations even effectively blocked military transportation from using Highway 10, the main road from Baghdad to the provincial capital of Ramadi to the west that passed right by Fallujah. In time, to most soldiers in the coalition, the city became just a dark spot on the map in west-central Iraq. Meanwhile, all through the summer, the insurgents in the city slowly expanded their influence into the surrounding suburban areas, increased the level of intimidation to those who did not support their cause, and grew roots in adjacent towns until troop movement anywhere near Fallujah was observed and tracked by the enemy and its sympathizers. Inside Fallujah the municipal functions became increasingly dominated by the needs of the insurgents, who began taking over more and more safe houses as their numbers grew and building defensive works to improve their expanding stronghold. The city that had resisted the coalition assault in April was by August a new symbol of the strength of the insurgency.

Still, the growing influence of the anti-Iraqi elements in Al Anbar province was not unique to that part of Iraq. Baghdad witnessed ever more numerous acts of opposition to the post-Saddam government during the summer, as did several other cities. And, more ominously, these acts were not always Sunni inspired;

other groups were starting to take a more active role in the insurgency. Some of these groups were Shia supported, and the influence of Iran was suspected. This expansion of the opposition resulted in ever-increasing numbers of incidents of Iraqi-on-Iraqi violence. In other words, the insurgents were taking the fight to the Iraqi people, not just the coalition forces.

Then, during the first days of August, antigovernment Mahdi Militia[1] working in nearby Najaf took the attention of the world off of the infamous Sunni triangle and Fallujah. For a few weeks the attention of the world changed to focus on Shia opposition; this important change signaled yet another significant step in the ever-increasing development of the insurgency.[2] While the symbolism of the April battle that "turned back the Marine assault" continued to grow, the fighting in Najaf illustrated a more dangerous form of revolt and gave the coalition an opportunity to learn some important tactical lessons that would be important to planning the second fight in Fallujah.

THE INSURGENT VIOLENCE EXPANDS

These summer insurgent attacks need to be viewed in a greater context, however. As indicated, Fallujah and Najaf were not alone among Iraqi cities where unrest and violence was significant in the spring and early summer of 2004. At least 68 people had been killed in Basra on April 21, 13 died in Baghdad on June 14, and insurgents launched coordinated attacks across Iraq on June 24, killing and injuring over 300 people. Later in the summer, on July 28, nearly 70 Iraqis were killed in Baquba.

The specific types of violent acts were also expanding. Murdering hostages became a favored insurgent tactic during this period, beginning on April 14 with the death of an Italian security guard. Nick Berg, a young U.S. hostage, had been shown being beheaded in a video released on May 11.[3] During the same time frame coalition forces continued to fight insurgent groups and to bomb their supporting infrastructure of safe houses, training bases, and weapons caches, whenever and wherever they could locate them, particularly in the Sunni triangle north and west of the Iraqi capital.[4]

This expansion of the insurgency and its actions had complex causation. Terrorists were most certainly behind the most grisly acts, the beheadings and the large impact bombings. But, FRE members and Iraqi criminals were also at work, adding to the confusion by taking advantage of any weakness in the government of coalition. To many outside of Iraq, it appeared that the insurgency was growing significantly in size under their very eyes.[5] Certainly, as the months passed and the coalition military units did not leave the country, more and more Iraqis joined the fight with patriotic motivations. Still, the largest source of conflict inside Iraq remained internecine vendettas left over from years of abuse of power. Religious strife was prevalent. With a tremendous rise in prices and goods being brought into the country, incidents of crime rose as well. All of these facts made the summer of 2004 a very difficult period for the new Iraqi government.[6]

These circumstances would have been difficult for any established government, but they were even more challenging to a brand new management team with limited recent experience in Iraq. The United Nations, under the leadership of veteran diplomat, special envoy Lakhdar Brahimi, had only appointed the key members of the new IIG on June 1.[7] When it took office in late June, the focus of effort of this first new Iraqi government was designed to be directing the day-to-day affairs of the 26 national ministries, preparing the country for national elections in January 2005, and helping the coalition create Iraqi security services to eventually take full responsibility in the country, but the IIG was quickly dominated by battling the insurgency instead.

PRELUDE: IRAQI SOVEREIGNTY

One of the most significant events of the Iraq war occurred on June 27, 2004, when the American-led CPA gave up responsibility for governing Iraq to the newly selected Iraqi sovereign government managed by Prime Minister Iyad Allawi.[8] The formation of this IIG had been the subject of much negotiation during the late spring but had finally been formed through compromise among the three major religious groups in the country. Although the president, Sheik Ghazi al-Yawar, was a Sunni, the real power in the structure rested in the office of Prime Minister Allawi.

The transfer of sovereignty occurred at 10:26 A.M., 2 days earlier than had been announced, in part to throw off insurgents (who may have been plotting an attack on the announced day) and in part because the new government did not want to waste even a single day.[9] The establishment of a democratic administration in Iraq was certain to be a difficult task in the face of so much turmoil. Initially, even the functioning of the ministries remained inefficient at best; provincial governments were just being formed and the new national government, the IIG, needed to establish even the most basic of procedures, including the working relationships among the president, two vice presidents, and the prime minister.

Early on, it became clear that the prime minister was the pivotal position and Iyad Allawi was the key to success for the IIG effort. Allawi was a long-time leader of one of Iraqi's many anti-Saddam opposition groups. He had also been one of the most prominent members of the original Iraqi governing council after the fall of the Iraqi dictator. He was from a Shia family, and although trained as a doctor, his aggressive opposition of Saddam had made him a firm and forceful leader with a very strong understanding of security issues.[10] Allawi had a host of solid supporters from his many years as an opposition leader, but his new task as prime minister would require him to develop a government even as he had to determine policy for the fledgling state, fighting for its life while working to establish itself as an independent entity, with the coalition still a dominant force in the country.

Another key player in this demonstration of Iraqi sovereignty was the newly arrived U.S. Ambassador, John D. Negroponte. It was important to show that L. Paul Bremer, the former U.S. Administrator, was leaving Iraq and being replaced by a diplomat whose responsibility did not include the administration of the country. Negroponte[11] was a diplomat of great experience, having served as the U.S. ambassador to war-torn Honduras in the early 1980s and later representing the United States in the Philippines and Mexico and at the United Nations. His stature demonstrated a commitment to supporting the IIG and his skill would bring much to the table in the difficult year ahead.

The final leg of the new management team confronting the insurgency in Iraq was the newly appointed commander of the Multinational Force-Iraq (MNF-I), U.S. Army General George W. Casey, who assumed command on July 1.[12] Like Allawi and Negroponte, Casey brought great talent and stature to the task in Iraq. He had most recently served as the Vice Chief of Staff of the Army after having commanded the 1st Armored Division in Germany and serving as the Director, Strategic Plans and Policy, J-5, on the Joint Staff in Washington, D.C., before becoming its director in 2003. Casey's appointment as a four-star commander in Iraq, under the command of General John Abizaid, the commander of the U.S. Central Command, demonstrated a renewed commitment to strategic direction of the war effort and better coordination with the political element at the new U.S. embassy.

Allawi, Negroponte, and Casey formed a very effective team. Each knew well to stay in their own lane to fully empower the others, yet they worked well enough together to ensure that the three most critical elements of the counterinsurgency, the host nation government, international diplomacy, and military power, were all well synchronized. Such synchronization would prove critical as the ongoing turbulence in Fallujah grew more and more influential and problems elsewhere in Iraq continued to plague the new Iraqi government.

SHIA OPPOSITION IN IRAQ

The confrontation in Fallujah was strongly influenced by Sunni religious and tribal opposition to the MNF[13] and the new Allawi government. The Sunnis had been largely displaced as the power brokers in Iraq. In particular, Ambassador Bremer's de-Ba'athification policy and the dissolution of the Iraqi Army – both Sunni flagstones – had angered the Sunnis and turned them away from any significant involvement in the government. President Yawar remained a token without real power in the eyes of most Sunnis, and in 2004, the insurgency seemed to them the only real way of combating what they viewed as increasing efforts to exclude them and diminish their role in the country they so recently had ruled.[14]

Sunni opposition to the new government, and certainly to the MNF, was anticipated and well understood by most people working on the development of the new Iraq. What was potentially much more dangerous and concerned them most, however, was the slow but clear growth in Shia opposition to the IIG. That opposition was made clear in Baghdad through the continuing strife in the slums of the Shia areas known as Sadr City. It became even more dangerous with the growing demands of the Shia "holy man," Muqtada al-Sadr, and his demonstrations in the holy city of Najaf.

The Shia holy city of Najaf is located just over 150 kilometers southwest of Baghdad. Imam Ali bin Ali Talib, Muhammad's son-in-law, is buried there, in the world-famous Imam Ali Mosque. Because of its historical significance, Najaf has become one of the holiest and most important cities in Islam, and the spiritual center of Shiite Islam, because Imam Ali was not just the son-in-law of the Prophet Mohammad, he is also seen as the first leader of the Shias. The city holds such a revered place in Islam that even Iran's Grand Ayatollah Ruhollah Khomeini chose to live in exile there from 1964 to 1978.

Under normal circumstances, Najaf is a pretty city situated on a plateau "with boulevards lined by trees, arched brick buildings, and streets filled with bearded clerics wearing white or black turbans."[15] Its huge cemetery and the Shia shrines at its center mark the city physically and psychologically. Thousands of the faithful visit the city to pray at the breathtaking mausoleum of Hazrat Ali. In 2004, it was a city of over 550,000 people and, because of its religious importance, it became a significant flashpoint for non-Sunni insurgent actions against the new IIG and, even more unfortunately, the site of some of the most intense fighting of the summer.

Muqtada al-Sadr chose to fight in Najaf for a reason. His father had lived and taught there, becoming one of the most revered Shia leaders in Iraq before he was assassinated, along with two of his sons, by Saddam Hussein's henchmen. The elder al-Sadr's influence had always radiated from the city of Najaf, but his surviving son first came to prominence as the leader of the Mahdi Militia in the Sadr City area of Baghdad. Sadr City was an extremely poor Shia enclave in the capital city, where his words found fertile soil and his appeal grew to national significance.

Yet, on April 10, 2003, it was in much more prosperous Najaf that Muqtada al-Sadr's actions first became linked to the nascent insurgency.[16] On that date some of his followers allegedly assassinated the chief cleric of the Imam Ali Shrine in a dispute over the keys to the mosque. By September 2003, after coalition forces moved into the area of Najaf,[17] Sadr began calling for the overthrow of the CPA and had set up his own shadow Iraqi government in the Sadr City area of Baghdad. Coalition forces had their hands full in the huge, densely populated city of Baghdad, and in Najaf, a lack of reconstruction project funding and Mahdi Militia efforts combined to discourage pilgrims. The resulting downturn in tourism produced an economic slump and disappointment with the coalition.[18] Sadr took full advantage of these difficulties to press his agenda with the dissatisfied in both cities. By the following spring, in March 2004, his rhetoric had become so extreme that the CPA shut down his newspaper, which only served to worsen the situation.

As a result of Muqtada al-Sadr's continuing vocal opposition and the worsening economic conditions, open fighting broke out between Mahdi Militia elements and government forces in early April in Najaf, Sadr City, and even in Basra. Ambassador Bremer declared Sadr an outlaw the next day, based largely on his alleged participation in the murders of two prominent Najafis, Imam Abdul Majid al-Khoei and rival Shia leader Ayatollah Sayed Mohammed Baqir al-Hakim. The conflict in Najaf soon proved too great for the local Iraqi Security Forces to handle and the Multinational Corps-Iraq (MNC-I) commander, General Metz, assigned the 2nd Armored Cavalry Regiment (2ndACR) to the region for over 2 months. Najaf province is too large for even an armored cavalry regiment to maintain order, so 2ndACR concentrated its operations on security of the main supply routes outside the old city of Najaf and countering the Mahdi Militia.

Luckily for the coalition, Grand Ayatollah Ali al-Sistani[19] stepped in to effectively mediate the violence caused by al-Sadr's militiamen, and a truce was developed on June 4. The truce permitted the Mahdi Militia to remain in the city and called for restrictions on the employment of coalition forces in the area.[20] Similar to the truce that had ended operation Vigilant Resolve; these conditions satisfied few and permitted antigovernment forces to retain the initiative.

Under the guidance of the most respected of Shia leaders, and with certain rights provided by the truce agreement, al-Sadr went to ground for nearly 2 months, resurfacing only in early August, after stating yet again his opposition to the government. Sadr publicly boycotted an important Sunni conference, signaling his renewed effort to gain attention, and the Mahdi Militia stepped up their activities against local security forces around Iraqi. Sadr's spokesman called for revolution and claimed his supporters controlled four provinces in the country.[21] They even attacked a newly arrived element of the 11th Marine Expeditionary Unit (11th MEU) on Monday, August 2.[22] The situation peaked again when Iraqi policemen and MNF forces were forced to surround al-Sadr's home and counterattack enemy forces on August 5 in response to a significant attack by Mahdi Militiamen on the main Najaf police station the night before.[23]

When attacked by members of the Mahdi Militia, the Najafi police called for Iraqi Army support, and by the early hours of Thursday morning, U.S. Marines from the 11th MEU were called in by the provincial governor as well.[24] Officially, the Mahdi Militia claimed the altercation was instigated by the police, but regardless of the real cause (the Mahdi Militia had been operating outside the exclusion zone, kidnapping members of the Iraqi security forces and conducting harassing attacks in violation of the truce,[25] acts they claimed to be defense of the city against coalition encroachment), the confrontation resulted in heavy gunfire, mortar, and grenade blasts – significantly more resistance than the local police could handle.

In response to the militia attack on the police station, the Marines had first deployed an antiarmor team and then a mechanized quick reaction force, including

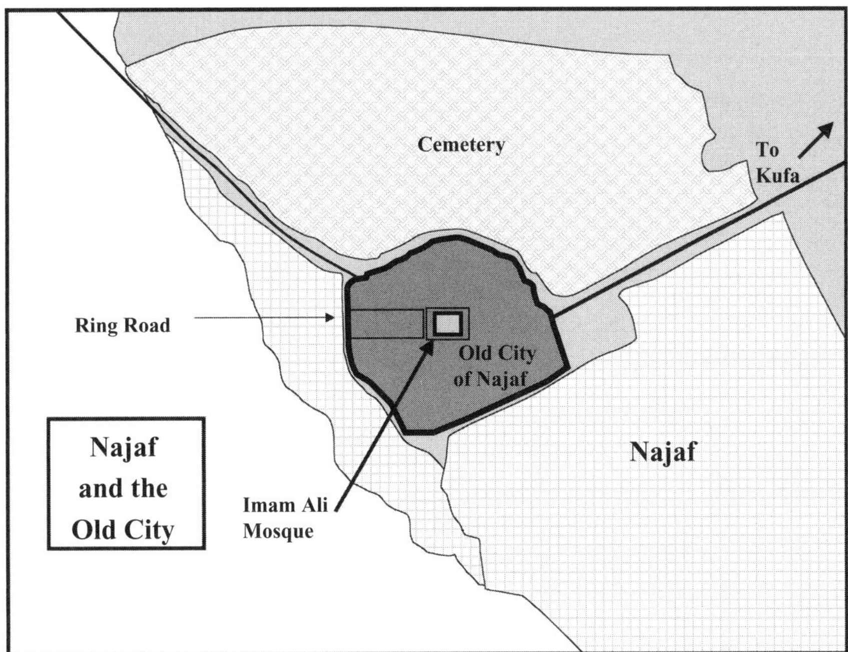

Map 4. Najaf and the Old City

armored vehicles and tanks. When the fighting continued to escalate, a section of AH-1 Cobra and UH-1 Huey helicopters was assigned to provide close air support. A UH-1 helicopter was soon shot down by the militia and a reinforced infantry company was then quickly deployed to reinforce the Marines in the fight.[26] A lesson well learned previously by the Marines was the need to act rapidly and decisively in combat, charging "to the sound of the guns." Finally, provincial Governor Adnan al-Ziruffi ordered the local Iraqi National Guard and police forces to seal off Kufa and Najaf in response to reports that busloads of Mahdi Militia were traveling from Baghdad to fight in Najaf.

Some thought the use of such force would intimidate al-Sadr and deter his continued antigovernmental rhetoric, but in fact his followers grew ever more militant as additional force was applied. Al-Sadr himself urged a cease-fire as had occurred in Fallujah in April, but Governor Ziruffi rejected al-Sadr's call. Ziruffi, along with many others, had been soured by the failure to resolve the issue earlier and remained convinced that Sadr would respond only to force. "Once he was convinced the Interim Iraqi Government and the coalition forces were decisively engaged, he wanted the job finished."[27] Instead of folding, however, the Mahdi Militia mounted stronger-than-expected opposition and the level of fighting continued to increase.

COMBAT OPERATIONS IN THE SHIA SOUTH: THE LION OF NAJAF

Back at Camp Fallujah, the MEF had not anticipated such hard fighting in Najaf province. Outside of al-Sadr's actions, that part of Iraq had been relatively quiet, and the Spanish contingent of the coalition based there had encountered little trouble with the local Najafis after the fall of the Saddam regime. Yet, in reaction to the significant threat posed by the antigovernment Mahdi Militia, the 11th MEU was soon called on by General Metz to conduct full-scale offensive operations to defeat al-Sadr's forces in Najaf and restore normal civil authority in the city. Normally, the MEF would have had only a fatherly interest in the MEU's taskings, as 11th MEU worked directly for General Metz, but with the potential of significant combat operations, General Conway recommended that the MEU and indeed the entire province of Najaf be "chopped"[28] to MEF control.[29]

Over the following weeks, in the first sustained urban combat since the previous April operations in Fallujah, MEF and coalition forces under the tactical control of 11th MEU eventually destroyed or expelled the well-entrenched elements of the Mahdi Militia from Najaf and did so without damaging the holy Imam Ali Shrine and Mosque complex. Perhaps most importantly, the fighting in Najaf showed a new Iraqi military capability for the first time and witnessed several other improvements that would prove critical to all future operations in Iraq, including those to come in Fallujah.

The 11th MEU had only just begun getting established in the province when the confrontation with al-Sadr exploded into large-scale fighting.[30] At the time, it included only one battalion of infantry, the 1st Battalion, 4th Marines (known as BLT 1/4 once the normal compliment of Marine reconnaissance, tanks, and armored vehicle units were integrated with the infantry) commanded by Lieutenant Colonel John L. Mayer. The MEU commander, Colonel Tony Haslem, soon understood that he needed more "boots on the ground" to deal with the ever-worsening situation in such a large city.

Combat continued through Thursday, August 5 and into August 6, resulting in a company-size attack by Alpha Company, BLT 1/4, in the Najaf cemetery.[31] The combat in the difficult terrain of the cemetery was intense and unforgiving. The site was huge, the Mahdi Militia were fanatical defenders, and the hundreds of monuments (many of which were busted and broken) made fighting there hell, foot by dirty, terrible foot. Understanding the importance of the fighting in Najaf, General Metz approved the reinforcement of the MEU by forces from the 1st Cavalry Division in Baghdad.

On August 7, Task Force 1-5 Cavalry (TF 1-5) arrived from the Iraqi capital to reinforce the 11th MEU and its single infantry battalion. Meanwhile, the local Iraqi National Guard forces led a second Iraqi operation to raid a Sadr safe house in Najaf. This engagement resulted in four enemy killed and the capture of two other members of the Mahdi Militia. Downtown, BLT 1/4 reached its limit of advance, and John Meyer was able to pull Alpha Company out to rest and refit after the horror of the initial cemetery contest.

Through its immediate and aggressive fighting, the BLT seemed initially to have broken the back of the most organized resistance by the Militia. The next day, TF 1-5 cleared the remainder of the Najaf cemetery and encountered little to no resistance moving into the central area of the city. On Monday, August 9, the MEF officially assumed control of 11th MEU and the other coalition forces with the arrival of the MEF forward command element, commanded by the MEF deputy commanding general, Brigadier General Dennis J. Hejlik. Upon his arrival, and for the duration of operations in and around Najaf, General Hejlik and Colonel Haslem conducted rounds of sustained peace negotiations with representatives of the IIG and Mahdi Militia officials while still planning and supervising smaller-scale combat operations. The goal was to minimize the effects of the confrontation on the people of the region. An initial cessation of hostilities was planned for the following Wednesday, August 11.

As further reinforcement, TF 2-7 Cavalry arrived at Forward Operating Base Duke outside of Najaf on August 10. On August 11, the MNF units were again engaged by AIF in the southwest, northwest, and northeast portions of the city.[32] It was clear that the Mahdi Militia would not adhere to any peace. General Hejlik put TF 2-7 into the fight resulting in a three-battalion advance on the Imam Ali Shrine complex at the heart of the symbolic city beginning at 6:45 in the morning. On Thursday, August 12, after 1 full week of combat, units from BLT 1/4 and members of the 405th Iraqi National Guard Battalion conducted another raid near al-Sadr's house to destroy known AIF in the area and gather intelligence information. They attacked and cleared four buildings against a platoon-size enemy armed with small arms, sniper rifles, and mortars, resulting in 3 enemy killed and 18 militia wounded.[33] Later analysis of the information found in al-Sadr's house (numerous documents, computer hard drives, and other material) produced much valuable intelligence implicating him and his key leaders in the worst acts of the Militia.

Also on Thursday, the 11th MEU, in support of the Iraqi 36th Commando Battalion and the new Iraqi Counter-Terrorism Force (ICTF), conducted a direct action mission in the Sahlah Mosque in nearby Kufa. Marines from BLT 1/4 provided an exterior cordon around the site, while members of the 36th Commando and ICTF established an inner cordon around the mosque and conducted the actual assault into the building, killing three and capturing eight Mahdi Militia.

A second cessation of hostilities was directed by General Metz on Friday, August 13 and some reports indicated that al-Sadr had been wounded in the fighting the day before, so most thought the uprising would wind down by the weekend. But that was not to be. Clearly, religion and anticoalition fervor served as an effective motivator for the Mahdi Militia, and the conflict in Najaf demonstrated true commitment on the part of Allawi's IIG. On the first meeting day of the new Iraqi National Assembly, the government ordered the reinforcement of the coalition in Najaf province with a battalion of the new Iraqi Intervention Force (IIF).

On Sunday, August 15, both TF 1-5 and TF 2-7 were engaged numerous times by direct and indirect militia weapon systems.[34] Both U.S. units returned fire, killing or wounding a host of the enemy. Later that day, Governor Ziruffi announced that the Provincial Council had voted to oust the Mahdi Militia and had demanded that al-Sadr's forces leave Najaf. Sporadic fighting continued with members of the Mahdi Militia intentionally using mosques and the Imam Ali Shrine area as safe havens from which to attack coalition forces. In response to the increasing combat and the need for maximizing the effects of firepower in the city, a Restricted Fire Area (RFA) was created by the MEF to ensure the protection of the holy sites in the center of Najaf. By creating such a fire control measure, aviation and artillery fires could be employed with greater precision, yet enemy fighters could still be freely engaged elsewhere.

On Tuesday, August 17, Alpha Company of BLT 1/4, back in the fight and attached to TF 2-7, conducted a destruction raid on a suspected enemy weapons cache site in Najaf, while Charlie Company, TF 2-7, conducted a second destruction raid on another suspected enemy stronghold nearby. These raids resulted in the capture of one militiaman and discovery of another significant weapons cache. The same day, at the request of Army Lieutenant Colonel Jim Rainey, the commander of TF 2-7, Marine fixed-wing aviation assets engaged an enemy mortar position near the hotel district within the Old City of Najaf.

The combat intensity increased again on August 18, which saw sustained engagements involving every battalion attached to the 11th MEU. TF 1-5 was engaged with enemy RPGs in the cemetery. Alpha Company, TF 2-7, received heavy machine gun, small arms, and RPG fire from a building just inside the ring road. After Bravo Company of BLT 1/4 was engaged by mortar fire, aviation assets surgically destroyed the mortar system, which been located within the RFA.[35] Reinforced by Iraqi National Guard, the local Iraqi police established a TCP for all traffic approaching the ring road and finally succeeded in containing the Mahdi Militiamen inside the center sector of the city. On Friday, August 20, in response to enemy mortar fire directed at TF 1-5 in the cemetery, an AC-130 Specter gunship was employed with telling effect to accurately destroy the enemy position. The AC-130 soon became the fire support system of choice inside the tightest zones of the city.

The following day, Alpha Company of BLT 1/4 conducted a raid in Kufa to clear a former Iraqi police station that had been taken over by insurgents. In support of this raid, Bravo Company attacked by fire into a nearby Mahdi Militia checkpoint. The 2nd Platoon of Alpha Company and BLT 1/4's reconnaissance platoon established a screening line to prevent any enemy egress from Kufa to the south. Again, an AC-130 gunship, in coordination with attack helicopters, put extremely effective fire on the target during the attack. Both objectives were secured with an estimated 45 enemy killed and another 30 captured.

Why the Mahdi Militia continued to fight against such continued coalition success is difficult to determine. They may have been emboldened by the earlier success in Fallujah, or they may have benefited from a higher level of organizational cohesion inspired by their religious fervor. In any case, al-Sadr did not try to limit the combat and the members of his militia continued to fight day after day, taking serious losses without a major victory. Slowed encircled and then cut off from outside support, al-Sadr's forces had no fighting chance against the combined efforts of the Marine and Army units and those of the Iraqi military and police. Even worse, the local Najafis, who had never been very supportive of the militia's activities, grew increasingly opposed to their actions. Changing popular support is of course the key to success in any insurgency, and after the weekend of August 21 and 22, al-Sadr's hopes in Najaf were pointless without popular support.

Sunday, August 22 saw TF 1-5, reinforced by elements of BLT 1/4, conducting a probing attack on the western portion of a prominent parking garage near the shrine that had been used continuously as a base by the Mahdi insurgents. The probing element encountered heavy resistance, centered mainly on the buildings to the southwest of the parking garage. The trusty AC-130 aircraft, which had been prosecuting targets of opportunity on the western end of the parking garage and surrounding buildings, was used to engage a mortar position. After TF 2-7 received sniper fire from four buildings to the east of the RFA, aviation assets destroyed those targets also, killing several more members of the Militia.

Despite rumors of Iraqi peace talks, the fighting continued on Monday, August 23, with TF 2-7 receiving both RPG and heavy machine-gun fire from the northern end of the Old City. The AC-130 Specter was again employed to destroy the enemy fire. Following an RPG and small arms fire attack on TF 1-5 from west of the Imam Ali Shrine, artillery fire destroyed a second target close by. The following day TF 2-7, TF 1-5, and BLT 1/4 all conducted limited-objective attacks in their respective zones inside the city. They were supported by 155-millimeter artillery, AC-130 gunships, AV-8B Harrier aircraft, F-18 fighters, and AH-1W Cobra helicopters. TF 2-7 came in contact immediately and executed numerous close air support (CAS) missions. Hellfire missiles and several rockets helped the TF take buildings in the eastern portion of the Old City of Najaf. TF 1-5 engaged the enemy with tank main gun, 25-millimeter chain gun, and heavy machine-gun fire. Following those attacks, TF 1-5 moved south into the Old City to conduct a reconnaissance by force. TF 1-5 encountered a deliberate obstacle with imbedded IEDs and sporadic RPG and small arms fire. Again, an AC-130 aircraft was brought in to engage the obstacles, which resulted in a large secondary explosion and the partial reduction of the enemy obstacle. The AC-130 gunship also engaged a bus near the garage complex. BLT 1/4 successfully cleared their zone with little contact, forcing a Mahdi Militia retreat south and east, where the 36th Commando conducted preplanned ambush, resulting in numerous enemy casualties.

On August 24, a UH-1N Huey helicopter employed a Bright Star laser designator in Najaf for the first time in combat. The aircraft designated a building that housed 5 to 15 Mahdi Militia and a possible antiaircraft gun. The building and enemy were destroyed by Hellfire missiles, from an AH-1W Cobra helicopter, which were employed in conjunction with the Bright Star laser. On August 24, TF 2-7 established attack by fire positions around the eastern side of the ring road to support the pending BLT 1/4 attack south through the cemetery and into the northwest corner of the Old City. Two key buildings were seized, followed by systematic clearing of Mahdi Militia forces throughout the night. In support of this attack and the final assault planned for August 26, 2004, several key targets were engaged by fixed-wing aviation assets. To help shape the conditions for the final assault on the shrine and mosque, GBU-12s (500-pound bombs) and GBU-31s (2,000-pound bombs) were delivered on key buildings that housed Mahdi Militia with superb results. During this final decisive assault over 50 enemy fighters were killed, and the coalition forces suffered 13 wounded in action (WIA).[36]

Sporadic fighting continued throughout the morning and into the early afternoon of Thursday, August 26, 3 weeks into the fighting. BLT 1/4 again attacked the Mahdi Militia through the northwest corner of the Old City. Alpha Company attacked toward the east and tied in with TF 1-5 near the intersection of the ring road and Route Nova. TF 2-7 attacked from east to west in its sector of the city. By 3 P.M., the Imam Ali Shrine and Mosque were surrounded and final planning continued on decisive actions to storm the site.[37] However, General Metz, the new commanding general of MNC-I, released an order directing MEF to cease offensive operations in Najaf to allow Iraqi political and religious officials the opportunity to peaceably resolve the removal of Mahdi Militia from the Imam Ali Shrine and Mosque complex. On August 27, the Grand Ayatollah Sistani received the keys to the Imam Ali Shrine and Mosque complex, finally signaling the end of hostilities in Najaf.

THE SCHOOLHOUSE OF NAJAF

The combat operations in Najaf were characterized by intense and close combat. Infantry fought at close range through a huge cemetery, honeycombed with tunnels, crypts, and other concealed positions. Even so, close air support and main tank direct fire enabled ground units to dislodge Mahdi Militia from improved fighting positions in the cemetery and buildings around the mosques. During the entire 24 days of combat in Najaf, MEF forces suffered relatively light casualties but killed an estimated 1,500 of the enemy.

The defeat of the enemy in Najaf represented the beginning of the end for the organized Mahdi Militia insurgency and the marginalization of a dangerous militant Shia insurgent movement, a strategic outcome that later helped shape future combat operations in Fallujah and encouraged Shia support for a national election to follow later in the year. It was particularly significant that the Iraqi security forces played such a prominent role in the action. The combat operations in Najaf demonstrated conclusively that some Iraqi military units could hold their own in high-intensity combat alongside their American counterparts. In fact, they could be entrusted to conduct limited independent operations – to secure mosques and other sensitive targets. The 36th Commando Battalion and the ICTF proved themselves in combat.

Integration of U.S. Marine and Army units also proved easy and powerful. The two Army Task Forces integrated very well into the MEU operations and were highly interoperable with BLT 1/4. MEF command and control, using the forward command post over the full distance from Camp Fallujah, also worked very well. Finally, although the urban combat in Fallujah had proven the effectiveness of the U.S. weapons systems, it was really in the tight quarters of the cemetery and Old City of Najaf that coalition, combined arms tactics, and techniques really proved their viability.

Muqtada al-Sadr had attempted to spark Shia opposition to the newly formed IIG and set fire to Iraq. He did so at a very weak period for the IIG in the war, but his movement failed to gain decisive support among the people because he chose to employ tactics that only brought more death and destruction to the country. He wanted to become a religious lion in a very holy city and remake the future. But he was firmly and decisively confronted by the coalition, and his methods were sufficiently exposed by Prime Minister Allawi so that his fellow Shia rejected the vision he proposed for the future of Iraq. Al-Sadr never became the "lion" of Najaf, and his failure helped prepare the government's path and reinforced Allawi's conviction for decisive action in Fallujah.

SUMMER HEAT IN FALLUJAH

The situation in and around Fallujah had only grown worse during the summer months.[38] In fact, a major shift in the coalition's approach to the city occurred when Lieutenant Colonel Suleiman of the 506th Iraqi National Guard was kidnapped and killed by insurgents in downtown Fallujah. Suleiman was one of the two local National Guard battalion commanders and was the first truly aggressive Iraqi officer to make a mark through his efforts to return order to Fallujah. When he confronted Omar Hadid in early August over the abduction of one of his officers, Suleiman was kidnapped and tortured to death. It was clear at the time that Abdullah Janabi and Hadid were collaborating with Zarqawi to establish a jihadist state in Fallujah.[39] The murder caused the MNF leadership and a few key members of the IIG to determine that no local success was likely by Iraqis in the city. From that point forward the MNF focus of effort was to restore the peace through military means. The concurrent operation in Najaf had demonstrated for the first time that some Iraqi forces would fight against insurgents, but only if they were recruited from other areas of Iraq and only if they were closely integrated with MNF units. This was an important lesson that would play significantly in the success of operations in Fallujah in the fall.

Chapter Four

Shaping Operations Prior to the Assault

With the clear lessons of operation Vigilant Resolve and the combat in Najaf in mind, the MEF realized that the continuing threat from Fallujah might never be solved through negotiations and that plans for a second, more decisive, military assault needed to be refined. From the MEF's operational perspective, two key improvements desired in any future operation would be an effort to split the AIF from their popular support base and a parallel, reinforcing effort designed to draw the civilian population out of the city in advance of any fighting to save innocent lives and minimize negative reactions from the international media. Over the fall months, splitting out the enemy and protecting the civilian population became just as important in preparing for combat as more traditional actions, such as building logistics stockpiles and developing actionable intelligence.

If the population of Fallujah voluntarily left their homes, it would benefit the MNF in three critical ways. First, the incidence of civilian casualties would be lowered significantly, and that would in turn reduce the chances that political leaders in both the United States and Iraq would be pressured to stop the assault prior to accomplishing all of the objectives of the operation. Second, the AIF forces would be increasingly less well hidden and less well sheltered by innocent civilians. Thus, precision targeting could have a greater effect during operations in the city. Finally, the "shaping actions" (unit feints around the city, probing operations, loudspeaker activities, and even public statements by key officials) had a tendency to draw out enemy fighters so that they could be positively identified and attacked. On many occasions ground forces would make feints along the south and eastern sides of the city to draw out the enemy defensive forces and allow the MEF to identify their key leaders, defensive structures, and command and control nodes.

Finally, the shaping actions of the MNF would help deceive the enemy as to the actual point of the attack. The key members of the insurgent leadership could have no doubt that the attack would come, but the constant probing effort of units night after night during the shaping phase helped convince them that the main attack would come again from the south and east, as had been the case in operation Vigilant Resolve the previous April.

STRATEGIC TIMING

By mid-September, the level of insurgent opposition in Fallujah was so visible and so defiant that something had to be done if the IIG of Prime Minister Allawi was to have any credibility as a partner in the war on terror and any claim of returning security in Iraq. The irony was that the Fallujah terrorist enclave was so prominent that it called attention to itself as a symbol of terrorist opposition to the United States and its coalition partners. Its success spelled its own defeat. If Allawi was to direct the action against Fallujah, and it appeared he had the guts and political power to do so, then the coalition military leadership needed to give him advice concerning the timing and scope of the action required to purge the city of the enemy.

It was clear to most military planners that the operation to free Fallujah had to take place during one of three different periods of time, each driven by different but equally dominant strategic reasons. The U.S. elections in early November, the Iraqi elections in late January, and the Ramadan Islamic holy period were unrealistic times for combat operations to start. Political leaders were just not likely to order an attack during those sensitive periods of time. This fact made the last week of September, the second week of November, and the last week of December the only times that an assault of over 2 weeks in duration could be conducted without having a direct and negative effect on one of the elections. With a possibility that the attack could be directed as early as the first period in late September, the MEF stepped up its targeting campaign at midmonth to increase the pressure on the insurgent leadership and begin to shape the tactical fight.

One of the most significant problems facing the MEF planners was a lack of useful, recent intelligence concerning insurgent actions in Fallujah. Because they were not patrolling in the city and could not fly over or insert human intelligence agents into the city, their understanding of the exact locations and activities of the enemy were severely restricted. In fact, members of the MNF had far less information about what was going on inside Fallujah than they had concerning the actions of the Republican Guard under Saddam in the first phase of the fighting. Over time, the MEF G2, under the leadership of Colonel Ron Makuta, developed some Iraqi sources of intelligence inside the city, but the most valuable source of information about insurgent actions over the fall turned out to be the insurgent's responses to the MEF's shaping campaign.

One of the most difficult challenges of the battle was the effort to separate the residents of the city from the insurgents who were living there by night and attacking the multinational forces by day. It is certainly true that many Fallujahns supported the insurgency, at least passively. The city had always been a hotbed of unruly conservatism; many of the residents were unhappy with the displacement of Saddam Hussein, and many more were opposed to any presence of foreigners in there city. So there were many who would be inclined to support the insurgency at least with giving information, shelter, or material to individual insurgents. Certainly, too, several well-known leaders of the insurgency, among them Omar Hadid, Abdullah al-Janabi, and Abu Mousab al-Zarqawi, were known to live in and have free run of the city. Their supporters brought money and business to the city. The leaders of Fallujah appeared to side with the insurgents. They had frequently negotiated for the insurgents during the spring and provided other forms of low-level support for the anti-MNF operations.

Still, many residents of Fallujah were not active in the insurgency and even those that did provide passive support frequently did so simply as a means of livelihood. Iraq by the summer of 2004 was a sovereign country, and although some discount its freedom of action, the IIG was making the majority of the key decisions in the day-to-day management of the country. The MNF and the U.S. embassy wanted very much to keep public support for the IIG strong and to demonstrate the de facto Iraqi control of the nation's affairs. The law of war clearly requires the safeguarding of innocent noncombatants from the destruction of war. One of the lessons learned most painfully during the April fighting in the city was the power of the international lobby and the negative impact of images of civilian injuries during modern urban warfare. Finally, the support of the local residents would certainly be crucial for any posthostilities reconstruction effort and the eventual return of the region to normalcy. Therefore, there were many practical reasons to spare local residents of the city from the risks of fighting.

Although the rationale for sparing the residents was evident to most senior coalition leaders, the actual process of protecting them from lethal firepower was much more difficult to develop. The devil was always in the details. No one really knew how many Iraqis lived in Fallujah; estimates ranged from 240,000 to nearly 400,000. No census records existed and the normal baseline for estimating population in Iraq (the family food card system resulting from the Oil for Food program) was wildly inaccurate. The Iraqi Ministry of Trade (MOT) had issued some 24,000 food cards to families who claimed Fallujah as their home city. Notionally, these cards were designed to allocate food to all the members of an Iraqi family living in one "household," but even very senior ministry representatives used different numbers when they were asked how many people lived in an average household. In the west most families range in number from 4 to 6 members, but in Iraq the planning figure varied from 10 to 16 members per household. Even this large variation did not accurately account for the "residents" of Fallujah who actually lived in other cities and were driven into the anti-MNF enclave by the insurgency itself.

Using a midrange planning figure of 300,000 residents, it quickly became obvious that caring for so many civilians would tax the resources of the whole nation. Although many believed that Iraq would return to being a prosperous nation soon after the fall of Saddam because the country was rich in oil natural resources, the facts were that in Iraq in 2004 the infrastructure was too old and poorly maintained to support event the most basic needs of the Iraqi people. Electric service was intermittent, fuel was in short supply, and even food and medicines were often lacking in parts of the country. So it would have been a huge burden on the government if it had to care for the residents of Fallujah for long. The dramatic increase in the availability of luxury items such as cars and cell phones only increased the burden on the archaic systems that provided basic, essential services.

The fractious Iraqi cultural and religious climate only added complexity to the situation. Sunnis were still out of favor and resented by the majority Shia population. Fallujah was a symbol of Sunni influence and the near Taliban-like approaches of the religious leadership of the city (under the influence of Janabi) only increased the reluctance of the national government in Baghdad to work with the Fallujahns. Prime Minister Allawi did maintain a dialog and even negotiated directly with key members of the city "leadership," but even he was frustrated with the lack of progress toward a reduction in the opposition rhetoric. The "leaders" of the city were in reality just frontmen for insurgents who had no desire to produce anything other than death and destruction.

Once the requirement to spare the population became an accepted planning factor, the MEF had to consider practical ways of shielding the population from the effects of battle. The easiest way to do that would be to force the residents from their homes and leave only the insurgents in the city. This concept was legally dubious and impractical. Any effort to force the population from the city would not only result in a very negative international reaction but would also place the onus for sheltering and feeding those "displaced" by MNF direction back on the coalition. Although widely assumed to have excess capacity for personnel support, in fact, the MNF barely had enough resources to support even 10,000 displaced civilians, and that support would be provided largely by contracted agencies at exorbitant prices. Thus, it was not feasible for the military to simply direct an evacuation of the city because the MNF did not have the resources to care for the population that would be forced from its homes. Additionally, any forced evacuation would undoubtedly give the insurgents a huge target and easy escape from the city, not to mention painting the MNF as a brutal occupier.

MINIMIZING DAMAGE

Any modern military action requires the judicious application of combat power, but combat in an urban area demands a great deal of effort if damage to civilians and nonmilitary infrastructure is to be prevented. This is most complex when airpower and indirect (artillery and mortar) fire are concerned. The fight in Fallujah involved some of the most extensive firepower in recent history, so the development of the targeting process deserves to be explained.

The MEF targeting process was designed to integrate both lethal (kinetic) fires and nonlethal fires. Lethal firepower most normally included aircraft delivered bombs, artillery[1] and rockets, artillery and mortar fire, and less commonly used tank and machine-gun fires delivered from the immediate outskirts of the city. Nonlethal fires included all those things the military could use to influence the actions of the enemy, but most commonly involved media statement and communications.

The MNF had been firing on targets in Fallujah for months, and even with a shortfall in quality intelligence by September, had built a fair database of both potential targets and places that needed to be protected. Unfortunately, the earlier fighting in April had resulted in some very extensive restrictions on the employment of indirect fires into the city. Partially because operation Vigilant Resolve ended in a cease-fire and partially because of the huge degree of international scrutiny Fallujah had generated, most artillery- and aircraft-delivered fires into the city had to be personally approved by the senior U.S. military commander in Iraq – General George Casey. Even then each proposed fire mission had to be gauged against criteria for collateral damage. If the damage from a chosen weapons system on a given target was too high, regardless of the importance of the target, approval was required from the U.S. Secretary of Defense.[2] Given current planning technologies, these restrictions would not have been too onerous on static preplanned targets; however, many of the emerging targets revealed in Fallujah occurred on very short notice. With no visibility at the street level and little reliable overhead observation, when an enemy weapons system or cell leader was discovered, the permission to attack that target was required very quickly.

The G3 operations section of the MEF staff, lead by Colonel Mike Regner, was the center of the MEF targeting coordination and approval process. By September, his staff was highly skilled, as much had been learned during the fighting in April and later in Najaf that helped make the fires section of that staff particularly responsive. Due to his recent experience in Najaf, with its complex urban fires issues, it made great sense to have Brigadier General Hejlik lead the command's coordination of fires efforts and chair the nightly 8 P.M. MEF targeting board, where all subordinate commands of the MEF contributed to develop the most effective plan for the employment of both kinetic and non-kinetic fires. Late every night, once all the targeting coordination was done, the MEF commander, General Sattler, formally approved the targets scheduled for the next day. Although he was frequently wakened during the night for required modifications, or to seek higher command approval of unanticipated or emerging targets, overall this system worked very well for the entire MEF.

A classic example of this system in action was the berm attacks on suspected IEDs buried in earthen embankments in Fallujah. Although initially the MEF commander had to seek higher approval for fires inside Fallujah, over time the MEF demonstrated such expertise with the targeting that greater and greater freedom was earned. The earthen berms that were being constructed in the city were clearly efforts by the insurgents to fortify their positions, and they would have become great obstacles if, early in the October shaping period, General Sattler and his targeteers had not chosen to attack the berms as threats. As time passed the MEF gained valuable intelligence from the secondary explosions that resulted from taking the berms out all around the city of Fallujah. After these strikes the insurgents had many fewer defenses and the attacking battalions knew very well to expect IEDs inside insurgent defensive networks.

Of course, these strikes, particularly the ones on emerging terrorist targets in the city, were bound to have negative information value for the enemy, who had demonstrated a facile ability to use every bit of negative publicity to limit the MEF's freedom of action. With each strike, there was always a chance of Iraqi casualties and the terrorist-supportive staff at the Fallujah General Hospital was always willing to publicize any injuries, no matter how loosely related to the MNF fires.[3] In one case an ambulance from the hospital was used to ferry weapons inside the city during a feint. As the ambulance, when used uniquely to transport weapons, was a lawful target, the MEF commander approved a strike on the vehicle. The insurgents later showed photos of a bullet-ridden ambulance with many wounded Iraqis, when, in actuality, the weapon system used to strike the ambulance was a laser-guided bomb.

There were instances when innocent Iraqis were injured or killed as a result of MNF fires in the city. Although all targets and weapons systems were carefully weighed, warfare is so unpredictable that no process designed to minimize collateral damage can anticipate everything. On at least one occasion the MEF was able to identify a known terrorist and some bodyguards staying nightly in a local house. The insurgents were monitored for several days and permission was obtained to use a laser-guided bomb to destroy the house in the early hours of the morning after the insurgents returned there one night. Although the resulting attack did not damage any of the homes flanking the dwelling where the insurgents were sheltered, the target planners had no way of knowing that a few other Iraqis were being kept in the house by the insurgents.

SHAPING THE BATTLESPACE –THE PLANNING PHASE

Formal planning for an assault on Fallujah began on September 10. The MNC-I staff at Camp Victory in Baghdad conducted a video teleconference (VTC) with key MEF and 4th Civil Affairs Group (CAG) planners. The stated objective of the VTC was to pass down Fallujah mission analysis products from MNC-I and discuss the commander's planning guidance provided by Lieutenant General Tom Metz (III Corps and MNC-I commander and Lieutenant General Sattler's immediate operational boss). That conference was immediately followed by a detailed collaborative planning session between MNC-I and MEF staff members, including representatives from the MEF subordinate commands.

By September 13, the critical tasks for both combat and posthostility stabilization operations had been roughed out. Given the experience of the April attack in Fallujah, the planners identified requirement for a "branch plan" to address the high potential for civilians in the battlespace. Information operations was acknowledged as a weak capability and the knotty problem of isolating the insurgents while keeping MEF supplies flowing was also identified as a concern.

From the very beginning, the planners put their cultural perspectives and lessons learned during previous combat operations into effect. Every critical task identified had to pass a four-question test: (1) How do the Iraqis view this action? (2) Is it culturally acceptable? (3) Can the Iraqis sustain this effort? And, finally, (4) does it help in a transition to full Iraqi control of their country? With such questions as a guide, all the work that went into developing the military situation in Fallujah was aimed at an eventual return of the city to an Iraqi municipal government free of terrorist influence. The MEF leadership had clearly modified its focus of effort to ensure all MNF military actions in the area were developed with Iraqi solutions in mind.

In the third week of September, key military planners from around the MEF had conducted mission analysis for operations in Fallujah and had developed a draft-protected target list to ensure key infrastructure was shielded from both intentional and unintended fires throughout the duration of the planned operation. The CAG had developed 10 conditions to turn over Fallujah to local control. On September 25, MNF-I released its order 306, entitled "Integrated Operations Prior to Ramadan." It stipulated that the MEF, in coordination with the Iraqi Security Forces, should conduct full-spectrum counterinsurgency operations to counter and neutralize FRE and foreign terrorist networks and eliminate their sanctuaries. That direction clearly made Fallujah an objective and pushed for decisive action prior to the end of November. General Sattler immediately flew to Baghdad to brief General Metz on phases two and three of the operation, then named Phantom Fury.

For 4 days after that briefing, the MEF staff took the follow-on guidance provided by Generals Metz and Sattler to develop an even more detailed concept for posthostilities in Fallujah. The 4th CAG civil affairs planners had a leading role in envisioning what the requirements for the interim government and security conditions needed to be to set conditions for the eventual transition of the city back to local Iraqi government control.

By the end of September, the MEF and its subordinate commands were clearly focused above all else on preparations for the fight for Fallujah. Although many other smaller operations were being conducted throughout western Iraq, the primary focus of effort was shaping the major fight around Fallujah and linking all other operations to support that goal. Because fighting an insurgency is much, much less precise than fighting a conventional campaign, significant effort was expended making sense out of the ever-changing mosaic of insurgent actions in the Al Anbar province and the adjoining areas of southwest Baghdad and Najaf that made up Area of Operations (AO) Atlanta – the MEF's area of responsibility.

Each morning at 7:30, the MEF commander, General Sattler, and his staff would meet in the combat operations center at Camp Fallujah for an overview briefing of the events of the previous 24 hours and any planned events for the day and in the near future. This brief not only informed the commander and helped focus the staff on the key issues from among the hundreds of details that had to be coordinated everyday but, most importantly, it also provided perspective from which to assess the effectiveness of the MEF counterinsurgency campaign. Sattler would enter the operations center and sit with his trusted deputy Brigadier General Hejlik on one side and his chief of staff Colonel John Coleman on the other. Filling out the first row were his intelligence chief, Colonel Makuta, and his director of operations, Colonel Regner. The brief began with quick summaries of the weather and the latest intelligence, and then rapidly covered the actions and readiness of the major subordinate units within AO Atlanta.

Thus, every day the MEF commander would review the actions of the enemy and those of his own units to analyze patterns and opportunities, risks, and concerns. Activities in and around Fallujah were only a portion of the brief, but as the weeks passed, the city received increasing attention. Of note, General Sattler maintained a particular focus on four less traditional military efforts that helped frame the campaign. These were (1) the progress of Iraqi security force development, (2) information operations, (3) media and important visitors to the area of operations, and (4) civil–military operations.

The enemy had been far from passive during the early days of September and maintained an unrelenting series of attacks on Marine positions throughout the month. Mortar rounds and rockets fell on Camp Fallujah, Camp Blue Diamond, and other Marine bases on a regular basis. Four Marines had been killed in western Iraq on September 3, and seven others died just north of Fallujah on September 6.[4] A solider assigned to the MEF, Army Private First Class Jason L. Sparks, was killed in Fallujah by insurgent fire on September 8[5] and two other Marines, including First Lieutenant Alexander Wetherbee, died in combat on September 12.[6] Two more Marines died as a result of hostile fire the following day, putting September well on its way to becoming one of the deadliest months of the war.[7] Even major bases were not immune from enemy attacks; as an example, one of the key ground commanders in the region, Colonel Larry Nicholson, was severely injured and his communications officer, Lieutenant Colonel Kevin M. Shea, was killed, by a rocket that penetrated their headquarters on Camp Fallujah on September 14 – the very day Colonel Nicholson had assumed command of the regiment from Colonel John Toolan.[8] Seventeen more Marines would die as the month wore on.[9]

General Sattler received a detailed brief on the operational planning from his key staff on October 1, during which he made some key decisions concerning command and control and the phasing of the operation. Among other issues, he agreed to assign the 4th CAG under the tactical control of the 1st Marine Division to ensure that the transition from active combat to posthostilities could be directly managed by the ground commander, in concert with the "three-block war" construct. He also concurred with the employment of the 31st MEU in the operation. Although some were disappointed that September had passed without an order to start the assault on the city, most members of the higher-level staffs knew well that much more work remained and that any available time was needed before any cohesive attack would be completely prepared.

One of the innovations of the Fallujah battle plan was the incorporation of the 31st MEU (which was still not in country) as the headquarters in charge of western Al Anbar and the border region, freeing up the 7th Marines headquarters, under Colonel Craig Tucker, and one of his battalions (1st Battalion, 8th Marines) to join in the tactical assault on the city. The infantry battalion assigned to the 31st MEU would also be brought to Fallujah for the attack and the aviation and combat service support elements of the MEU were integrated into the operations of the Marine Air Wing (MAW) and the Force Service Support Group (FSSG). Although such flexibility was not new, it brilliantly demonstrated the Marine Air Ground Task Force flexibility touted by the Marines.

The next day MNC-I released its Warning Order 15 for operation Phantom Fury, officially tasking the 31st MEU [which had been the U.S. Central Command (CENTCOM) theater strategic reserve] to support the operation. On October 3, MNF-I released its order outlining the required "Preconditions for Operations in Fallujah." Thus, the basic forces were assigned and the stage was set for more detailed planning in the first days of October.

The focus of the planning effort remained on the crucial transition from combat to posthostilities. MEF, CAG, MAW, FSSG, and Division planners met at Camp Blue Diamond to refine the combat tasks and build in requirements addressing the safeguarding of the civilian population. The planners recognized early the need for much more coordination with higher headquarters and the IIG, so a series of coordination meetings were scheduled to ensure all the supporting efforts needed in Fallujah were synchronized with the assault plan. While this planning effort continued at higher levels, everyday combat continued to take its horrible toll.[10]

On October 7, Colonel John Ballard and Lieutenant Colonels Mike Paulk and Kevin Hansen flew to Baghdad to brief the MNC-I and MNF-I civil–military operations staffs concerning the phase four requirements that had been developed by the planning effort at Camp Blue Diamond. Presenting key elements of their plan in advance to members of the MNC-I (III Corps) and MNF-I staffs permitted those staffs to accurately synchronize and leverage national resources and to begin an informed dialog at the staff level with certain key members of the embassy and Iraqi governments in Baghdad. These efforts in turn permitted the CAG and 1st Marine Division staffs to hone their expectations of civil–military action during the Fallujah operation.

With this additional level of detail established, MEF subordinate commands further expanded their plans. The Division refined the sequence of major operations and the key objectives to be secured along with the actions required of supporting forces around Fallujah. A key shortfall in military police and security units along with major road network outside of Fallujah was referred through the MEF to MNC-I for sourcing. A critical infrastructure review meeting was held at the CAG headquarters to finalize a protected target list with the input of the other MEF subordinate commands to include the MEF Engineer Group (MEG), the critically important Navy Seabees, and the Army Construction Engineers. At this point, because of sparse intelligence and civil information, the MEF still did not understand fully how the critical infrastructure inside Fallujah worked. This was important to make critical decisions concerning what could be targeted and what might need to be immediately reconstructed as the battle was ongoing. For example, the MEF submitted a request for additional information concerning the 10 water lift stations in the city because planners did not understand how they worked together to keep the city free of the waters of the Euphrates River, the level of which was higher than sections of southern Fallujah.

BATTLE PREPARATIONS

By October 18, the key elements of the plan had been completed and the 1st Marine Division commander, Major General Natonski, was able to conduct a rock-drill synchronization meeting of every action to be conducted by each of his subordinate commanders. After Natonski outlined his intent for the operation, his primary tactical commanders, Colonels Shupp and Tucker, walked through their regimental sequence of actions and supporting assault objectives. These descriptions of assault objectives were followed by Colonel Ballard's overview of the civil affairs effort and how it would be integrated to support the assault commander's objectives. Then the operations officer of the U.S. Army's Blackjack Brigade of the 1st Cavalry Division, which had recently been tasked with a supporting mission by MNC-I in response to the MEF's need for additional security forces around Fallujah, discussed how his brigade would assist in sealing off the objective area. This meeting, orchestrated by Lieutenant Colonel Joe L'etoile, the very capable Division G3, was the first time all the tactical commanders had met face to face to pull together the individual parts of the plan.

The result of this synchronization effort was 1st Marine Division fragmentary order number 363-04, released on October 21. It specified that at H-hour on D-day, the Division, reinforced by the CAG and the Blackjack Brigade, would attack "to destroy insurgent forces in Fallujah in support of the ISF in order to establish legitimate local control." The main attack was planned for November 8, and initial operations to set conditions for the main attack were scheduled to begin 24 hours prior to that on D-day, November 7.[11]

MNC-I fragmentary order 891 followed 2 days later, confirming the mission and adding emphasis on the role of the IIG.[12] It also included reference to the need to safeguard the Iraqi people, which became the next major planning issue to be addressed. The next day, October 24, the 4th CAG released its operations order, focusing on conducting CMO in support of the 1st Marine Division to minimize civilian interference in military operations, minimize human suffering, restore essential services, and establish the foundation for local Iraqi governance. Over the next few days, key planners met at Camp Fallujah to develop a concept of operations for handling dislocated civilians (DC) from Fallujah. This effort resulted in MNC-I accepting responsibility to build and run a displaced civilian camp near Fallujah, should large numbers of the population need food and shelter during the battle.[13]

During the final few days of October, the pace of events picked up even more. The MEF issued its final operations order for operation Phantom Fury stating the objective of "clearing enemy forces in order to allow legitimate governance, security, and reconstruction of the city." The 7th Marines headquarters and one infantry battalion had moved to nearby Camp Baharia, and the Blackjack Brigade had established its units at Camp Fallujah. That same day, the 4th CAG transferred to the tactical control of the 1st Marine Division, which shifted its forward command post to Camp Fallujah. General Natonski had another coordination meeting with his commanders inside the old base auditorium, where he was to remain throughout the major combat phases of the fight.

With a great deal of furious activity, it was obvious to the enemy that something was imminent in Fallujah. As a consequence, insurgent activity in general and probes, mortar attacks, and vehicle-borne IED strikes all increased significantly near the end of the month. During this build-up, in one of the most horrific attacks of the year, a suicide bomber in a luxury car detonated his vehicle inside a convoy of the 1st Battalion, 3rd Marines, while that battalion was moving into the Fallujah operations area. The resulting fireball killed eight Marines, wounded many others, and saddened everyone in the coalition camp.[14]

Camp Fallujah was the scene of a classic wartime event on November 1. The MEF conducted a final Phantom Fury confirmation brief in the base theater, during which all the MEF subordinate commanders walked through their plan with Generals Sattler and Metz. There were still some notable shortfalls, among them a complete lack of Iraqi military staff members to coordinate activities and no Iraqi police to establish law and order inside Fallujah, but the exchange of information was extremely valuable and General Metz left with a true sense of confidence in the MEF's plan.

With the confirmation that the plan was sound and approval delegated to hit targets inside the city, the MEF really began operation Phantom Fury on November 2, conducting nightly targeting boards and monitoring unit movements with a huge critical events log in the MEF combat operations center. One major issued remained: the integration of Iraqi forces.

IRAQI FORCES FOR THE FIGHT

If the fighting in Fallujah was to meet the critical four tests set by the MEF for operations, then Iraqi forces had to be fully integrated into the MEF. To assist in that effort, and in response to the shortfalls addressed in the November 1 confirmation brief, Iraqi Major General Abdul-Qader and his deputy, Brigadier General Kassim, arrived at Camp Fallujah on November 3. They were sent not only to form the Iraqi component of the multinational force set for Fallujah, but also General Abdul-Qader had been empowered by the Prime Minister of Iraq to serve as the military governor of Al Anbar province. This gave him the authority to establish law and order in the city during combat operations.

Even with the fortuitous arrival of General Abdul-Qader, Iraqi forces still had to be moved to the Fallujah operations area, supported with basing and essential supplies, and fully integrated into the Division structure. This huge effort (which was conducted simultaneously with the reception and basing of 10,000 additional U.S. forces around Fallujah) was monumental in scope and importance, but it was understood from the beginning to be of greatest importance, for the assault on Fallujah had to be made by an integrated U.S. and Iraqi force.

General Sattler made the reception and integration of the Iraqi forces one of his highest priorities. To facilitate their integration, the MEF constructed what came to be known as the East Fallujah Iraqi Camp (EFIC). From broken buildings with no power and water, the MEF engineers (Army, Navy, and Marine), with the help of every available "free hand" in the camp, built sufficient basing to accommodate and train all eight of the Iraqi battalions sent to the fight. By the time these Iraqi units arrived in camp, they had shelter, food, and water and training equipment for the fight staged in unit sets and were met by representatives of their "parent" MEF units so that they would be immediate melded into the force. Once in camp, each Iraqi unit was paired with an American counterpart, liaison officers were exchanged, and integrated training began in earnest.

ISOLATION

Overnight on November 6, most units of the 1st Marine Division and their Iraqi counterpart units shifted out of their home bases and began movement to the assault positions that were chosen around the city. By that time, the Blackjack Brigade had already begun active patrolling of the highways around the city. The next day, on November 7, coalition forces began the fight for Fallujah by seizing the Fallujah General Hospital at the western end of the old bridge – effectively sealing off the city from insurgent reinforcement in a bold opening move on the site where Fallujah became infamous 7 months before.

The attack on the hospital was launched because MEF intelligence officers knew that site was home to one of the insurgents' most important command and control nodes, and the hospital itself was key terrain controlling access to the old bridge. By taking the upper peninsula the MNF could control egress from both of the city's western bridges. The insurgents believed that the MNF would not attack hospitals, not fully understanding that by using one as a military command facility they had sacrificed its protected status. Still, rather than attacking the insurgent command and control node with fires, which would destroy much of the hospital, the MEF had determined to accomplish the objective using the Iraqi 36th Commando Battalion and elements of its own Task Force LAR, built around the 3rd Light Armored Reconnaissance Battalion, commanded by Lieutenant Colonel Steve Dinauer. To prevent reduction of its ability to provide essential health care services, an attached civil affairs team led by Captain (Doctor) John Williams, MC, USN, delivered a New Emergency Health Kit – a 30-day package of medical supplies procured from Sweden. This small tactical action received much attention in the press as the first act of the battle. Eventually, it was seen as a strategic information operations win, protecting an important Fallujahn civic capability.

The same night as the attack on the Fallujah General Hospital, November 7, reconstruction teams from the CAG and MEG moved in immediately behind the lead assault battalions. The CAG coordinated with the Iraqi Ministry of Electricity through Lieutenant Colonel Steve "Wildman" Walsh to shut off the power to Fallujah. Walsh and a very small team removed critical parts to the main generators, so the power could not be reenergized by the insurgents.

In the immediate hours prior to the start of the assault on Fallujah, the MEF concentrated its efforts on isolating the city from the insurgency. This isolation was critical to prevent to escape of the insurgents in the city and to ensure that AIF would not be able to reinforce their people in the city. Using the Blackjack Brigade, the 1st Marine Division controlled all the roads leading to Fallujah from the south and east, assembled the main attack force of two regiments along the highway bounding the northern side of Fallujah, and then moved the light armored task force, including the Iraqi 36th Commando Battalion, up the peninsula west of the city to effectively seal it off. Once the city was surrounded[15] the main combat forces of the 1st Marine Division moved into place all along the northern edge of Fallujah. The combined force was set.

Lieutenant General James T. Conway, commander of MEF during Iraqi Freedom I and the first 6 months of Iraqi Freedom II.

Lieutenant General John F. Sattler, commander of MEF during operation Al Fajr.

General Mattis during negotiations after Vigilant Resolve.

Marines fighting inside a building during Vigilant Resolve.

A company commander in Fallujah during Vigilant Resolve.

Soldiers fighting in the cemetery in Najaf.

Lieutenant General Abdul-Qader (center), with Brigadier General Hejlik (far left), Brigadier General Kassin (left), and Colonel Ballard (far right).

Major General Richard Natonski in the Fallujah CMOC.

Colonel Mike Shupp, commander of RCT-1.

Destruction in the city of Fallujah. The old green bridge across the Euphrates is in the background.

Marines during the assault into Fallujah.

A Marine walking the old green bridge after it was captured during Al Fajr.

The tank, bulldozer, and attack aircraft were all used as necessary and with great effect.

Iraqi soldiers of the 36th Commando Battalion erecting an Iraqi flag in Fallujah.

Residents of Fallujah waiting to reenter the city in November.

The Iraqi Minister of Municipalities discussing the rebuilding of Fallujah during a visit to the city in February.

Iraqi women waiting in line in Fallujah for $200 payments from the MEF.

The Monday Fallujah Reconstruction Meeting in the CMOC. At the head of the table are Deputy Minister Muhammad Abdullah and Director General Basil Mahmoud of the Ministry of Industry.

Residents of Fallujah standing in line to vote on January 30, 2005.

Iraqi election workers being transported to polling sites.

Iraqi soldiers trained and ready in Najaf.

Chapter Five

Assault Operations

By the evening of November 7, 2004, the 1st Marine Division was arrayed in its attack positions around Fallujah and the city was effectively cut off from insurgent support from the outside world.[1] The Division's order of battle included two Marine Regiments and the 1st Cavalry Division's Blackjack Brigade, but each of those formations were fully joint and combined, with Marine and Army units cross-attached and Iraqi forces integrated into all the U.S. formations for the duration of the fighting in Fallujah.

On the northwestern side of the city, Colonel Mike Shupp's 1st Marines (RCT-1) included the 3rd Battalion, 1st Marines (commanded by Lieutenant Colonel Willy Buhl); the 3rd Battalion, 5th Marines (commanded by Lieutenant Colonel Patrick Malay) and Mechanized Task Force 2-7 Infantry from the U.S. Army (commanded by Lieutenant Colonel Jim Rainey); as well as two battalions of the Iraqi Intervention Force (1/1 and 4/1 IIF) and a small battalion of the Iraqi Specialized Special Forces (SSF). On the northeast side of Fallujah, Colonel Craig Tucker had the 1st Battalion, 8th Marines (commanded by Lieutenant Colonel Gareth Brandl); the 1st Battalion, 3rd Marines (commanded by Lieutenant Colonel Michael Ramos); and the U.S. Army's Armored Task Force 2-2 (commanded by Lieutenant Colonel Pete Newall); a battalion of the IIF; and even a battalion of the new IAF, plus another battalion of SSF, all rolled up within Regimental Combat Team 7 (RCT-7). Covering the southeast side of the battle space was the 2nd Brigade of the 1st Cavalry Division, the Blackjack Brigade, which for operations in Fallujah included the Marine 2nd Reconnaissance Battalion and the 6th Battalion of the 3rd Brigade of the IAF.

In advance of the fight, the Division staff had divided the city into grids and retitled almost all the crucial streets with first names (such as Elizabeth, Cathy, Dave, and Donna in the north) for ease of understanding. Some of the other names, such as Michigan (the label for the main highway bisecting the city from east to west), had been retained from the period of operation Vigilant Resolve. As all the key leaders had rehearsed the execution of the plan numerous times, the street names and grid locations had become almost a current slang, unintelligible to anyone other than the warriors of the MEF. The plan called for the assault forces to infiltrate into their battle positions under cover of darkness late on November 6 and wait there all of D-day (November 7) without movement, as if the positioning was just another in the series of feints that the Marines had been conducting since October. Then, the actual attack would begin before first light on the following day – a time when they knew that insurgents would be unlikely to respond effectively from their beds and when most of the residents who had not left would be safe in their homes. The assault concept was for both Marine regiments to attack from the north on parallel axes of advance slicing through the northern half of the city, smashing the insurgents against the Army brigade in the south.

OPERATION AL-FAJR COMBINED OPERATIONS

Although the MEF had been calling the operation Phantom Fury for weeks, just before it began, the Iraqi Minister of Defense renamed the operation Al Fajr ("new dawn" in Arabic) to highlight the Iraqi nature of the operation. This change showcased a uniquely important element of the assault on the city: the formation of a functional command and control mechanism for the Iraqi forces operating in Fallujah. It was a working-level, coalition command and control (C2) process that facilitated unity of effort at both the tactical and operational levels of war. The most influential part of this structure provided the MEF some coordinating authority over Iraqi units and institutions, while still maintaining Iraqi direction of the operation. It was formed when Iraqi Major General Abdul-Qader Mohammed Jassim was appointed military governor of Al Anbar province by Prime Minister Allawi immediately prior to the commencement of combat operations on November 5.[2]

When General Abdul-Qader arrived at Camp Fallujah to assume his duties as the provincial military governor, he was assumed to have authority over all MNF forces in the province, and, more importantly, everything in the city of Fallujah, to include law and order. This was a huge assumption given the fact that he arrived without any written charter from the prime minister[3] and with only a few officers to form a staff. Luckily, General Sattler and the members of his MEF staff understood the critical importance of Abdul-Qader's role and he was immediately hosted by (and his meager staff was supported by) the MEF headquarters in an impressive conference facility rehabilitated literally overnight by Colonel John Coleman and a bunch of his command group Marines. The newly "combined headquarters" arrangement on Camp Fallujah made complete integration of the Iraqi Security Forces within the MNF structure possible.

By that time, the Multinational Security Transition Command-Iraq (MNSTC-I) had been formed to assist in the development and training of all the Iraqi security forces. It provided two liaison officers to General Abdul-Qader but had no real staff resources to provide him and neither did his own government. In particular, General Abdul-Qader needed a broad range of administrators and representatives from the various national ministries to function effectively as a military governor. For example, he needed immediate support from the Ministry of Interior (MOI) so that he could manage police and local security issues. Because he did not get any real support from the MOI for several months, he had to formulate many basic security policies, such as weapons handling, curfew, and vehicle-use rules, without Iraqi legal advice.

General Abdul-Qader proved to be a brave and cooperative commander who soon was a strong advocate for the operation with his government; he even became a spokesman for the operation's success with the international media. He worked closely and well with the MNF chain of command, yet always retained an independent decision-making role. Because he was not completely dominated by the MNF[4] and had the respect of his subordinate Iraqi brigade commanders, he accomplished many difficult tasks that would have been impossible for the MNF commanders to do on their own.[5] He also worked well with the MEF staff to develop a host of important policies to include rules of engagement during the battle and eventually the civic rules that the Fallujah residents were required to follow on their return.[6]

With General Abdul-Qader's concurrence, before any forces moved on the city, thousands of leaflets were dropped to urge the remaining residents to leave. Other leaflets would also outline the new rules for the residents of the city to observe over the coming weeks, mostly in a continuing effort to separate insurgents from residents and protect the residents from accidental injury. One last appeal was also made for any members of the Fallujah police or Iraqi Security Forces still working in the city to come over to the coalition – where they would be allowed to retain their jobs. No one volunteered.

FIRST TO FIGHT

Colonel Shupp's 1st Marines had the most difficult approach on D-day because they could not get direct access to the critical Jolan area of Fallujah without showing their hand. But they could and did establish an attack position in the dominating terrain of the Saklawyiah Apartment complex, several eight-story buildings just 200 meters across the train tracks for their initial objective. They did so by actually going door to door, paying the residents who were still in the apartments $200 to leave and "rent" their homes for the period of the battle. But that did not make the Marines of the regiment safe from enemy fire. The apartment complex was key terrain because it allowed the Marines to look down into the city; once they took the apartments the Marines moved up to the rooftops and began engaging

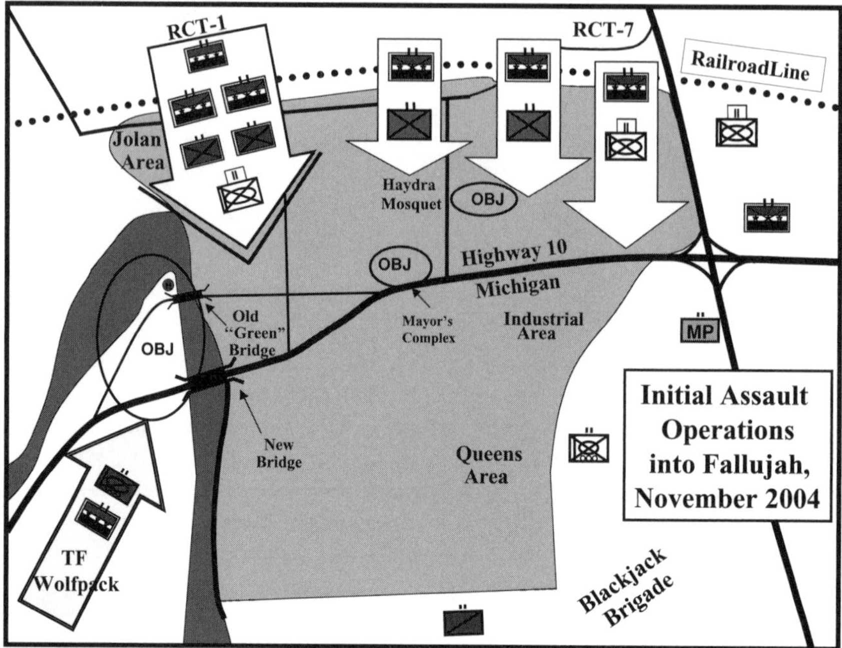

Map 5. Initial Assault Operations into Fallujah, November 2004

insurgents who were trying to move toward their fighting positions. No one wanted the enemy to see the extent of the MNF attack force.

The view on the apartment rooftop was choice, but it also attracted a lot of enemy fire. Machine-gun teams were carrying guns and boxes of ammunition up eight flights of stairs in full Kevlar body armor, while Marine snipers engaged the enemy to keep them inside the city proper. The whole time insurgents were also firing mortars and rockets at the apartments.[7] It was a dangerous move, but every study of the attack had indicated the apartments had to be taken and held before the assault could begin.

Craig Tucker's 7th Regiment was able to move almost into the city from the northeastern road on the night of D-day. The northeastern corner of Fallujah was outside of enemy observation and had a far less congested approach, but Tucker's men were still very exposed through the long first day because their attack position was largely open desert with very few buildings. It was separated from the city only by a major rail line and the Fallujah city train station. With the forces in position, the commanders and troops had to wait out a very long and nerve-wracking day within easy rocket and mortar range of the enemy.

The tactical attack plan called for the two Army mechanized battalions to penetrate as quickly and deeply into the city as they could from north to south. The Marine infantry battalions (having more actual infantrymen per battalion than the Army mechanized units) and their Iraqi counterparts would follow in immediate trace of the armor, clearing pockets of resistance and searching for remnants of insurgent groups blown wide open by the plunging mailed fist of the Abrams tanks and Bradley fighting vehicles. All the feints and the historical precedent of the April attack had convinced the enemy that the primary attack would come at Fallujah from the south. The MNF senior planners were hoping that the two regiments could push south to the main east–west highway, known forever to them as Route Michigan, within 48 to 72 hours, quickly pushing the insurgents into the less well developed and less inhabited southern half of the city where they could be decimated by fire.

Along the way there were a series of tactical objectives that had been chosen because they were either known insurgent command and control nodes or suspected weapons stockpiling locations. Several of these were located in mosques or other normally restricted locations, again because the insurgents believed that the MNF would not attack them in such places. For example, the famous Hydra Mosque, along the main north–south route, nicknamed Ethan, was a well-known insurgent headquarters. These sensitive objectives were assigned to the Iraqi Security Forces, so that non-Muslims would not have to enter such holy sites.

Although many outside Iraq had a very poor opinion of the Iraqi troops, their past experience fighting alongside Iraqis in Najaf had given the Marines a more open mind as to their abilities in combat, and their esteem grew as the Marine and Army leaders worked with them in the immediate days preceding the battle. So by D-day, commanders felt confident in assigning the Iraqis important objectives like the Hydra Mosque. Colonel Shupp had such confidence in one of his assigned Iraqi battalions that he gave it its own axis of advance up front with his lead battalions. Clearly, the Iraqi forces had not only proven themselves in Najaf but also improved their tactics and unit cohesion at the battalion level by November.

One of the locations assigned to the Iraqi forces was the single operational objective that had to be secured immediately before the main assault on the city could begin: the Fallujah General Hospital. For weeks prior to the attack, the Marines had observed insurgents using the hospital on a peninsula formed by a bend in the Euphrates, across the old green bridge, as a communications and command and control node. Because the location had good observation of the entire western side of the city, and restricted access in and out of Fallujah by dominating both bridges leading to the west, it had to be controlled by the MNF in the very early stages of the attack. But, as a hospital, and a hospital well known for giving anti-coalition comments to the press, "controlling" it posed a very delicate problem.[8]

After much debate (during which time some MEF planners wanted to simply blow the building up), it was agreed that the Iraqi 36th Commando Battalion would be given the mission of securing the hospital at a time during the night when most of the staff would be off duty. The Iraqis were accompanied by elements of 3rd Light Armored Reconnaissance Battalion (Task Force Wolfpack) and a U.S. Navy medical team from the CAG composed of Captain John Williams, M.D., and Chief Chester Painter, who were assigned to assess any patients in the hospital needing care and to drop off a container of medical supplies that would keep the facility in operation for several weeks. Without firing a shot, the Iraqi Commandos burst through the doors of the facility and rounded up nearly 40 military-age males in the hospital who were neither staff nor patients. In fact, very few of the hospital beds were occupied and only one patient was in serious condition.[9] Once the hospital was secured, the Iraqi soldiers raised the Iraqi flag in the compound as a symbol of things to come. The 36th Commando and Task Force Wolfpack also secured the two bridges that connected the peninsula with the city and established blocking positions on each, completing the isolation of the city prior to D-day.[10]

Based on input from General Abdul-Qader and the MEF staff, Prime Minister Allawi had placed the entire country of Iraq in a state of emergency and put a round-the-clock curfew in effect in Fallujah, where he also banned the carrying of weapons and the use of private vehicles. Once the Fallujah General Hospital and its nearby bridges were under coalition control, Colonel Mike Formica's Blackjack Brigade took positions on the southern and eastern approaches to the city to restrict any insurgents from escaping and to prevent any insurgent reinforcements from entering Fallujah. Units from RCT-1 and RCT-7 completed movement into their attack positions just north of the city, with RCT-1 poised against the western portion of the city and RCT-7 assigned to the east. With MNF leaflets covering the city streets, and Iraqi radio and television announcing the national curfew, all civilian vehicle traffic was stopped and the area turned eerily quiet. The battlespace was set for commencing the main attack just after nightfall.

Still, after the units had waited the long day in their attack positions, many uncertainties remained in the leader's minds. How many civilians were left in the city? Would the insurgents use civilians as human shields? Would they use gas or biological agents in the fighting? Would the lead battalions get bogged down in the densely packed urban blocks of the city? How many insurgents were waiting for them? The insurgents inside Fallujah certainly knew that the battle they had anticipated for weeks was primed to start. They had no idea what kind of brawn was about to hit them.

A-DAY, NOVEMBER 8

Phase III (Decisive Operations) in Fallujah began at 7 P.M. on Sunday, November 7 (which was actually A-5 hours, as A-day was November 8), with the lead companies pushing into the northern edges of the city under the cover of darkness. Everyone in the MEF knew that the Army battalions' mechanized punch was key to the tempo of the main assault. Lieutenant Colonel Dave Bellon said of the attack by 7th Marines, "2/7 became our wedge. In short, they worked with 3rd Battalion, 1st Marines. We were limited in the amount of prep fires that we were allowed to fire on the city prior to the invasion. This was a point of some consternation to the forces actually taking the city. Our compensation was to turn to 2/7 and ask them to slash into the city and create as much turbulence as possible for 3/1 to follow. Because of the political reality, the Marine Corps was also under pressure to 'get it done quickly.' For this reason, 2/7 and 3/1 became the penetration force into the city."[11]

In the northwest, RCT-1 used a similar approach. Bellon recounted, "Immediately following 3/5's attack on the apartment buildings, 3/1 took the train station on the north end of the city. While the engineers blew a breach through the train trestle, the Cavalry soldiers poured through with their tanks and Bradley's and chewed an opening in the enemy defense. 3/1 followed them through until they reached a phase line deep into the northern half of the city. The Marine infantry along with a few tanks then turned to the right and attacked the heart of the enemy defense. The fighting was tough, as the enemy had the area dialed in with mortars. 3/5 then attacked into the northwest corner of the city. This fight continued as both Marine rifle battalions clawed their way into the city on different axis."[12]

The attack started a bit more slowly than many had hoped because access into Fallujah had been significantly constrained by insurgent defenses, but very soon after the lead infantry companies breached the defensive belt the armor took any vestige of control away from the defending insurgents by plunging down the city streets and destroying anything that posed a threat. Abrams tanks and Bradleys chewed through every vehicle, wall, berm, and defensive barrier they encountered, streaming south and leaving enemy dead and small fractured enemy units in their wake. The infantrymen rushed in right behind them to kill every enemy remaining in the fight.

Initial press coverage of the operation was uneven, with early confusion on the part of the media about the real focus of the fighting understandable, given the need for operations security. Still, Jackie Spinner of *The Washington Post*, Patrick McDonnell of *The Los Angeles Times*, and several other embedded reporters soon began to reveal the battle in great detail. They were purposely allowed full access, and commanders at all levels took care to provide them regular updates once the battle unfolded so that the truth about the operation could be told. Spinner quoted Prime Minister Allawi's revealing comments authorizing the attack, "I have reached the belief that I have no other choice but to resort to extreme measures to protect the Iraqi people from these killers and to liberate the residents of Fallujah so they can return to their homes. . . . I gave my full authority to the multinational forces, Iraqi forces. We are determined to clean Fallujah from the terrorists."[13] For their part, the insurgents in the city let it be known that they too would support reporters and provide them transportation and housing; they fully intended to tell their story as well.[14]

Once started, the MNF penetration went even faster than the Marines had hoped. Afterward, from studies of the battle and debriefs of those insurgents captured, it became clear that the shaping strategy had worked exceptionally well to manipulate the battle. First, the enemy forces arrayed along the northern side of the town were almost exclusively less well-trained, local fighters, paid well by the city leaders only to man barricades and defend the outskirts of the city.[15] They fought, but were no match for the coalition, and they broke and ran quickly in the first hours of the fight; they were killed or wounded in significant numbers during the slicing penetrations of the MNF assault battalions, but many continued to fight in ever smaller and more determined numbers as they were pummeled by the determined MEF infantry squads.

The majority of the "hard core" foreign fighters were posted in the southern section of the city, where the earlier Marine feints had made it appear that the attack would originate. The enemy had placed well-trained insurgents in well-prepared interlocking fighting positions there, with huge ammunition stockpiles nearby. Many of the insurgents in the southern part of the city were holding foreign passports and most were dedicated ideologues. They were prepared to fight to the death – and most did just that.[16]

Even more significantly, the good news was that the coalition forces found the city nearly deserted of civilians. Of the over 200,000 estimated inhabitants of Fallujah, initial assessments revealed fewer than 20,000 people had remained in the city as the assault began. This near absence of civilians not only made the battlefield much easier for the MNF to work in, but it also ensured that meeting the needs of the few people remaining would be much more manageable. It was evident also, early in the fight, that there were very, very few casualties among the civilian population, who had heeded the MNF call to stay at home and remain out of sight.

On November 9, 2/7 was pushing to the west toward the Euphrates with 3/1 clearing through the Jolan district in the northwestern quarter of Fallujah. Embedded reporter Kevin Sites caught the somber mood as elements of India Company, 3/1, continued the attack against the fleeing enemy down one of the main thoroughfares of the city, studded with ambush sites in building after building:

> The Marines turn the corner onto a main street they've tactically dubbed, "Elizabeth." . . . A squad from India Company passes by an alleyway with a spray painted rocket propelled grenade launcher – a real RPG round explodes against it. One Marine's face is burned by the powder and the gas – another has caught shrapnel in the leg, a third has been shot in the finger by the small arms fire that followed. . . . The Marines turn their M16s on the building to the west where they believe the shooter is hiding. But that is just an appetizer. A gunner in the armored turret of a Humvee fires 40-millimeter grenades non-stop into the building. . . . Staff Sergeant Terry Mcelwain of Burden Texas is pissed. He grabs the bazooka-like AT-4 rocket launcher from the back of another Humvee. Its fire zips into the now smoking building. Macelwain wants Weapons Company to fire a TOW missile into it as well, but low hanging electrical wires make it impossible – so he calls up the tanks instead. Two Abrams lumber towards the target. They stop and fire main guns in unison. The explosion shakes the street.[17]

Even with all their firepower, the insurgent defenders continued to shoot at the Marines with rifles and RPGs. Then other insurgents opened fire from the Marine's front, boxing them in. Later, the same platoon would call in the AC-130 gunship to use its mini-guns against the well-dug-in enemy. Sites continued, "The Marines know they are being hunted. Boxed from the east and the west in a treacherous kill zone by an enemy they can feel – but can't see."[18] Everywhere in the north half of Fallujah it was the same. A treacherous and unpredictable enemy used the natural defenses of the city and hard-bitten zeal to snipe and claw at the coalition forces even as they were decimated every time they were caught in the open.[19]

On the east side of the city, Pete Newall's 2/2 was already poised on Route Michigan and looking to press into the south of Fallujah. 1/8 had taken the Hydra Mosque with Iraqi Security Forces and was driving on toward the mayor's complex in the city center. Even as the assault battalions were still in close combat a few blocks away, civil affairs teams from the CAG began delivering humanitarian assistance supplies to the few Iraqi civilians assembling in the vicinity of the Saqlawyiah Apartments. No dislocated civilians or resulting humanitarian problems were immediately observed inside Fallujah proper, but the MEF had humanitarian supplies staged well forward to assist should they be required. The attack by RCT-7 continued into the night, with the assault battalions pressing into the western and southern sectors of the northeast quadrant. The Army's 2/2 mechanized task force held up and began to reinforce its battle positions along Michigan – the main route bisecting the city from east to west. In the northwest, where the buildings were more densely packed, the going was a bit slower but still well ahead of expectations.

By November 10, the Marine Corps' birthday, 1/8, working for Craig Tucker, had fully occupied the mayor's complex, a main objective in the heart of town. This was a key event signaling real progress in the fight. Although the enemy was still raining down fire on the Marines inside the buildings of the complex from higher structures all around the central square, the area was the political and symbolic heart of the city and it was firmly under Marine control. Occupying the square demonstrated that the insurgents no longer dominated the city; it was from that square, too, that the new Fallujah would begin to be rebuilt. Understanding the significance of the action, the Iraqi forces in the square again raised the Iraqi flag – a symbol of the new dawn for the city.

Even while the battle to secure the centerpiece of Fallujah continued, the 1st Marine Division began to prepare for the eventual return of the city to its people. Major Tim Hansen, the civil affairs team leader assigned to 1/8, remembered,

> As I sat using a piece of broken cinder block for a chair, I saw what I thought was another rifle squad double timing around the corner toward me. The squads usually went out a hole in the wall near me because the wall gave them protective cover until the last minute. The protection was needed because the 100 yards of open field between the wall and the next building had become known as "Snipers Alley," a place where a sniper had a good 10 seconds to get a bead on you if you dashed across the field and 30 seconds or more to pull the trigger if you walked. I looked at the squad again and my eyes fixed on the flak jackets of the two lead Marines. One had two silver stars! Holy smokes, it was a Marine Corps major general and a bunch of colonels; I then recognized two of them as Major General Natonski and Colonel Ballard, the CO of 4th CAG. They were on a leader's recon mission for a CMOC headquarters. After a brief cordial greeting, the "fire team" stacked up along the wall

> and waited to make the dash across "Snipers Alley." As the junior Marines present, Lieutenant Shuford and I thought it prudent to offer to provide cover fire to the 0-6 fire team. He and I looked at each other, popped up over the wall and searched for possible enemy snipers as the general and colonels zigged and zagged across the field, which at the end of the run turned into a pile of soft dirt and a muddy swamp. Once they were across the field and next to the four story high rise, the sniper fire resumed in the direction of the government complex. It all turned out well as the CMOC was eventually established at the Youth and Sports Center, the fire team's final destination that day.

The following day, Bravo Company of the 445th Civil Affairs Battalion (attached to 4th CAG) established the CMOC on that site, the former city recreation center in the mayor's complex in the center of Fallujah.

SENDING A MESSAGE

On the evening of November 10, Generals Sattler and Abdul-Qader provided the first joint press briefing of the operation to the assembled media in Camp Fallujah and the pool of reporters of the global press corps via VTC. General Sattler knew that the world needed to understand why the attack was taking place and should also know that it was exceeding all expectations. So he began the briefing by confirming the mission was "to liberate the city" so that the rule of law and conditions for reconstruction could be established. Although Sattler was his usual ebullient self, it was General Abdul-Qader who made the biggest impression on the listeners. Instead of merely nodding to confirm General Sattler's statements, he made his own heartfelt commitment evident, saying, "we wanted the Iraqi armed forces to say what the Iraqi dream is all about. We wish the people of Iraq to live in peace like any other nation."[20] He continued as follows:

> Our armed forces are just at the beginning of their formation. For that we need the friend, the multinational friends, to help us in this respective. And we work shoulder to shoulder with our friends to minimize casualties on both sides. . . . With all that we are also giving guidance for the civilians how to be safe, secure during the operation. And our Iraqi armed forces and the friends, we are trying to minimize collateral damage as minimum as we can. We are using weapons according to the enemy situation.

The press conference was an important part of the information campaign conducted by the MEF to ensure the world understood the reasons for the operation, but General Abdul-Qader's forceful and personal role in the briefing set a new standard. He had been in the thick of the fighting earlier that day with General Sattler and he saw then for the first time that the future of Iraq could start in Fallujah. From that day forward, General Abdul-Qader remained a proud and public spokesman for the operation, and with every passing day he grew in stature as a commander of the first Iraqi-directed operation to take the country back from the insurgency.[21]

The first horror stories of the insurgent occupation of Fallujah also began to be circulated during that initial press conference. Marines had discovered one Iraqi chained hand and foot to a wall in northern Fallujah earlier that day. They had also found several homes that appeared to have been used as human slaughterhouses for insurgent kidnapping victims.[22] It was well understood that Zarqawi had operated out of Fallujah, and most intelligence officers expected that such sites would be discovered; however, no one anticipated the extent of the organized killing in the city. Computer information on multiple murders, passports for illegally entered foreign nationals, chemicals that could have been used to make dirty bombs, many IED factories, and weapons cache sites too numerous to count filled the city. Although the gruesome appearance of the killing rooms got most of the media attention, it was the sophistication and the size of the insurgent war-making machine in Fallujah that concerned most of the commanders.

As the days passed, more and more evidence of insurgent terror tactics was revealed in the city. Underground prison cells with dead Iraqis were discovered in one house, and in another, five bodies with bullets in the back of their heads were found. Then, a few days later, Marines discovered the headless corpse of a mutilated Caucasian female, with her hands and feet cut off.[23] Along with the booby-trapping of dead bodies, the misuse of "protected" sites and equipment (e.g., mosques, white flags, and ambulances), and the "killing rooms" and other terrorist material, these discoveries made it very clear that the insurgents had been victimizing the local population, as well as using techniques that violated the usual convention of armed conflict in the city. To confirm the worst suspicions of some planners, a chemical agent was even found in the city that could have been used as a small weapon of mass effects, killing thousands.

In Baghdad on November 10, it was revealed that the key leaders of the insurgency, including Zarqawi, probably fled the city prior to the assault. Even so, everyone knew that the fighting would still significantly reduce the power of the insurgent movement, and with the mounting evidence of their unlawful acts, no one involved doubted the need to finish the operation thoroughly. As a sign of the desperation of the enemy, that same day, three of Prime Minister Allawi's relatives were kidnapped and threatened with beheading – the insurgency's symbolic method of death – if the assault on the city was not stopped.[24] Unlike the situation in April, Allawi was not deterred; he was determined to go the distance all along; in fact, the kidnapping most likely only cemented his conviction to fight until the city was cleared of the terrorist enemy.

GOING THE DISTANCE

On Thursday, November 11, Veteran's Day in the United States, the assault battalions stepped off on the next phase of the liberation of the city. Leaving some units to begin the all-important detailed searching to clear pockets of resistance from the north, Lieutenant Colonel Joe L'etoile, the division operations officer, recommended to General Natonski that the two assault regiments reconfigure forces and continue the attack even more aggressively than originally planned. Instead of sweeping west to the Euphrates, both RCT-1 and RCT-7 were directed to continue the attack to the south, all the way to the bottom of the city. This continuation of the attack would pin any remaining insurgents against the Blackjack Brigade, which was positioned in the south of the city.

As before, the Army mechanized task forces led the attack south, with 2/2 blasting through the industrial area occupied by the Marines of 1/5 back in April and with 2/7 attacking in parallel between 2/2 and the river. 1/8 pushed out of the mayor's complex to clear behind 2/2, and 3/1 did the same for its sister Army battalion in the western zone. As the assault units penetrated into the bottom third of the city, they began to find even more sophisticated defensive positions and a much more determined enemy.[25]

The "Queens" area was where the enemy had built up its best forces and fighting positions in anticipation of the Marine attack, and it was there in the bottom third of the city, trapped by the Blackjack Brigade further south outside the city limits, that the most devastation would result from a cornered enemy fighting to the death. Luckily, because the insurgents had anticipated that attack would come from the south, when 2/2 blasted its way down from the north, it encountered the rear of most of the insurgent positions and surprised most of the enemy defenders. They had not benefited from a unified command system inside Fallujah, and the insurgents in the south were largely caught unaware by the attack, without being informed of the advancing MNF forces by their fellow fighters in the northern half of the city.

After 4 days of fighting, Shupp's RCT-1 was able to turn the security for the Jolan neighborhood over to the Iraqi Security Forces on November 11. Although Jolan had been the first area attacked and was not as well defended as initial estimates had concluded, it was still significant that Iraqi forces could take on the security mission in an area of the city that had traditionally been a center of the insurgent movement. It was also near the location where the regeneration of the city would begin, so giving the Iraqi Security Forces the first role in that effort was particularly fitting.

It was also on Thursday that the rumors of a humanitarian disaster began to be circulated in Baghdad and through the Arab media. With the MNF claiming control of more than two-thirds of Fallujah, and the insurgents also saying they were still in control of the city, people began to imagine the worst for the residents. A spokesman for the National Islamic Resistance in Fallujah, Abu Shams al-Fallujy, told *Al Jazeera* that, "the situation in the town is very critical. The U.S. forces began a retreat under intense resistance fire. They are conducting a ferocious aerial bombing and artillery barrage. They have not accomplished any advance towards the edges of the town."[26] According to *Al Jazeera*, the Red Cross and Iraqi Red Crescent Society were extremely concerned that "tens of thousands who fled were ill and living in cramped conditions" and implied that because "up to half of the population of 300,000 may have stayed behind" there must be many wounded and dead residents in the city under MNF bombardment.

Al Jazeera had started discussing a humanitarian disaster the night before in an article entitled, "Mosques Bombed in Falluja Fighting," and continued the same line of reasoning in another article 2 hours later, "Falluja Facing Humanitarian Crisis."[27] With claims from people inside the city that "hundreds of families needed help" and "from a humanitarian point of view, it's a disaster, there's no other way to describe it," Iraqis in general and Sunnis in particular began to put great pressure on the Allawi government to stop the fighting as had been done in April. In November, the difference was that Allawi was firm in his control and his convictions. He had previously negotiated with the leaders of the city and by this time had lost all respect for them. In addition, he had his own commander on the ground, and General Abdul-Qader was just as firm in his support of the continuing fight.

Still, reasonable assertions of a humanitarian problem in such an urban fight were legitimate, and the MEF had to continue a full court effort to address claim after claim over the following weeks that the postulation was being supported and that no crisis existed. The MNF flew helicopters over all the outlying cities to look for displaced residents and stepped up an aggressive plan to provide all manner of supplies to the Iraqis who were found in shelters and camps in the southern half of Al Anbar province.

Most of this humanitarian coordination work was accomplished by the MEF staff and the CAG, so even as the battle raged in the city, things continued apace back at Camp Fallujah. On November 12, the MNF-I medical staff and the CAG surgeon, Commander Lou Tripoli, established an ambulance exchange point aboard the camp to evacuate any injured Iraqi noncombatants to hospitals in Baghdad and to the MNF military hospital at Abu Ghraib. Also, on November 12, civil affairs teams began to deliver humanitarian assistance (HA) supplies and provide medical care to local Iraqi residents at one of the many mosques in Fallujah. Although over 400 Iraqis were evacuated for their own safety, only about 20 individuals needed medical care.

On Friday, the assault regiments in Fallujah pressed the attack to the far corners of the city.[28] The concept was to first break up all large concentrations of enemy forces remaining in the city and then establish local control by searching out and destroying enemy pockets of resistance seeking refuge in individual buildings and homes in the various neighborhoods. The Marine and Army commanders had expected some decentralized fighting because they understood that the enemy was a loose coalition of groups from within and outside of Iraq, but they had not expected the insurgents to shift to a determined resistance movement in Fallujah once the city was dominated by the MNF forces.

The MEF staff estimated that by that point some 150 insurgents had been detained, over 300 had surrendered, and over 600 had been killed in the city. General Sattler estimated that the MNF controlled about 80 percent of Fallujah, but he made it very clear that the process of clearing the city, searching "each and every house," would take time and would certainly result in more combat.

The attack forces continued to employ the AC-130 with telling effect, as well as fixed-wing aviation, as they closed on the southern limits of Fallujah. Some three to four dozen insurgents tried to break out of the city to the south but were pushed back by the Soldiers and Marines assigned to Blackjack. Even in the northern half of the city, the fighting remained intense. General Natonski noted, "Today our forces are conducting deliberate clearing operations within the city. . . . In almost every single mosque in Fallujah, we have found an arms cache. We have found IED-making factories. . . . We've been shot at by snipers in minarets."[29]

One of the most significant contributions to the fight in the city was made by a unit that never deployed from Camp Fallujah – the U.S. Navy's Bravo Surgical Company, the "cheaters of death." Bravo Surgical was one of many medical support organizations in the province and was but a way station along the medevac route for seriously wounded personnel requiring extensive hospital treatment; but during the most intense combat in Fallujah it was where the vast majority of Soldiers and Marines were treated *and returned* to the fight! At a higher rate than ever before in history, many individuals were able to complete treatment and return to the fight within days.

For a Soldier or Marine who was seriously injured, after immediate treatment by on-scene unit medical personnel, they were normally medevaced back to Bravo Surgical, triaged, and then retransported to the main Army Hospital in Baghdad or Balad, Iraq. For some, their wounds would take them on to the Army Hospital in Landstuhl, Germany; for those with the most severe injuries, treatment would take place at Brooke Army Medical Center in Texas or at Walter Reed Army Medical Center or Bethesda Naval Hospital, both in Washington, D.C.

Still, it was while in the care of the "cheaters of death" that the vast majority of injured Soldiers and Marines received their most important treatment. Under most circumstances in previous conflicts, many more military personnel would have died in Fallujah. But with the advances in individual protective equipment (armored vests, neck and groin pads, helmets, and ballistic glasses) and the capability to get the injured to treatment within the first "golden" hour after the wound was received, the doctors and nurses assigned to Bravo Surgical were able to work wonders and prevent a host of normally catastrophic injuries from taking the Marine or Soldier out of the fight.

CLOSING IN

Unfortunately, the superb relationship that the MNF had cultivated with the media for the operation in Fallujah turned sour on Saturday, November 13, when an embedded reporter with 3/1 observed what appeared to be the purposeful shooting of a wounded Iraqi by a Marine corporal in that battalion. As with most units in the southern section of the city, 3/1 was pushing insurgents south, while also clearing important facilities and other known enemy locations within its area of operations. In this case, the Marine's unit had been assigned to clear a mosque that had been searched previously, yet where anti-coalition fighters had been seen reinfiltrating the area.

The corporal entered the building and shot three anti-coalition fighters, one of whom was recorded on videotape by embedded reporter Kevin Sites. Because so many of the enemy fighters in Fallujah had been using ruses and other illicit tactics, the shooting by the Marine was later found to be consistent with the rules of engagement in effect at the time because the enemy fighter appeared to be feigning death with his arm concealed behind his back.[30] The incident inflamed many Iraqis, who already held poor opinions of the MNF in the wake of the Abu Ghraib prison incident the previous spring. It also illustrated well the complexity of the combat environment and the stress placed on many individual Marines and Soldiers during irregular warfare, particularly in urban areas.[31]

Claiming "there is not going to be a stone unturned in the city," by Sunday, November 14, Colonel Shupp was able to state that the major clearing operation would only last another 4 or 5 days.[32] At the time, there was a band of 50 to 80 enemy fighters holding out in the southern area of the city, but no other firefights with large groups of insurgents were expected, although it was evident that the enemy had built a sophisticated system of tunnels linking many of the buildings in Fallujah. General Natonski noted, "We are sweeping back and forth, they are trying to get behind us. . . ."[33]

It was truly a "three-block war" in the city, where Marines and Soldiers could be required to walk police-like security patrols down one block, encounter a high-intensity firefight on the second block, and then be asked to provide humanitarian assistance to Iraqi residents in the third block they passed through. This had long been a Marine training construct, but was never more pertinent or challenging than in the rubble- and water-filled streets of Fallujah at the end of the first week of fighting.[34] It was a crucial validation of the training philosophy that had been bred into Marines since the tough days of their service in Somalia and Haiti in the early 1990s.

The MEF estimate of the number of enemy killed in the fighting had risen to 1,200 by that time, necessitating the construction of a makeshift morgue.[35] One of the civil affairs teams later determined that a potato factory just east of the entrance to the city was a suitable place to process insurgent corpses. The MEF commander then reformed his own mortuary affairs detachment within the Force Service Support Group (FSSG) to carry out this function for the enemy. This was important both to gather any available intelligence from the remains of the enemy and to show due concern for the religious practices of a Muslim enemy.

James Hider captured the tone in Fallujah during the weekend saying, "at midnight Fallujah looked like a scene from Stalingrad, with thick rubble on the roads and hundreds of severed power cables dangling between shattered buildings. Fog enveloped the smashed city in a silence frequently pierced by explosions and gunfire. . . . In the winding streets black-clad gunmen poured burning oil on roads

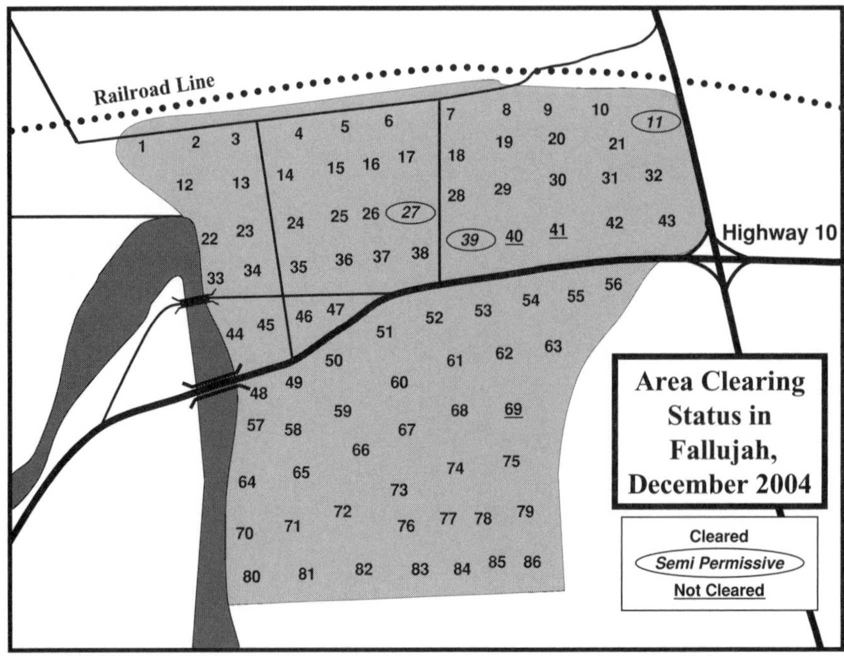

Map 6. Area Clearing Status in Fallujah, December 2004

to attract armoured columns into rocket ambushes, unaware that their actions were being filmed by unmanned American aircraft. . . . Abu Musab al-Zarqawi, the terrorist leader, issued an audiotape yesterday that confidently predicted victory for Fallujah's rebels. But after five days of fighting, U.S. forces are closing in on the men who have run the city as their own Islamist state for six months."[36] The insurgents in the south employed antitank rockets against U.S. tanks and Bradley fighting vehicles, and the enemy lured Marines and Soldiers into well-constructed ambushes inside houses and businesses all over the city, specifically focused to penetrate their protective equipment.

That Saturday, the city began to change. From the nearly continuous sounds of gunfire that had been the norm all week, Fallujah became much quieter and eerily still, except when increasingly isolated individual insurgents made violent contact with Marines and Soldiers and died. Fallujah smelled of death. Nearly all the structures in the city were damaged. Dogs and cats began to roam the streets in packs, feeding on the dead. The Marines and their Iraqi counterparts began to construct firm bases in the city from which to conduct normal security patrols. Task Force Rushmore (the CAG commander's jump command post) conducted the first of many visits through Fallujah to begin coordinating the process of restoring essential services. For the first time, the Marine and Army CA teams used Iraqi soldiers to distribute humanitarian assistance supplies to local residents.

And, on November 15, the Fallujah CMOC site survey was completed and the combined CAG/MEF Engineer Group (MEG) reconstruction team began its movement into the city center to begin the critical reconstruction effort in Fallujah.

Even more symbolic was the reopening on November 15 of the old green bridge across the Euphrates by the Marines of 3/5. After a solid week of the most intense urban combat that the Marine Corps had seen since Hue City in Vietnam over 25 years earlier, the reopening of the green bridge completed the action started so significantly way back the previous April.[37] As Major Todd Des Grosseilliers, the battalion executive officer, said, "For the Marines, this was a major victory."[38] The real issue remained: Could the MEF build on the great tactical victory to achieve a strategic success in Iraq by returning a free and functioning city to its residents?

Chapter Six

Clearing and Searching

Although fighting would continue sporadically for weeks, and despite the fact that there were still insurgents operating in the city, the MEF began to shift its focus at the end of the first week of combat in Fallujah to the resettlement and reconstruction of the city. With directions from the MEF on November 16 to relocate the CMOC from the Fallujah Liaison Team (FLT) site east of the city to the mayor's complex in the heart of downtown Fallujah, and the movement of the CAG operations cell downtown on the same day, the transition to a new phase of operations began in earnest.

Let there be no mistake, even as the MEF staff and the CAG began the reconstruction process, heavy fighting still occurred on a regular basis and its management still occupied most of Colonel Shupp's time – and would continue to do so for many weeks. News reports indicated that at least 38 Americans and 6 Iraqis had died to free the city, while the operation had taken the lives of nearly 1,200 insurgents and captured over 400 more.[1] There were some 20,000 buildings to clear in the city and the insurgents still fought in small pockets whenever they could marshal sufficient fighters.

On November 15, during one clearing mission in a house in Fallujah conducted by 3/1, Sergeant Rafael Peralta threw open a closed door to reveal three terrorists with AK-47s. He was hit in the head and chest with multiple bullets at close range and went down. As the fight continued, a "yellow, foreign-made, oval-shaped grenade" rolled into the room. Sergeant Peralta reached out, grabbed the grenade, and tucked it into his abdomen, where it exploded, taking his life.[2] In giving his own life, Sergeant Peralta saved the lives of the Marines in his squad. Dangerous, dirty, and terrifying combat continued every day in the city.

MEF COMMAND AND CONTROL CHANGES

During a December 15 coordination meeting between Brigadier General Hejlik, Rear Admiral Alexander, Colonel Shupp, and Colonel Ballard, the MEF developed a new cooperative arrangement for the reconstruction efforts in Fallujah. The MEF had never been responsible for reconstruction on a scale like that needed in Fallujah, and the normal combat command arrangements did not give the MEF commander the flexibility that he wanted in the reconstruction effort, so he directed that General Hejlik would ensure close coordination among Colonel John Ballard, the commander of the CAG, who was the MEF lead for phase four operations in Fallujah and the principle coordinator with Iraqi government officials; Admiral Alexander, the commander of the MEG; and the regimental commander who "owned" the tactical battlefield, Colonel Mike Shupp.

This structure was designed to balance force protection and combat requirements with the public works and civic action tasks needed to resettle the city under an overall timeline that was acceptable to the Iraqis. Every detail of the activities in Fallujah required coordination because the tactical situation remained fluid and the Iraqi government was very slow to respond to requests for support. The coordinating group structure also made establishing a priority of effort (for everything from supplies that were needed by both the military forces and the Fallujah residents to funding for major projects that could be accomplished by both governments) relatively easy. In practice, many other agencies, including both the MNC-I and MNF-I staffs and the various ministries of the IIG, hampered or frustrated decision making, but at least the key leaders of the MEF could easily pulse together and develop a quick response to an emerging problem. This structure did alter the normal reporting chain within the MEF as it brought the 1st Marine regiment into a closer direct support relationship with the MEF, but, like the shift of the CAG to the tactical control (TACON) of the Division earlier, these alterations were well accepted because all the key leaders worked well together. Flexibility and responsiveness were increased without much added confusion.

SETTING CORNERSTONES FOR RECONSTRUCTION

As valuable as he was as a military commander, General Abdul-Qader did not feel comfortable making civil decisions. He was not a Fallujahn and had no experience in civil administration. He was particularly reluctant to accept responsibility for financial and police functions because he had no experience in these areas of civil society. In the initial planning for the operation, the MEF staff had clearly stated the need for a new mayor and a new (local if possible) police force in the city – at the conclusion of offensive operations. Preparations for such capabilities in Fallujah should have started prior to or during the initial assault. Unfortunately, no mayor or police forces ever materialized and the structures put in place by the MNF to manage the combat operation and reconstruction of the city also had to be used for local administration. These included several critical tools, prominently among which were the Municipal Support Team (MST) and the CMOC.

Luckily, the CAG had previously created and trained its MST to assist in the initial civic reconstruction. The MST included a public administrator, a public works engineer, a security officer, a judicial officer, and a very clever veteran of the first phase of the war who really understood Iraqi culture, Marine Captain Brian Reynaldo. Although designed for work in the city, on November 13, the members of the CAG MST met with General Abdul-Qader to discuss the details of the reconstruction effort. The MST then began working as an adjunct to General Abdul-Qader's tiny staff, helping him formulate answers to civil problems that occurred during the fighting and to develop policies for the reconstruction period. These included the distribution of humanitarian assistance supplies, curfew regulations, access control, and the use of Iraqi Security Forces to prevent looting.

The CMOC was simply a coordination site for the military to interface with the local people and Iraqi and international aid organizations. But the Fallujah CMOC had been the only location where any meaningful dialog had occurred between the Marines and the leadership of the city, and it was also the only place that Iraqis felt comfortable to talk with the MNF about a host of issues, ranging from disappearing persons to employment opportunities to medical needs. Shifting the site downtown sent a clear signal that relations with the city were to be reestablished in a traditional manner, with the principal municipal functions taking place at the same site that the Fallujahns had always used to interact with their government. Of course, the city was in extreme distress by November 16, and the team of Marines that moved downtown that day took on the responsibility of managing all the major functions of a moderate-size city with every single process and service severely broken.

The director of the Fallujah CMOC, Lieutenant Colonel Dave Dysart, was a veteran civil affairs officer who understood well what was needed in the city. He and his key leaders, Lieutenant Colonel Scott Ballard and Lieutenant Colonel Gary Montgomery, established initial workspaces and security, powered up telephone connectivity, and put the towering presence of Master Sergeant Albert Blankenship in control of the physical site. The CMOC was fully operational on November 17. Dysart and his team stayed in the city without a break for most of the following 4 months.

Colonel Mike Shupp's 1st Marines regimental headquarters had also been established in the mayor's complex, located in the former education building less than 200 meters from the CMOC (which had been placed in the former city sports center). Therefore, the municipal "managers" had easy (if still very dangerous) access to the force commander responsible for coordinating the security of the city, and Colonel Shupp ensured that both processes – security and essential services restoration – were as well coordinated as two often diametrically opposed efforts could possibly become.

Although the MEF priority of work was shifting to reconstruction, the 1st Marine Division had to remain primarily concerned about stamping out insurgent fighting in the city. Less than one-third of Fallujah was deemed to be fully cleared of insurgent activity, and even those cleared areas proved to be easily "reinfected" by enemy fighters who moved house to house and through the sewer system at night to obtain weapons, food, and ammunition from previously emplaced caches.

Amazingly, with all these problems, the real fight in mid-November was for public and governmental perceptions about the plight of the Fallujahn people because the misconceptions concerning a humanitarian crisis simply would not end. Based solely on historical experience in other conflicts and no real understanding of the situation in the city, many outside Fallujah were convinced that the city was experiencing a humanitarian crisis of significant proportions. The United Nations High Commissioner for Refugees hosted a meeting in Amman, Jordan, on November 19 with several major relief organization to plan how to help the thousands they believed were in need. The image in many minds was of tens of thousands of people wandering the streets during active combat operations. The reality was that the city was nearly vacant. At most, a couple of hundred people were still living in Fallujah, mostly in their own homes, and by midmonth, the MEF had their locations well identified.

But so many concerns about a humanitarian crisis, unfounded or not, spurred officials in Baghdad to press for numerous updates concerning the plight of Fallujah's residents. In response, the MEF and MNC-I actually embarked on a major effort to find the local residents reputedly sheltering in numerous sites all around the eastern portion of Al Anbar province. This effort included helicopter overflights and even reconnaissance missions to a host of small towns in southern Al Anbar province.

Partially in response to the questions about internally displaced persons on November 16, the CAG had coordinated the delivery of HA supplies from the Iraqi government and Red Crescent Society to residents of nearby Saqlawyiah and Habbiniyah. Two days later, MEF representatives attended the first in a series of senior meetings in Baghdad designed to address the Fallujah situation. In the Iraqi capital, the lack of real coordination among the national ministries became painfully evident despite all the answers that had been requested before the combat operations had stared. General Sattler regularly stressed with General Abdul-Qader the necessity to get Iraqi Ministries involved, and the Iraqi general wholeheartedly agreed, but his requests for support seemed to fall on deaf ears inside the various Iraqi government ministries.

The military structure in Baghdad had been adapted by General Casey to support the reconstruction effort as well. Casey had tasked his deputy, British Lieutenant General Sir John Kiszely, with chairing the coordination effort. General Kiszely was a hard-driving force among the Baghdad crowd and never hesitated to call Iraqi representatives to task against specific objectives identified by the coordination group. He visited Fallujah on several occasions and became a true advocate for the city's restoration. He was often difficult to deal with and did not always support the MEF's plans, but he always had the big picture in mind and effectively broke through several logjams to get decisions made.

Of interest, the MNSTC-I staff also had a British deputy commander at the time, Major General Andrew Farquhar, later Major General Mark Mans, who with Canadian Major General Walter Natynczyk also played an important role in supporting requests for resources in the fighting for Fallujah. Although the major actions in the city were accomplished with U.S. and Iraqi forces, the multinational partners in Iraq did support the effort and reinforced it with their actions in other sections of the country. In particular the Black Watch Regiment was assigned to the 1st Marine Division during the winter of 2004, and it played an important role in closing one of the avenues through which insurgents could have escaped Fallujah for Baghdad.

Still, the transition from active combat to reconstruction continued, and on November 19, the CAG and the 1st Marine Division conducted a reconstruction planning meeting to correlate time and resources for the eventual return of citizens to the city. The return of residents was then to be based on a prerequisite of establishing a safe and secure environment with minimal basic services restored. As an innovative technique, the Division planners developed a sector map of the city, color coding the 17 principal resettlement areas. This diagram gave specificity to the process and helped immensely in coordination of effort. At that time, few military planners expected a significant political push to return residents early to the city, but such a push soon began to drive the priority of work in Fallujah.

In a groundbreaking event on November 20, the working-level members of the Iraqi "Fallujah Reconstruction Committee" from Baghdad agreed to meet at Camp Fallujah, and on the next day, under the leadership of General Abdul-Qader, the ad hoc group met at the camp and agreed to form several standing work groups to prioritize and coordinate Iraqi government reconstruction activities within the city. This was a critical first step toward real coordination for the future of Fallujah and Al Anbar province overall.

Improvements in the city infrastructure also began on November 20, when several electricity crews from the Ministry of Electricity finally entered the city and began working to repair the maze of tangled and fractured electrical wiring in Fallujah. The electrical network in Fallujah had suffered from years of abuse before the fighting and was a jury-rigged combination of several older and a few more modern electrical arrangements. Electricity was a key element of life in the city, as it would be in any other modern urban area, but the damage the network had received during combat broke the back of an already insufficient system. It was readily apparent that the electrical services would require rapid and extensive improvement to return full functionality to the city.

Also on that day the MEF began to conduct regular contractor coordination management meetings. Civilian contractors were linked up with security escorts at vehicle checkpoints on the outskirts of the city and brought into Fallujah to work. This process sounded simple but proved very difficult to execute in practice. Contractors often failed to link up with security at the coordinated time or place.

Eventually, the still well-known FLT site proved functional as a contractor staging and link-up area, but even this required a team of on-site managers and coordinators to work through a host of daily issues, such as security, fuel, movement control, and storage of material.

The previous day one of the infantry companies in the city has discovered a terrorist command center and VBIED workshop believed to have been used by Zarqawi. The command center included computers, letters from the terrorist leader, and a large sign titled, "Al Qaeda Organization."[3] Eleven Marines, one American, and one Iraqi soldier had been killed in continued fighting in Fallujah since November 15.[4] It was still a very dangerous place.

In a critically important step toward the city's recovery, the IIG sent some more senior ministry representatives to Camp Fallujah to attend the very first Fallujah reconstruction meeting on November 21 with General Abdul-Qader. Initially, the Iraqi attendees were extremely reluctant to even visit Camp Fallujah, preferring instead to meet in the cement plant operated by the MOI located a few kilometers northeast of city. (The Iraqis were reluctant to enter Camp Fallujah because they feared for their lives if the insurgents identified them as working with the MNF.) But, over time, it became evident that the meetings could only function as desired if they occurred inside Camp Fallujah and a regular series of meetings was designed for each Monday.

To support these meetings and entice the Baghdad representatives to work from Camp Fallujah, the MEF created additional sleeping quarters outside the conference building used by General Abdul-Qader for his command center. The Iraqi ministry representatives were flown by military helicopter from Baghdad to the meeting site on the camp to ensure their safety. The first group of Iraqis to arrive at Camp Fallujah for the meeting were a scared and ragged bunch who had not been told by their ministry officials that they would be staying overnight in the camp. No one knew for certain who the key members of the Iraqi contingent were or how much authority they had been given by their individual ministers. In fact, the MEF staff had to trust that all the men who arrived were indeed opponents of the insurgency.[5]

General Sattler began the first meeting with an appeal for unity of effort and dedication to the task of restoring Fallujah to its residents. Colonel Ballard provided a briefing on the MEF's posthostilities planning and proposed some initial priorities of work. Then General Abdul-Qader spoke for the first time before his fellow Iraqi civil leaders to push for an aggressive and diligent approach to restoring security and services such as electricity and water. As with many initial interagency meetings, the November 21 get-together lacked any form of decision-making process and no one knew who the real influential personalities were. Still, the first meeting did develop a high level of concurrence on the need to prioritize MNF-I efforts and thankfully set a good precedent for dialog and cooperation.

The MEF was not the only organization working to assist the Fallujahns. The host of NGOs that many expected to arrive with humanitarian supplies never materialized, but the Iraqi Red Crescent Society (IRCS) did establish an office in

Fallujah on November 24. Although the IRCS was soon proven to harbor insurgent supporters, the establishment of its office in the city did help allay some concerns of a widespread humanitarian disaster and opened a useful "window" into the city for nonmilitary members of the Iraqi government to gain an appreciation of what was really happening there.

The MEF and 1st Marine Division planners had by that time developed an innovative plan to manage the flow of returning citizens. They understood that the proper management of the flow of people and the information they needed to return to their homes safely would be keys to success. So the Marine planners had identified information required to inform the residents of conditions inside Fallujah, printed pamphlets for distribution all over the province, and developed a scheme of entry control points, an identification badge policy, and even new citywide rules of conduct required for a municipality that still had no police or traffic officers. Security inside the city was still the driving factor, and the Marines did not want thousands of people to reenter the city all at once because shops and businesses were still filled with goods that presented the temptation for looting, as did the household items that were remaining after the owners left the city. Almost every door in the city was open as a result of the clearing operations that were required to ensure the insurgents had been evicted from Fallujah.

Additional evidence of the dangers of entering the city before it could be made secure was illustrated by the discovery of a massive weapons cache, the largest up to that point in the city, inside the Saad Bin Abi Waqas mosque. This mosque was the location where Janabi had been known to preach. It contained artillery shells, heavy machine guns, antitank mines, and even some surface-to-air missile components. On the same day in the southwestern part of the city, a suspected chemical laboratory was also discovered by forces searching for buried weapons. That lab contained some vials of cyanide and manuals for producing anthrax.[6] There was no doubt remaining that the city had hosted all of the worst elements of the insurgency.

Debris removal contracts were let starting on November 26, although getting contractors into the city still proved to be a painfully slow and difficult process. Unexpectedly, a host of coordination issues concerning security requirements of the MNF, residual insurgent intimidation efforts, and fear of the unknown kept contractors and laborers away from many very lucrative opportunities. By the end of the month, standing water in the city posed a real threat, so water removal contracts were let to assist the MEG engineers with the monumental effort to dry up the numerous areas of the city that were under water. Water tank installation contracts were also let as the MEG determined that what remained of the water treatment system was insufficient for the needs of the city. Food and construction material contracts were also formed to build stockpiles in advance of the return of residents.

The military labor provided by the MEG finally began to reduce flooding in Fallujah on November 27; 3 weeks after major combat began in the city. The Navy Seabees started generators and operated three lift stations, producing the first noticeable drop in flood water levels in the city. Pumps had to be operated daily

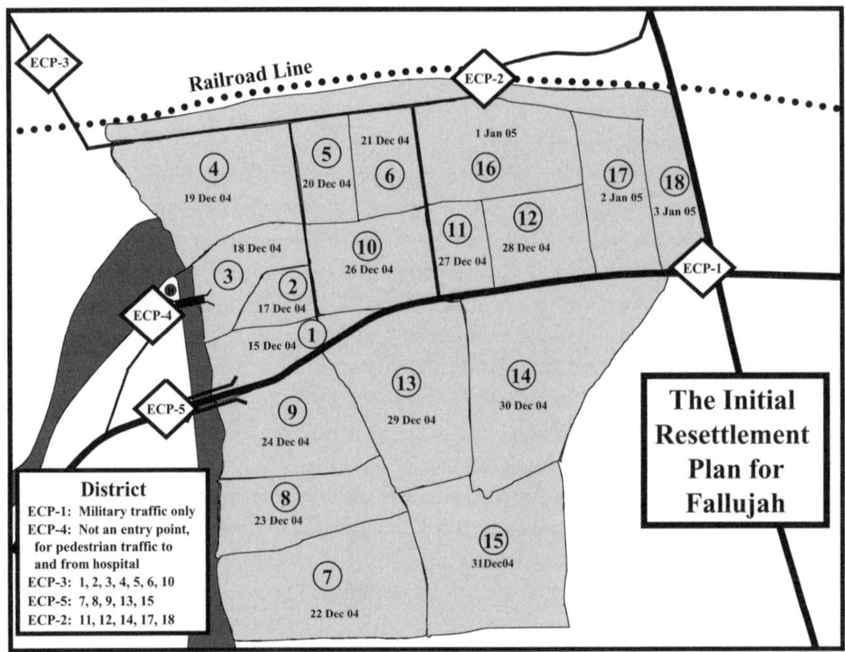

Map 7. The Initial Resettlement Plan for Fallujah

to keep ahead of the water table; even so, the dewatering effort would remain an ongoing challenge for many more weeks. Many feared at the time that had the Navy Seabees not been able to rid the city of standing water, Fallujah and its residents might have been prone to an insect-borne disease outbreak. Later, on December 1, a U.S. Navy Forward Deployable Environmental/Preventive Medicine Unit (FDPMU) arrived in Fallujah to conduct a survey addressing the potential public health threats in the city. Although its members did not detect any significant insect-borne disease vectors, they did recommend ridding the city of the large number of feral dogs and cats that were living amid the rubble.

That same day, Ambassador John Negroponte and Ambassador Bill Taylor, the head of the Iraqi Reconstruction Management Office (IRMO), both visited Fallujah along with the Iraqi Minister of Industry and Minerals, Hajim Al-Hasani, who had been assigned by Prime Minister Allawi as the chief Iraqi coordinator for the city's reconstruction. Ambassador Negroponte felt strongly that the Iraqis needed to support the reconstruction effort in Fallujah more strongly, so he toured the city with Minister Hasani to understand the extent of the destruction and to impel Hasani to greater activity. Both men spoke to reporters in the Fallujah CMOC and discussed reconstruction plans with the CMOC team.

During the second weekly Iraqi reconstruction meeting held on Camp Fallujah on November 28, the Iraqis chose December 15 as the resettlement date for Fallujah residents. In part, this was a signal of their urgency and although the date would slip slowly to the third week of December, it was still an important target for all the key players to focus their efforts. Even more importantly, during the same meeting, Engineer Basil Mahmoud of the Ministry of Industry and Minerals was appointed as the Iraqi civil manager of the reconstruction effort for Fallujah. General Abdul-Qader quickly began to defer all civil decisions to Basil and focus his efforts solely on security issues once the civil coordinator had been acknowledged by the other ministry representatives.

Ambassador Negroponte's push for greater Iraqi energy bore real fruit on November 30, when Prime Minister Allawi arrived in the city and visited the CMOC. Allawi traveled with just a few subordinates, including Minister Hasani and Allawi's close advisor Adel Hillawi, but made a quick and decisive study of the situation. He spoke in very specific terms in the CMOC with Basil Mahmoud and the Iraqi officials working downtown in Fallujah to press for a town council and fuller involvement by the residents of the city in the reconstruction process. Prime Minister Allawi lent his full support to the reconstruction effort, and his visit stimulated a stronger effort on the part of his government and resulted in newfound sincere interest on the part of several ministries that had not been sufficiently engaged prior to his visit. The one outlier among the ministries in active coordination remained the MOI, which had still made no effort to develop a new police force for the city.

It is important to remember that in November the IIG was still a government in development and that even in a mature, functioning democracy coordinating a national effort for something as extensive and complex as the reconstruction of Fallujah was a monumental task. Similar to American efforts to coordinate the national response following a natural disaster, the various parts of Allawi's government were loathe to expend resources outside their specific areas of responsibility and no "contingency" funds were available in Iraq for such an expensive proposition. Therefore, particularly in the early weeks, reconstruction coordination for the effort in Fallujah required a great deal of personal commitment from leaders at all levels and, indeed, forceful persuasion by the prime minister and his staff director, Adel Hillawi.

CHANGES IN MEF FORCES

Colonel Craig Tucker's RCT-7 had only been shifted to the Fallujah operations area for the assault portion of operation Al Fajr. He and his battalions were needed back in the northwestern part of the province to relive the 31st MEU and tighten controls on the border entry points into Iraq. Tucker's battalions had begun turning over their sections of Fallujah to their sister units in Mike Shupp's RCT-1 soon after the first week of combat operations.[7] By the first week of December, RCT-7 had turned over all of its responsibilities in the city and RCT-1 provided the command and control of all forces assigned for security operations in the city – both United States and Iraqi.

Under normal circumstances such a rapid turnover and reduction in forces in the city would have produced a gap into which the enemy could attack the MNF. But the interoperability among the MEF forces (from commands all over the Marine Corps) was so well honed that no noticeable reduction in coverage was evident. Added to this efficient turnover, the Iraqis provided a newly organized Public Order Brigade to replace the Marines and soldiers of RCT-7.

The Public Order Brigade, commanded by Major General Mehdi, was so new that the individual units did not even have basic items of equipment such as cold weather boots and gloves (it was December and even Iraq gets quite cold in the evenings). They did have new weapons but did not have the level of training necessary to carry out even small unit maneuvers unassisted by U.S. forces. This meant that the MEF was required to provide both basic equipment and small unit training to the Public Order units prior to employing the Brigade inside Fallujah.

Most of the equipment was issued and the training accomplished in the East Fallujah Iraqi Camp (EFIC), a training site built from nothing east of the main MEF camp specifically to support the Iraqi forces in the operation. In the camp, each Marine unit in Fallujah was linked to an Iraqi unit of similar size, with which it would be paired in the city. Both units lived and trained together and worked as a team inside Fallujah. This innovative mentorship technique significantly accelerated the improvement in the readiness of the Public Order Brigade and gave Colonel Shupp the additional forces he needed to replace the departing RCT-7 battalions.

Colonel Shupp and General Mehdi also had to work hand in hand. Although they began the relationship as skeptical partners, over time, they both began to value the other's contributions. In particular, General Mehdi soon saw how dedicated Colonel Shupp was to the Iraqi people and their welfare and he then began to step up his own role as the senior Iraqi security officer in the city. As with Generals Abdul-Qader and Sattler, the mentorship program succeeded again through the personal dedication and professionalism of the people involved.

SLOW START TO IRAQI RECONSTRUCTION

Even in early December 2004, military labor still shouldered the full burden of reconstruction and cleanup in Fallujah. The municipal workers of the city were slowly coming back to work, but the civilian contractors that were the only source of the manual labor required were still not showing up to assist. Intimidation, fear, and access coordination were all to blame. Water removal and rubble clearing remained the top two priorities – both preconditions to the return of the residents. (Rubble clearing was not just a beautification issue; the Marines feared many IEDs and items of unexploded ordnance lay beneath the mounds of rubble.)[8]

On December 3, 3 weeks after the initial bids were announced, the first three contractors arrived in Fallujah to begin water and rubble removal. Of greater import on December 5, the Seabees were finally able to turn over 3 of the 10 water lift stations to returned municipal employees.[9] The water contractor also began installing large gray water cisterns in the city to compensate for the damaged pipes and provided washing water to residents after their return.

During the December 9 Fallujah reconstruction meeting in Baghdad, the U.S. representatives stressed the risk involved with an earlier-than-acceptable return date for the population. It was clear to those who were working in the city every day that a rapid increase in the city population would easily overwhelm fragile civil support structures then in place. Given the possibility of an early reopening of the city, on December 9, the CAG staff prepared a plan to backstop Iraqi reconstruction efforts for an early return date. This plan identified MNF resources required and also illustrated the cost of an early reopening without essential Iraqi support to assist in informing the Iraqi decision makers.

The same day, in a press conference, General Sattler outlined the generic plan for returning residents to Fallujah. The plan was based on the Division's desire to limit access only to heads of households, at least initially, and to control the resettlement by opening only certain districts of the city on a gradual basis. The plan also included using a limited number of entry control points and iris scanning to produce identification cards for certain residents (mostly military-age males) and no privately owned vehicles. General Sattler indicated that 90 percent of the city's buildings had been cleared, but some unexploded ordnance might still remain so returning residents needed to be very cautious. The information needed to get out to the residents of Fallujah so that they could understand what to expect and how long it might take to get the city resettled. The MEF depended on the IIG to get the information out to the Iraqi population, but General Sattler also wanted to ensure that the media was well informed about the plan and the need to manage expectations – it would not be a headlong dash to return.[10]

By December 11, the first four entry control points and associated humanitarian assistance sites had been constructed by the Marine battalions in the city and the Seabees. The Marines needed to have the sites in advance of the actual return – still expected for December 15 – so that they could train and rehearse a variety of scenarios prior to the arrival of the first waves of returning residents. The entry control points were designed to shield residents from an attack while they were being checked through security, in case of the number one threat – the vehicle-borne IED (VBIED).

The Director of the United States Agency for International Development (USAID) and Ambassador Taylor, the American director of the Iraqi Reconstruction Management Organization (IRMO) both visited Camp Fallujah on December 12 to get an update on the reconstruction efforts in Fallujah. General Sattler sat in on the meeting to signal the importance of the construction effort, while Colonel Ballard briefed the Fallujah resettlement plan to USAID Director Natsios, Ambassador Taylor of IRMO, and a host of Iraqi ministry representatives. USAID had provided funding for two large electrical generators in Fallujah and had promised much more support but was not at the time very forthcoming with personnel and materials.

As a painful reminder of the severity of the fighting that still occurred in Fallujah, five Marines lost their lives in a single day as a result of combat that broke out on December 12. Every day, Marines and their Iraqi counterparts continued to risk their lives patrolling the streets of the city. Although the enemy had by mid-December been decisively defeated, there was evidence that some insurgents were returning to the city to continue the fighting. Slowly the Iraqi security forces were taking on the role of the municipal police, but the process was a difficult one. It was only the establishment of such local "beat cop" security that could effectively ensure the safety of the people inside Fallujah, allowing the Marines to focus singularly on the insurgent threat.

During the Fallujah reconstruction meeting held on December 13, each Iraqi ministry representative was asked to brief their plan for the support of returning Fallujah residents. Unfortunately, the members from the important Trade and Oil ministries did not have executable plans to support the returning populace. Because the Trade Ministry was responsible for providing the monthly Iraqi food allocation and the Ministry of Oil was to distribute fuel oils, their planning and resource shortcomings could have posed a real threat to an otherwise successful return effort. In such cases, only the MNF remained to compensate for any shortfalls, but even the MNF did not have the food or fuel to support 100,000 residents simultaneously with ongoing operations in Iraq.

During the 2-day period from December 13 to 14, significant combat action in the city of Fallujah slowed reconstruction efforts and closed the main supply routes to contractor traffic. It was the last gasp of the main body of the insurgents that had started in the city a month before and the pooled resources of those who had reinfiltrated, but it was a futile attempt to lessen the MNF control in Fallujah. By mid-December, the local residents were strongly behind the MNF's efforts and they were reporting on violations of the rules and on any weapons caches they found. There was no longer any real indigenous support for the insurgency in the city.

Also, on December 14, the MEF released its operations order 001-04, entitled "Phase IV, Operation AL FAJR." That order delineated the functional responsibilities among the MEF major subordinate commanders during the next phase of the operation and designated the 4th CAG as the main effort. The Deputy Commanding General, Brigadier General Hejlik, was designed as the MEF's Executive Agent to oversee the security, stability, reconstruction, and resettlement efforts in Fallujah. The 1st Marine Division was tasked to provide security within the city, as well as manning entry control points and using the Biometric Automated Toolset System (BATS) to identify every military-age male who returned to the city. Both the FSSG and the MEG were directed to provide engineering support to the reconstruction effort, and the FSSG was required to oversee the functioning of the HA sites.

Even with all the military planned completed, on December 15, the Fallujah resettlement date was eventually postponed on the very day planned for the reentry of its residents. The security situation and lack of ministry preparations forced the IIG to postpone the date. This gave the MEF additional breathing room to fully prepare and rehearse the entry control process it was so feverishly developing.

Overall, the city was improving, if very slowly. By December 16, water and rubble removal efforts continued to make good progress. A significant decrease in flood water levels was noticeable for the first time as a result of the MEG's removal efforts throughout city. Based on the original return date, on December 17, bus routes were established in the city to move Fallujahns about without permitting privately owned vehicles free access within the city. And, the following day (December 18), electrical restoration efforts brought the Fallujah General Hospital back on city power and local Iraqi municipal leaders begin meeting with one another at the CMOC without prompting to do so from the CAG.

That same day, the 1st Marine Division released its FRAGO 453-04 (Operation Al Fajr Phase IV) to give guidance to its major subordinate commanders for the return of residents to Fallujah. That order formally set the parameters for Phase IV of operation Phantom Fury (now called Al Fajr) to begin from the MNF perspective. Unfortunately, it was the Iraqi ministries that still had much to do to make the return successful.

By December 20, a noticeable change in Iraqi support in Fallujah was illustrated by the Ministry of Oil's effort to restock the fuel station outside the city of Fallujah and the Ministry of Minerals efforts to stockpile food and household necessities in the cement plant. The next day, IRAQNA cellular phone service was restored after IRAQNA workers were brought into the city to make necessary repairs. Late in the day, the IIG announced from Baghdad that December 23 would be the resettlement date – the date for the residents to return. The next day, contractors were finally given unescorted access to work in the city to make final repairs.

During the period of major combat operations in Fallujah, the Marines discovered a vast amount about the enemy they were fighting. They also found over 450 weapons cache sites, 24 IED factories, 13 command and control (headquarters) locations, 2 VBIED construction sites, and numerous execution sites. The 1st Marine Division also located 4 known hostage locations. Along the way, Marines and Soldiers identified numerous violations of the law of armed conflict, including instances where an IED was placed in a human corpse, insurgents faked surrender with a white flag, and multiple occasions when the enemy used schools, hospitals, and ambulances to stage attacks.[11]

Given the news about December 23, the MEF issued a modification to its previous operations order 001-04 (Fallujah Resettlement). The modification set the new date and specified that MEF forces would support the IIG in the resettlement of the city of Fallujah and the reestablishment of governmental control and essential services. It also required the MEF subordinate commanders to provide emergency supplies and services as required and provide security in coordination with the IIG to hasten the city's return to local control. From the military perspective all the controls were in place to begin resettlement.

THE RETURN TO FALLUJAH

On December 23, the real objective of the operations began to be realized when nearly 1,000 residents returned to a Fallujah free of organized insurgent influence. They lined up in cars, from the entrances to the city to the visual horizon, not knowing what they would find once inside but anxious to restart their lives. Once inside the shattered city they traveled by their own cars (the requested prohibition on private automobiles was disapproved as too harsh) toward the Andalus section of the city very near the old green bridge. From that small part of the city, Fallujah would slowly be reborn over the coming weeks and months.

A few days later, Osama bin Laden had a speech published on the Internet that paid homage to the fighters in Fallujah who were "standing firm and refusing to submit" in the face of the MNF attack.[12] He certainly knew the truth. Overall, the speech was a clear acknowledgment that the battle had been lost, yet bin Laden still praised the insurgent fighters who fought bravely "bareheaded and with chests uncovered" against the Americans.[13] As in many other elements of the Al Qaeda media campaign, bin Laden attempted to turn the tactical defeat into a rallying cry for more support for his overall campaign of jihad.

He used the speech to declare Zarqawi the Emir of Al Qaeda in Iraq and Baghdad the capital of the Islamic Caliphate he desired. In another section of the speech, he also demonstrated that Prime Minister Allawi, along with President Karzai of Afghanistan, were apostate supporters of the infidel. The leader of Al Qaeda used the fight for Fallujah to urge even greater steadfastness against the besieging and bombarding American invader. Even as the defeat of the insurgents in the city was sealed by the peaceful return of the city's residents, the strategic importance of Fallujah was not lost on bin Laden.

Chapter Seven

Civil–Military Operations: The Bridge to a New Fallujah

Once the decision was made to reopen the city to all its residents, the focus of effort by military forces in Fallujah had to change as well. The transition from combat operations against the enemy to a focus on the restoration of essential services and humanitarian assistance in Fallujah was envisioned to be spatial, not time based. In other words, although fighting was continuing in some areas of the city, where possible, MNF and Iraqi forces would be rebuilding pump houses and electrical substations in an area not far away, and, in other locations within the city, military forces would also be providing humanitarian relief supplies to the remaining Fallujah residents. Under this construct, conflict in the city would be terminated and livability would be restored sector by sector.

In practice, this conditions-based conflict termination and resettlement process worked rather well on the ground, but it did suffer from some significant challenges. First, the agreed-on prerequisites for restoring normalcy to the city were never completely met. The IIG did appoint a military governor, but General Abdul-Qader's authority in the city was never made clear. Perhaps more importantly, the Minister of the Interior flatly failed in his commitment to bring in police forces from outside the city to restore civil order. Iraqi and coalition soldiers, to include two battalions of newly formed public order troops, were used instead to provide the necessary police functions in the city for several months. Finally, both the MNF and the IIG did commit funds for the city's restoration, but initially there was no coordinating mechanism to determine who should accomplish which essential project and in what order civic and public works projects were to be completed. It will surprise no one to know that the MNF and Iraqi priorities for restoration were different.

THE INTER-MINISTERIAL FALLUJAH WORKING GROUP

The second key mechanism for the coordination of effort in Al Fajr was an interagency working group that operated at the operational level and linked issues in Fallujah with intergovernmental support through the MNF military headquarters and the U.S. and UK embassies. This Inter-ministerial Fallujah Working Group operated through twice weekly meetings. The first was always held in Fallujah, initially on Camp Fallujah while combat operations continued, and then later within the old Fallujah mayor's complex at the MEF CMOC. The second was always held in Baghdad, normally at the Ministry of Industry and Minerals, whose minister was appointed as the lead agent for Fallujah reconstruction. Although many individuals attended both these meetings, their focus and authorities were quite different. The local Fallujah meeting was designed to provide the administration and technical expertise to manage the city's affairs. It was led by Engineer Basil Mahmoud of the Ministry of Industry and Minerals, who for several months was in effect the city manager of Fallujah. He had the authority to establish priorities and direct local reconstruction activities by the various Iraqi government institutions. He was assisted every day by members of the MST. During November, MEF Civil Affairs officers effectively directed the affairs of the city while combat operations were the focus of effort, but by January, as the residents were beginning to return, Engineer Mahmoud had grown to be the key Iraqi figure in the city and the manager of daily activities.

The Baghdad meeting was normally chaired by the Deputy Minister of Industry and Minerals, Mr. Mohammed Abdullah Mohammed. Minister Mohammed Abdullah was a career bureaucrat of real skill, who had survived under Saddam Hussein and into the IIG. He ensured that the policymakers within the council of ministers were executing the work and following the priorities required in Fallujah. Using personal authority alone, he managed to gain resources from many of the resource-poor ministries in Iraq to help the reconstruction in Fallujah. Military representatives attended both meetings and acted as a sort of connecting file at the local and national levels. The one gap in coverage of this two meeting process was at the provincial level.

Like most nations, Iraq has a strong provincial government function, where national policies are adapted to more local needs. For the operation in Fallujah, the provincial government was in Ramadi, only 30 miles away, yet unfortunately, the appointed governor there was never very well integrated into the coordination process. Initially, the civilian governor was so repressed and intimidated by insurgent threats that he played no visible role; afterward, Prime Minster Allawi appointed a new governor, Sheik Fassel al-Goud, but he attended only one meeting in Fallujah and did nothing to assist in the reconstruction effort. His provincial Directors-General could have added much to the recovery process but was effectively isolated from the most pressing issues because the governor was not interested and the national government in Baghdad was absorbed by it.

Another important shortfall in this structure was the lack of any functioning Iraqi civil–military coordination. It took the prime minister's personal involvement to get the Ministry of Interior or Ministry of Industry to work directly with the Ministry of Defense for any of its subordinate command elements. In practice, this meant that the MNF pulled together any inter-ministerial coordination that did not occur in either the local Fallujah meetings or the Baghdad Reconstruction Working Group. With no forcing function behind the scenes, it was extremely difficult to develop in any real consensus in the early months. Only after some reconstruction headway was developed and significant funding was made available did any proactive ministry coordination begin on the part of the Iraqi leaders. Publicity certainly helping this as Fallujah was on every media outlet in the country, but it was progress and money that really made the difference.

THE NEWLY REOPENED CITY

On December 24, long lines at the city's four primary Entry Control Points (ECPs) begin the start of what would seem to the Marines as an endless series of complaints about access to Fallujah. Government officials, contractors, and workers all wanted special high-speed access to the city, but with every improvement in access some improvement in security had to be made and the risk in not maintaining security was unacceptable to the MEF, so speed of access became a sort of a governor on entry to the city.

Finally showing some interest, Governor Fassal al-Goud attended the Fallujah reconstruction meeting at the CMOC on December 27. By his own statements, the governor was clearly out of touch with current reconstruction efforts and progress. He would continue to remain disengaged with Fallujah governance. Intimidation was still rampant in Al Anbar province overall, however, and the murder of the Al Anbar vice governor at the end of the month effectively halted key leader engagement at the provincial level. This barbaric act had no tangible effect on Fallujah reconstruction though, as government involvement in Iraq had traditionally bypassed the provincial level and only occurred significantly at the national level.

The good news was that the national government of Iraq was improving its support significantly day by day, and the city was mostly clear of the major pockets of debris. By December 28, food and fuel deliveries from the Baghdad ministries were occurring regularly in Fallujah. The Ministry of Trade (MOT) was trucking food and welfare supplies such as heaters and cooking fuel into the city once or twice a week. Initially, they were off-loading the trucks at mosques around the city, but the government quickly decided to distance itself from the traditional support through mosques and began to shift their deliveries to the humanitarian assistance sites created by the Marines. (The IIG expressed concern over the practice of distributing food from mosques because it did not want to associate government action with religious sites.)

The first of these humanitarian assistance sites to be constructed was in Jolan on the location of a children's amusement park; it was named Jolan Park. The second site was in the southern half of the city in an open area near a flour factory – it later became known as Brahma Ranch. The final site was Dave's Field in the eastern sector of the city, located behind a small strip mall, near some soccer fields.

All three of these locations were ringed with protective wire and well guarded by the individual infantry battalions that had responsibility for the sector of the city in which they were located. Although the civil affairs Marines assisted with overall coordination, they were normally run day to day by Marines from the 1st FSSG, and Iraqi soldiers always played a part in the distribution of aid. These humanitarian assistance sites were eventually turned over to the MOT in the second week of January, when the MOT began to take full responsibility for the distribution of food from Jolan Park. The MEF continued to operate two other HA sites at Brahma Ranch and Dave's Field for several more weeks, but they soon outlived their usefulness as the market system in the city began to take new root.

Fuel deliveries were more challenging because of the special handling required and the value of fuel on the black market. Luckily, the Ministry of Oil controlled two storage sites in Fallujah and was able to make special provisions to keep three fuel stations fairly well stocked with automobile fuel (which in Iraq is benzene). Cooking and heating fuels were also distributed in the city, although initially the Marines provided much of it by contracting tanker trucks to roam the city permitting residents to fill containers street side.

These distribution efforts were possible only because the MEG and groups of contracted workers had put a priority on clearing the city of debris immediately after the heaviest fighting was reduced in late November. Using military labor (dump trucks and drivers) initially, over December more and more contracted workers and ministry assistance contributed to the effort until all the streets were clear of obstructions; downed power lines were removed, and the barriers and obstacles constructed by the insurgents (which many feared still contained IEDs) were removed to a dump site north of Fallujah.

The new year closed out a chapter in Fallujah with the cost of one more Marine's life in the continuing clearing effort by RCT-1. Lance Corporal Jason E. Smith of Phoenix, Arizona, died on December 31 during a patrol in support of operations in the city. He was assigned to 1st Light Armored Reconnaissance Battalion, 1st Marine Division. Smith's death showed that the city remained a dangerous place even after nearly 2 months of security operations.

A NEW YEAR BACK IN FALLUJAH

During the first week of January, drinking water was restored to the northwest quadrant of the city. Although without electricity, the water pumps used by Fallujah residents to lift the liquid from the pipes at street level could not be operated to pump the water to cisterns on the rooftops of residential homes. The first evidence of markets and shop owners opening up also began to appear in that first week of the year. The Marines first witnessed a vegetable market doing brisk business in western Fallujah, just east of the new bridge and near the Green Mosque. This area, the Andalus, was the first to be repopulated and was the origin of most of the economic growth in the first weeks.

At the end of the week, several local Iraqi officials met with former presidential candidate and serving U.S. Senator John Kerry, at his request, during an official visit to Camp Fallujah. The conversation focused on the upcoming elections, stability, and compensation but was not tainted with bitterness on the Iraqis' part, as many might have expected. Overall, the officials understood about the challenges of returning life to the city and were thankful for the U.S. assistance. The general population, however, still had a wait and see attitude.[1]

During January, the management arrangements inside Fallujah began to shift. First General Abdul-Qader was appointed the new commander of all Iraqi land forces in early January. He moved to his new headquarters in Baghdad with General Kassim and neither officer was replaced. Although Basil Mahmoud was serving admirably and was in fact growing more and more influential as the city's reconstruction coordinator, he did not want to make decisions about resident's legal issues. As had always been anticipated by the Marines, there was a growing need for a municipal council or mayor in the city.

Consequently, on January 11, the CMOC staff met with former Fallujah mayor Ra'ad Hussein, who appeared supportive of coalition efforts. He had been mayor in late 2004, before the last insurgent-supporting mayor (a man named Al Joorusi) had occupied the post. Al Joorusi had tried to lobby for his old job and title back during the initial days of the operation, even presenting himself at Camp Fallujah as an IIG coordinator, but he was so tainted by his association with the insurgents that he was completely rebuffed by the IIG.

Ra'ad Hussein was not completely above suspicion either, and the Marines started to work with him as an authority figure very much with a wait and see attitude. Colonel Shupp knew that he had some dangerous ties with the sheiks of the city, and members of his staff were implicated with anti-coalition activities (one was later arrested for plotting to kidnap a Marine officer). But Mayor Ra'ad seemed to have the best interests of the people at heart and was a hardworking man who remained closely involved with every issue of reconstruction and resettlement, so he performed a very useful service and became gradually accepted as the municipal chief.

By midmonth it was apparent to General Sattler that the city needed an infusion of funds to jump start the individual family reconstruction needs in the city. He pushed hard for the Iraqi government to contribute $100 to each family that had returned, but the Iraqi bureaucracy, even using the national food card system as a template, proved too unwieldy to produce payments in short notice. After pushing formally several times, General Sattler decided to use his own authority and obtained MNF-I permission to pay the families using coalition funds. This tactic definitely inspired the IIG to match his offer of a payment, but the Iraqi government still suffered under such mismanagement that this first significant cash payment shipment was intercepted and stolen within hours of its arrival in the provincial capital of Ramadi.[2]

On January 13, the MEF through RCT-1 began paying a $200 humanitarian assistance payment to all Fallujah heads of households. That same day, the Ministry of Trade doubled its food shipments into Fallujah, and on the following day all neighborhoods in Fallujah were finally opened to residents. The gradual resettlement plan was complete on schedule on January 14, although it seemed to the Marines on the ground as though it was a rush to fill the city much faster than seemed prudent. Again, it was the sense of urgency in Baghdad, not Fallujah, that drove events, from a fear that delays could reflect badly on the IIG.

The MST's role in bringing the sheiks, imams, and other Fallujahn leaders of various groups together to develop some sort of a city council was crucial. The prime minister had pressed for a city council rather than a single mayor so that broad-based support could develop in the city. Over time the MST became the motive force within the city for this effort and, through its town hall meetings, it reached out to touch a host of additional issues that were of local concern. Although the effort started slowly, after midmonth it began to engender ever-greater local involvement once it became clear that the reconstruction committee was responsive to requests by residents.

The MST mentored Iraqi technocrats and municipal leaders and assisted Basil Mahmoud, the appointed Iraqi reconstruction director, in his many varied tasks. With the addition of U.S. Navy Seabees and their construction engineering expertise on several working groups, the MST played the critical tactical role of developing governance, consensus, and progress in the city.

TRANSITION TO A NEW FALLUJAH: NATIONAL ELECTIONS AND COMPENSATION

By the second week of January 2005, Fallujah had become a very different city. Reconstruction was still modest, but the MNF and the IIG had compensated for the basic city essential services and more and more residents were staying overnight in the city. Although the entire city was open for resettlement and incidents of combat had been nearly extinguished, Iraqis were still very hesitant to go to the scene of so much heavy fighting. Still, everyone in the government knew that the burden of so many displaced people would be hard for Iraq to bear and the national election scheduled for the end of January would be difficult to conduct as long as the Sunnis viewed Fallujah as a battlefield.

Food, fuel, and water were being provided in the basic ways throughout the city. Food was still distributed to locals in two humanitarian assistance sites (one at Brahma Park in the south and the other at Dave's Field in the northeast quadrant of the city). Electricity was still problematic, with the only source of power being provided by generators spread around the various city districts. Because household water was lifted from ground level by electrical pumps, drinking water was not flowing in individual homes but was still furnished by tanker trucks moving daily along the major streets. Large gray cisterns with ground-level outlet valves supplied nonpotable cleaning water to the residents that had returned. Still, long lines of cars still built up along the five major roads leading into the city; nearly 1,000 cars transported an average of over 7,000 people into the city each day. Government food distribution – normally supplied by ration cards through the Oil for Food program[3] – had yet to be reestablished, and markets remained barren except for a few fresh vegetable stands at the base of the western bridge. Normal life had not yet returned, but it was clear that the foundation for the new, safer city had been laid.

The number one priority of the MNF for Fallujah was pushing through an Iraqi compensation package for housing reconstruction in the city. General Sattler and his key staff knew that normal life in the city could only return once the residents were able to rebuild their homes and markets were reopened in the city. For that to occur, Fallujah needed an influx of capital. The MEF was so concerned about the state of the city's houses that it started planning a process to pay each head of household $200.

No one thought it would be possible to pay each Iraqi family inside the city. Yet, in characteristic fashion, the Marines never considered that the effort would fail. They obtained the funds and used the same humanitarian assistance site in Brahma Ranch that had been used to dispense food early in the operation as a secure location. Information was broadcast throughout the province to ensure all the families on the Oil for Food ration card rolls for the city were able to request the money. Each head of household was eligible to get the $100 by showing proof of residency. (Each also received an ink stamp on the hand to prevent applying multiple times.)

In a matter of a few days, over 32,000 residents of Fallujah were paid the "humanitarian payment." They stood in long lines, they were orderly, and they understood what the money was intended to do. Their own government had promised to match the payment, but it took weeks for that effort to reach the hands of the needy (although for the IIG payment, eligible residents were able to get the money at several national banks in Al Anbar and in Baghdad).

Still combat casualties punctuated the daily efforts of the MEF as it conducted a series of clearing operations in Ramadi and the northern half of the province.[4] These operations were designed to keep the insurgents who had been cleaned out of Fallujah on the run and prevent the supporting elements of the terrorist network from picking up from the cell that had been destroyed by Al Fajr.

ZARQAWI'S CALL FOR PERSEVERANCE

In an effort that was clearly linked to Osama bin Laden's Internet speech on December 27, Abu Musab al-Zarqawi had a similar announcement released on

January 20 that provided a great deal of insight into the results of the fight for Fallujah from the perspective of the insurgent leadership.[5] Zarqawi made eight major points in his announcement, which was clearly aimed at inspiring his subordinates and other Muslims to continue the fight against the MNF and the IIG, but his major theme throughout was perseverance. The loss of Fallujah had been a heavy blow to his movement, but he sought in this announcement to rally those remaining loyal to his cause and inspire them with the sacrifice of those who had been martyred in the city.

Zarqawi claimed that the fighting in Fallujah had produced a "significant military and strategic victory" by forcing the United States to fight in close combat in the streets of the city and suffer increased casualties. He believed that such losses would produce in turn a "major psychological defeat" by causing President Bush and the entire U.S. leadership to suffer from "moral confusion." Zarqawi's text indicated that the martyrs in Fallujah had taught new lessons in perseverance and would inspire others to take up jihad.

Among his major points, Zarqawi also testified to the importance of Prime Minister Allawi's involvement in the effort in Fallujah, although he claimed that Allawi's actions had merely striped him of his "cloak of deceit" supporting the United States and Israel in Iraq. Among the most outlandish diatribes in the taped version of the statement was Zarqawi's claim that 800 Israelis had participated in the battle, along with numerous Jordanians.[6]

Of note, Zarqawi also chose this January message to insult the Grand Ayatollah al-Sisatani by calling him "the imam of infidelity" on the tape. Zarqawi claimed that 80 percent of the Iraqi security forces in the city were Shia and the remaining 10 percent were Kurds, in an effort to show that the other Iraqi sects were allied with the United States against the Sunni minority there. Zarqawi obviously was a proponent of increased violence between Sunnis and Shia in Iraq.

Although much in the tape was incorrect, the text did demonstrate that Zarqawi's information was uneven at best. His assessment of the role and composition of the Iraqi forces was not far off target, but his own confirmation of the death of Omar Hadid in the tape showed he did not have all the facts concerning his own forces. The tape also showed that the strategy of the insurgent leadership would continue to be based on long-term attrition of the MNF forces and would remain dependent on keeping up the perseverance and religious righteousness of the effort in the eyes of Sunni Muslims.

Zarqawi made his allegiance to Osama bin Laden clear and expressed his commitment to the overall terrorist campaign. He called for all Muslims to join with him even if many more would be martyred for the cause. The tape also demonstrated that even Zarqawi understood the importance of the impending Iraqi national elections on the success of the insurgency. In the tape he called strongly for Iraqis not to participate in the voting, for he knew that a strong turnout would significantly reduce the support for the insurgency among non-Sunnis and would further isolate and minimize the influence of the Sunni minority in the country.

NATIONAL ELECTIONS IN AL ANBAR PROVINCE

The IIG had announced plans to hold national elections during the previous summer of 2004, and an Independent Electoral Commission for Iraq (IECI) had been created to plan and conduct the electoral process. The IECI was an independent body, set up and run using funds allocated in the Iraqi budget "to prepare for and conduct elections in Iraq in accordance with the highest international electoral standards."[7] From its inception, supporters of the IECI knew that it had to be completely impartial and thoroughly professional to help ensure the credibility of any election.

The IECI began its work by recruiting a national staff, which was later augmented by a host of regional staff members. There were to be three separate elections on January 30: one to select an Interim National Assembly, one for a Kurdistan National Assembly, and another in each province to select the eighteen governorate councils. Operating independently of the Iraqi government, the IECI was empowered to develop all the regulations and polling procedures necessary for the conduct of the elections.

The MEF staff understood that these elections were perhaps the most significant event that would occur in Iraq in 2005, so key members of the staff began election planning even before the assault on Fallujah began. It was a real credit to the strategic vision of the MNF as a whole that such a "nonmilitary" task as election support received any focus at all in violence-prone Al Anbar province in 2004. Yet, the commitment of the MEF and its commander General Sattler were even more noteworthy given the huge task of resettling Fallujah and fighting the insurgency in the rest of Al Anbar province simultaneously.

Over time, the MEF staff developed a very detailed security and logistic support effort to support the IECI and its international contractors prior to and during the elections. A very small group of planners had started developing an elections concept of support as early as September 2004. Lead by a few officers in the MEF operations and plans sections and the CAG, these planners tackled the difficult challenge of supporting an election completely *indirectly*. In other words, they could not influence the policies and procedures of the IECI even though they understood very well that the voting in predominately Sunni Al Anbar province would have to be conducted very differently than elsewhere in Iraq. For example, if they announced the location of any polling center in advance of the election, the insurgents in that area would most certainly either destroy the site or set explosives to kill voters on polling day. Having identified the number and locations of centers, the MEF staff began obtaining essential protective concrete barriers and radio communications sets to equip the polling center sites.

Naively, the IECI had envisioned that elections in Al Anbar would follow the same model as elsewhere in Iraq, but most Iraqis and Americans in Al Anbar province understood that would not be true. The first indication the IECI leadership had that the Sunni heartland would present unique problems to their efforts was when the provincial representative they hired in December refused to occupy his office in Ramadi. Without a provincial representative, no voter education program would be developed for the province and no polling center locations would be chosen. The MEF obtained permission from the IECI to offer suggestions for the polling center locations, but the IECI was very reluctant to allow the MEF any involvement in voting education or media. The commissioners of the IECI and its director, Carlos Valenzuela, were very suspicious of the MEF's motives and, as they did not understand the dynamics of the Sunni triangle, they delayed approving any MEF involvement in the process to the eleventh hour.

Although the MEF representatives put as much pressure on the IECI as they could to incorporate a more aggressive approach to polling, nothing improved over the months preceding the election until the IECI finally revealed in late January that it might not be able to hire sufficient polling center workers for Al Anbar province by Election Day. In most of Iraq, local residents were hired to operate polling centers in their own neighborhoods; in Al Anbar, residents did not understand the election process well and were actively being discouraged from voting – at the threat of their lives if they visit a polling site – by the insurgents still in the province.

The real problem was that Sunni leaders in the province were either intimidated by the insurgents or were unconvinced of the value of the election. Many who did understand that the election gave them a chance to determine the future of Iraq were so fearful that they would be punished for voting that they planned to stay away. It was extremely hard to choose risking one's life for democracy when most Iraqis in the province had no real experience of voting. Sunni leaders felt that any election that would reflect majority rule would necessarily work against the objectives of Sunnis and favor the preferences of the majority Shia electorate.

As it had with locations for polling centers, the MEF again offered support with the needed polling station workers. Within days, the MEF's subordinate commands, through coordination with community and government leaders, assembled hundreds of Iraqi citizens from Al Anbar to work for the IECI in polling centers. On January 25, for example, Marines from the CAG and Kael Weston of the State Department hired a large number of election poll workers in Fallujah. This group included over 100 Iraqis from the city who would end up working in polling centers all across Al Anbar province.

Two days later in Fallujah, the CMOC staff held a series of elections-oriented discussions with local sheikhs. One of these events was even covered in detail by ABC's *Nightline* news program. Such discussions were critical to an understanding of the process and the value of elections. As few residents of the city had ever voted in a meaningful election, there was understandable mystery associated with the process. It was also quite unclear from the IECI-produced literature what effect the election could potentially have on the area, so the CMOC staff put special effort into a local education program to inform and empower the residents of the city that they had by that time come to care very much about.

In a huge logistical feat, the FSSG and the MEG provided thousands of concrete barriers and other polling station materials to the general locations of the proposed polling sites. Great resourcefulness and initiative was exercised to find products (walk-thru metal detectors, wands, barriers, and commercial phones, among other things) that could be delivered on very short notice to Al Anbar sites to support Election Day activities. Many of these items were purchased from civilian sources all over the world by the MEF to ensure the security of the polling process.

The CAG developed a reception and training program that picked up the IECI polling center workers at Baghdad International Airport and transported them to a hasty training facility at the Taqqadum Air Base west of Fallujah. There near the runway, the CAG staff, lead by Colonel Miles Diamond, provided 3 days of basic polling center training prior to the workers' departure for the actual sites where they were to assist with the voting.

To support Iraqi polling center workers, the 1st Marine Division and the CAG provided Election Support Teams (ESTs) for each polling center. These ESTs consisted of a senior NCO or officer and a translator from the unit that was providing the security for the polling center assigned – most frequently, they were members of the CAG (supporting the unit) who interacted directly with the IECI workers. The ESTs had the responsibility to provide liaison with the IECI workers at their respective polling centers and to help coordinate security, daily support, and training for the elections.

The ESTs met their polling center workers at Taqqadum Air Base at the completion of training and arranged for their air transport from Taqqadum to various sites throughout Al Anbar province. Upon arrival at the MEF delivery sites, each EST and the IECI workers were transported to the designated polling centers and immediately began setting up the spaces to be ready by first light on January 30 for the arrival of the voters. For many Marine ESTs, this resulted in a 24-hour day and then another full day of working security issues for voters. On the morning of Election Day, these ESTs moved out of the polling centers along with the Marines and Soldiers who were providing outer cordon security. No Marines were present in the polling centers on Election Day.

As a collateral mission, the MEF sought to ensure that all polling center workers, both locally recruited and IECI provided, had a very positive experience. The MEF succeeded in sending all the workers home enthusiastic about their positive experiences with MNF and the democratic process. This extra effort was believed essential to support successful polling center recruiting for future elections in October and December 2005.

Another challenge the MEF faced was the lack of IECI-provided voter education on the election and the election process. The MEF information operations cell worked closely with IECI, producing and distributing hundreds of products released in concert with a deliberate education campaign in the weeks prior to the election. This campaign was designed to inform voters of the existence of the election, the date of the election, the importance of the election to

Iraq's future, and then in the last few days the exact locations of polling centers. Polling center locations were not released until January 28 for force protection reasons.

In conjunction with the information operations effort, the MEF leadership, supported by civil affairs Marines and Soldiers, and the Department of State's Kael Weston, engaged almost daily with local and provincial government leaders, sheiks, religious leaders, former military leaders, and business leaders to solicit their support for the elections. Battalion Commanders, Regimental/Brigade Commanders, as well as the Assistant Division Commander and Commanding General, promoted the elections message over and over again to the Iraqi people they dealt with every day. This multifaceted method of delivering the message proved highly successful, particularly in Fallujah.

All the MEF subordinate commands played important roles in supporting the elections. The Division continued to conduct a series of violent spoiling operations to keep the insurgents off guard and reduce their ability to intimidate the population.[8] The 3rd Marine Aircraft Wing (3rd MAW) safely flew over 500 sorties in support of the actual election movement, flying over 4,080 passengers and 83,570 pounds of polling materials in a 4-day period, spanning the entire MEF area of responsibility from An Najaf in the south to Al Qaim in northwestern Al Anbar province. During operation Citadel II, the 3rd MAW transported over 4,002 passengers and 80,880 pounds of cargo. This effort was conducted by over 455 carefully planned sorties. Finally, once the election was completed, the MAW and U.S. Air Force C-130s safely returned over 1,100 IECI election volunteers to their home cities in southcentral Iraq.

This helicopter movement in Iraq was no small feat. Flying around Al Anbar province was always a very dangerous and unpredictable action. This was brought home to every member of the MEF in the worst way possible, when on January 26, in the midst of repositioning the forces to support the election process, a CH-53 helicopter of the 3rd MAW crashed outside of Ar Rutbah in northwestern Iraq. Twenty-seven Marines and one Sailor were killed in the tragic accident.[9]

During the same period, the FSSG of the MEF built "Iron Mountains" of supplies and put infrastructure in place to receive, billet, and provide basic daily support to the over 1,000 IECI personnel in the province. Then, the FSSG identified and built life support requirements for 1,000 IECI personnel, and segregated, guarded, and secured the IECI polling materials and personnel at Camp Taqaddum. The materials were sorted, distributed, and staged at the forward staging locations; then the FSSG distributed the necessary materials to the polling centers.

The MEG placed over 200 concrete barriers at polling sites for the January 30 elections, reducing significantly the threat at high-density polling sites. It provided engineering support at designated polling centers for habitability and survivability of IECI workers and it provided several hundred Seabees as members of a provisional infantry battalion (the Spartacus Battalion) that was used to augment sparse Division resources spread throughout the province for the election.

On January 30, all Division polling centers opened on time and Iraqi citizens were able to vote at all centers in the province. Luckily, thanks to the huge force protection effort and the operations security emplaced by the MEF, the insurgents were caught unprepared; no injuries were suffered by Iraqis or Marines at any polling center in Al Anbar. Intelligence reports through Election Day indicated that the MEF's disruption actions [which included vehicle control points (VCPs), cordon and search operations, targeted raids, and presence operations] made it difficult for the insurgents to conduct deliberate operations or plan actions against the voting centers. The absence of attacks against polling centers on Election Day demonstrated the success of the MEF's offensive strategy and the quality of its execution. The MEF suffered only one Marine and one Soldier killed in action on Election Day.[10]

Of particular note, on January 30, Marines in Fallujah observed a very large voter turnout in the city. Over 7,000 Fallujah residents participated in the event, demonstrating conclusively the value of engaging with the local Iraqi population and the optimism that could be generated in even the most devastated of Iraqi locations. Voter turnout in the Shia environs of Abu Ghraib prison was the only other area where the election was actively supported by the people of Al Anbar province. In some areas, including the city of Ramadi, intimidation was so powerful that no voters visited the polls. The paucity of involvement elsewhere in the province gave even more significance to the turnout in Fallujah, where no one doubted that the high level of safety added greatly to the willingness of Iraqis to turn out to vote.

Following the polling on January 30, all ballots were tallied by the IECI, boxed, and returned to Camp Taqqadum without incident. The MEF's locally hired workers were paid on site, using IECI funds, and released in good spirits. Most of them were extremely encouraged by their participation in the election process . . . an important seed for Iraqi elections to come. Within 48 hours, as planned, all polling centers had been cleared of personnel, equipment, and barriers and returned to their original state.

These actions by the MEF ensured that the Iraqi national elections were conducted as scheduled on January 30. Nearly 1 million people voted in Karbala and Najaf at more than 430 polling centers. Unlike other areas of Iraq, the Marines, Sailors, and Soldiers in Al Anbar province were requested to provide unprecedented direct security and logistical support to the IECI. In addition to tight security around polling areas, the MEF accomplished the vast majority of all voter education efforts in the Al Anbar province. Also, the MEF was solely responsible for the unprecedented recruitment, outfitting, housing, and movement of the IECI workers at the various polling sites throughout the province. It had been a uniquely challenging effort so soon on the heels of the combat inside Fallujah, but given its strategic importance, it was an obvious priority of effort even while reconstruction of the city continued without pause.

HOUSING COMPENSATION

By the end of January, progress was obvious in Fallujah to anyone who visited the city. But for many officials isolated in Baghdad, the real needs of the people of Fallujah remained misunderstood. The MEF leadership realized, however, that the local success of the election in Fallujah could serve as a springboard to gain better support for the Fallujahns. In particular, this meant building support for housing compensation payments for the residents who had returned to the city.

General Sattler understood very well that money for individual homes was needed from the IIG to seal the reconstruction process as a success. The government could rebuild all the buildings in the city, but if the residents moved away from their shattered properties without rebuilding homes, Fallujah would die, and with it would die the symbol of a new Iraqi future. General Sattler first used his own chain of command to push the idea of $100 million in housing aid to the city. General Hejlik and Colonel Ballard engaged on the same issue every week in the reconstruction meetings and support was evident from General Kizseley and even Adel Hillawi, but for some reason the actual allocation of funds always seemed to be out of reach. The IIG did have a survey team in the city that had estimated the damage to the homes in each district and had developed a formula for compensation, but still the funds were not provided.

Finally, General Sattler took his appeal to the various Congressional Delegations that were so frequently visiting Camp Fallujah in the early months of 2005. By February, the MEF was giving escorted tours of the most needy areas of the city to visitors, including the Iraqi Minister of Municipalities. By early March, the logjam seemed to break, and after some very pointed appeals and complimentary offers by members of the U.S. Congress and Ambassador Negroponte, the IIG agreed to allocate nearly $100 million to the housing compensation needs of the residents of Fallujah.

The first compensation payments were made by Basil Mahmoud on March 17, less than 6 months after the beginning of combat operations in the city. At about the same time, the majority of the MEF's payments for damages and for rent of facilities started, so a large influx of money was available by month's end to stimulate the economic recovery of the city.

Chapter Eight

A New Dawn: Lessons in Modern Warfare

Operation Al Fajr (New Dawn) had for its objective the destruction of the terrorist element in the Iraqi city of Fallujah and the peaceful restoration of the city to its residents. It was designed very specifically to be a significant new start for one Iraqi city and the beginning of a new day for Iraq overall. The November battle resulted in the loss of 71 American lives and injuries to more than 600 more young men. It was the worst month of the war in terms of U.S. fatalities.[1] Estimates of insurgent casualties conclude that over 1,500 enemy fighters were killed in the fighting. Such a costly fight should bring an equally significant outcome, so what were the results of operation Al Fajr?

There is no doubt that the fight for Fallujah was important to the overall campaign in Iraq because the city had become a significant terrorist strongpoint with great symbolic significance; it was the most prominent place in Iraq that had resisted the combined efforts of both the MNF and the Iraqi government to cleanse it of anti-Iraqi influence the previous April. As the planning for the battle proceeded, it also gained importance as the first major military effort in Iraq directed and controlled by the newly installed IIG of Prime Minister Allawi. For these reasons, and its scope and degree of tactical success, operation Al Fajr provides a number of important lessons to be learned for any future multinational combat operation.

Even as the high-intensity combat in Fallujah drew to a close in mid-November 2004, it had already became clear that the battle had achieved both its tactical objectives and could illustrate a number of key facts that would be important for the future of the overall MNF campaign in Iraq. Included among these were indicators of the importance of information operations, the critical nature of integrated (MNF and Iraqi) force structures and command and control, and the decisiveness of precision fires in an urban environment. Yet something else was also becoming clear. Following the tactical victory gained by operation Al Fajr and the subsequent successful election held in January 2005, the great value of conflict termination planning and civil military operations to a counterinsurgency campaign also became very evident. In fact, the future course of the war in Iraq had changed significantly because of the fight for Fallujah.

Operation Al Fajr employed traditional tactics as well as some very innovative procedures and command structures. The MEF planners understood well the discontinuous nature of the modern battlefield and the need for flexibility in execution. Pre-assault rehearsals by the 1st Marine Division produced unity of effort and a great degree of cohesion during the assault.

It was planned that civil affairs teams and combat engineers would follow in trace of the lead combat battalions to begin assessment of critical infrastructure and to facilitate population and resource control for any civilians remaining in the city. Because operation Vigilant Resolve had been halted as a result of widespread negative media attention, the planners of Al Fajr wanted to ensure that collateral damage was minimized and civilians could be cared for or evacuated as soon as possible. This was one reason that the city general hospital was one of the first objectives of the attack.

Tactical civil affairs teams were also used with telling effect to manage detainees captured in the fighting and to facilitate burials for local fighters who were killed during the combat. An aggressive PA stance was also employed and found to be critical for the maintenance of popular support. This, in turn, helped assure the maintenance of Iraqi government's resolve to continue the larger counterinsurgency effort. As the first major battle directed by the IIG in its own defense, it could not have been a more important win.

THE COMBAT LESSONS OF AL FAJR

Continuity of Effort. The lack of any steady MNF presence in the Fallujah region following the fall of Saddam's regime clearly presented a gap for insurgents to exploit. Initial lack of security forces can be understood simply as a result of the paucity of troops on the ground in Iraq in the late spring of 2003. However, the ever-changing array of Army forces responsible for operations in Fallujah presented a weak and vulnerable front to agitators in Fallujah and clearly played into the hands of terrorists looking for a fertile zone to incite members of the local population to counter MNF initiatives.

Although it is too much to expect military planners and intelligence analysts to be able to address every seam in a modern battlefield, it is reasonable for commanders and their staffs to maintain continuity of effort in key areas of the battlespace. Fallujah should have been recognized as such by the Army planners as early as the summer of 2003. Forces assigned to the region should have done more to ensure tactical transitions and opportunities for the insurgents to infiltrate the city were minimized. Once Fallujah was identified as a trouble spot of great importance, the coalition/MNF should have focused long-term, concerted, and forceful actions on the city.

Information Operations. In ways few people understood at the time, information operations (IO) really shaped the battle. Perhaps most importantly, proper information techniques convinced the residents of the city to leave prior to the battle, reducing civilian casualties and permitting the assault forces much greater freedom of action. Almost as important, information tools help the MNF split insurgents from their base of support (the remaining residents) to reduce their freedom of action. There is even evidence that our information campaign turned many of the insurgents on one another as they grew fearful of informants within their ranks. There is no doubt that information could be employed as a weapon adding significant nonkinetic fires within the battlespace.

Information also played an important role outside the battle zone. Wide-ranging, aggressive, PA activities helped inform the people of Iraq and the American people about the real issues of the battle. The huge number of weapons caches and numerous IED factories, as well as multiple incidents when mosques were used as weapons storages sites, all helped reveal the techniques of the enemy. The real horror of the terrorist killing houses in the city only magnified the extent of insurgent culpability for crimes against innocents. Making these facts well known helped justify the risk and cost of the battle. The cumulative effect of these facts reduced pressure on the Iraqi prime minister to curtail the fighting. In the end it also made the residents more willing to accept their own culpability as unwilling supporters for these acts after they returned to survey the destruction of the city.

Robert Kaplan said it well when he wrote, "Because the battles in a counterinsurgency are small scale and often clandestine, the story line is rarely obvious. It becomes a matter of perceptions, and victory is awarded to those who weave the most compelling narrative. Truly, the world of post-modern, 21st century conflict, civilian and military public-affairs officers must become warfighters by another name. They must control and anticipate a whole new storm system represented by global media, media, which often exposes embarrassing facts out of historical or philosophical context."[2]

Military Operations in Urban Terrain. Fighting in cities has always been extremely challenging; historically, many of the most devastating battles in American history have resulted in high casualties because of the complex nature of urban terrain. Fallujah was clearly an urban fight and it showed us much about the current state of military operations in urban terrain (MOUT). Mechanized and armored vehicles were critical to the MEF's success in Fallujah. Both assaults into the city were spearheaded by armored vehicles, allowing rapid penetration to break up and get behind enemy defensive positions and break through the multiple layers of IEDs that were nested at key locations.

Still, the fight for Fallujah also proved the need for infantry, "boots on the ground," in significant numbers to clear the nearly 20,000 structures in the city.

Current tactics and building assault techniques serviced the MNF forces well, even when pitted against a determined enemy who was fighting to the death. Insurgents booby-trapped themselves, used armor-piercing rounds, established internal ambushes in homes, and worked through a network of interconnected defensive positions to hold off the MNF infantry attack, without success.

Joint Fires. Many felt that the risk of "blue on blue"[3] friendly casualties from the use of artillery in urban operations was too high to accept in modern warfare – particularly in an unconventional environment. However, operation Al Fajr clearly demonstrated that well-controlled fires, in combination with good target identification and well-trained forces, made artillery safe to use – and it proved itself invaluable. Although supported only by one battery of Marine M198 howitzers and one battery of Army Paladin artillery, the 1st Marine Division attack in Fallujah employed artillery fires to great effect even at extreme "danger-close" ranges within the same city block as attacking infantry. Firing nearly continuously during the assault and thereafter on-call, ready to rapidly respond for weeks afterward, artillery fires made a huge contribution to the fight and produced no friendly casualties.

Civil Military Operations. Civil Military Operations (CMO) include population and resource control, humanitarian assistance, and many forms of coordination with the host nation.[4] For operation Al Fajr, civil affairs forces were integrated within the assault echelon of the Marine Division so that the needs of the population could be addressed immediately and continuously throughout the battle. Even in the first days of the attack, civil affairs units were dealing with the local population to compensate them for damages, help them bury the dead, and provide them food and water, as needed. They also helped clarify the real goals of the operation for those living in Fallujah so the remaining residents of the city could help protect themselves. As the operation progressed, those same civil affairs forces turned their attention to the construction and management of sites providing humanitarian assistance.

Before the attack, civil affairs planners had helped identify locations in the city that should have been protected from MNF fires. During the fighting, they moved to assess the status and functioning of the many essential services areas (most were municipal government facilities such as water purification and sewage) so that any immediate repairs could be started. Without these actions the city would have been under water for months and largely uninhabitable.

The initial objectives of the attack were secured early and the entire city was under MNF control after 4 days of very hard fighting. Although small pockets of determined, even suicidal insurgents would continue to fight for nearly a month, the MEF staff began to focus on the vitally important transition to local control during the first week of combat. The city needed to be secure and made safe, essential services had to be restored to minimal levels, and the residents of the city had to have some semblance of normalcy in their lives before the promise of freedom from insurgents would have any meaning. This was the real test of operation Al Fajr and, knowing this, Generals Sattler and Natonski ensured that all their subordinate commanders valued and supported the CMO effort in the city.

Tactical Transitions. The basic concept of the Fallujah operation depended on a series of transitions: from high-intensity combat operations to restoration of security and essential services to resettlement, and, finally, to the return to local control by an Iraqi municipal government. Minimum requirements for conflict termination were identified prior to the beginning of combat operations. These included a nonlocal (therefore neutral) police force functioning in the city, a civilian or military mayor/city manager to direct the operations of essential services in the city, and a package of reconstruction projects and necessary funding designed to restore the city's infrastructure to preconflict levels as soon as possible after the terrorist influence was destroyed. These prerequisites were briefed all the way up the chain of command to the prime minister because, at that time in Iraq, all of these requirements depended on national-level decisions to be effective.

The transition from the combat operations phase to the period when restoration of security and essential services took priority was envisioned to be based on geographic (spatial) considerations, not time. In other words, even while fighting was continuing in some areas of the city, where possible, MNF and Iraqi forces would be rebuilding pump houses and electrical substations in an area not far away. And, in other locations within the city, military forces would also be providing humanitarian relief supplies to the few remaining Fallujah residents.

With the return of the residents to Fallujah, however, a distinctly different set of priorities was required. This was because the military forces would no longer have first use of the limited resources in the city once the residents reentered their homes. In fact, it was very clear that once the local people returned to the city, the priority given to the military effort to provide security would be challenged by the need to assist and support resident's requests. People would need regular deliveries of food, supplies of potable water, emergency medical care, and answers to a host of questions. . . . And, the more residents who returned, the more military resources would be needed to support civil requirements. In fact, with the exception of providing police functions [initially using Marine units, then Iraqi Public Order Battalions (POB) and limited numbers of newly recruited traffic policemen], most of the military resources in the city after December 23 were used to service the needs of returning residents.

Such a shift in priorities required a change of mind-set by everyone concerned. Every Marine and Soldier had to understand that the local population was the center of gravity in the city after December 23. It is a great credit to the leadership of General Natonski and Colonel Shupp, and later even of General Mehdi, the POB brigade commander, that this emphasis on the residents and not the insurgents took prominence down to the squad level in both American and Iraqi forces.[5]

Flexibility in Combat Execution. Operations around Fallujah validated the importance of tactical and organizational flexibility to a high degree. The short notice capability to reorganize and integrate forces from 31st MEU into the MEF and the easy integration of U.S. Army Task Forces at the regimental level and Army brigades at the division level were a testament to tactical interoperability honed and proven in Iraq. Finally the successful reception, staging, and incorporation of Iraqi units and staff within the MEF in the days prior to the battle was a noteworthy and eventually very significant effort that showed the world that the fight for Fallujah was as much an Iraqi effort as it was an American fight.

OPERATIONAL POSTCONFLICT ACTIONS

As with any issue of management, planning ahead is fundamental for successful multinational relationships. Without the creation of the MST, the effectiveness of the MEF's operations would have been reduced, with no real hub or mechanism for local control. Like every other facet of war, planning assumptions are never completely fulfilled during execution, but some structure and process is required to begin any coordinated activity on the scope and scale of the multinational postconflict operations in Fallujah.

In any multinational arena, an understanding of the local culture helps greatly to properly anticipate requirements. The MNF staffs knew well they needed to gain the buy-in of the sheiks and imams of Fallujah, the city of mosques, before any sustainable progress would be made. Local ad hoc working groups eventually proved to be the answer, but only after much trial mentoring.

In Baghdad, a structure to manage reconstruction was crucial at both the local (city) level and the national level, and a coordinating process linking the two was fundamental. As is often said, all politics is local, but in Iraq only leaders in Baghdad had any authority or financial power. Therefore, every important issue needed to be considered at both levels. Having several of the same members working at both the Fallujah (local) meeting and the Baghdad (national) meeting helped. But there were still many issues where no agreement was easy. Each ministry had different priorities and very different understanding of the real situation in the city of Fallujah.

One of the real values of the Fallujah meeting was its setting. No one who visited the city could fail to observe the situation there and be moved by the basic needs of the population. Responsibility and authority had to be matched for any management mechanism to work. Basil Mahmoud was appointed quite early in the process as the senior representative of the minister of industry and minerals. That minister was the government lead for Fallujah reconstruction; still, in the early days, Basil Mahmoud's real authority over other ministry functions (power generation, sewage treatment, fuel distribution) was uncertain at best and almost always too weak to generate real action. Without a single (Federal Emergency Management Agency-like) government entity and no real recent experience in the reconstruction of a city, the Iraqi government was extremely ponderous in its responsiveness. Only in March 2005, after Basil Mahmoud became first among equals and was empowered to spend national funds did he gain the authority that matched his huge responsibility.

Military-to-military and civil–military relationships had to be created where none existed before. In wartime, the civil aspects of any endeavor must be linked to security and the role of the military. In the case of operation Al Fajr, the Iraqi military was present in all phases of the battle and the reconstruction but in relatively small numbers. They were also plagued by a holdover from the former regime – reluctance on the part of the local residents to trust their motives.

As combat operations in Fallujah drew to a close in late December 2004, the tactical success of the Iraqi Security Forces and the MNF was clear, but the success of the reconstruction effort remained uncertain. Yet, at the end of the following month, the residents of Fallujah voted in greater numbers than in any other city in the province. Such voter participation in a city still under military control sent a strong signal to the national government. Soon Baghdad increased its level of effort in the processes of reconstruction, and by early March, had committed more than $200 million in reconstruction funding. Such success within less than 6 months after combat operations began was a clear testament to the value of the multinational command and control processes that facilitated the reconstruction of Fallujah. Those processes directly supported the MNF campaign in Iraq. The importance of integrated (MNF–Iraqi) force structures and command and control, and the great value of conflict termination planning and civil–military operations, were clear to everyone in the area of operations.

Nongovernmental Organizations. Many people believe, and in fact NGOs often advertise, that humanitarian assistance is made available across the globe to help those in need. In fact, NGOs do provide a great deal of aid to large numbers of people in many nations; however, very few aid organizations, and, in fact, few government organizations, will venture into areas of active combat or uncertain physical security. Only the Iraqi Red Crescent Society (IRCS) ventured into Fallujah during the winter of 2004–2005. And it did so more for its own reasons and provided a negligible amount of assistance to the people.[6] Other humanitarian organizations did provide relief to Iraq, and some of those resources did get to the residents of Fallujah who had moved into surrounded areas of the country, but even that aid was delivered with significant military and host nation governmental support.

The danger presented by overestimating the contributions from NGOs in war-torn areas of the world is that governments may assume they do not need to intervene in a humanitarian way and can leave populations at risk. Military forces should not be tasked to provide such aide either, so a realistic and well-integrated, combined effort of government, military, and NGO support (where it is available) is the only tenable answer in uncertain postconflict situations.

Civil-Military Operations Center . Although not well understood by most in the military, the small CMOC in Fallujah was critically important to the operational success of the fight. It served as the coordinating point for civil affairs and MEG reconstruction efforts in the city, the effective "seat" of local governance through the late spring of 2005, and the location where MNF biometric ID cards were manufactured, but perhaps more importantly, the CMOC itself served as the coordinating point for MNF and local Iraqi issues. It became the site of weekly and then nearly daily "town hall meetings" where issues, grievances, and communications errors were resolved. As the site for these town hall meetings, the CMOC served to bring together the then very disparate groups within the local population.

The CMOC-hosted effort to develop an Iraqi municipal council was strategically important. It not only bridged local gaps in the subgroups of the city, but also provided a venue for residents to witness their government in action. Numerous key Iraqi government leaders, including the prime minister, the minister of industry, and the minister of public works, all met with and discussed issues with local residents at the CMOC. Even the U.S. Ambassador and key congressional leaders traveled "downtown" to the Fallujah CMOC to gain an understanding of what was happening in the city. For all these reasons, the CMOC concept needs to be better understood by military leaders, and a rapidly deployable CMOC kit needs to be developed for use on short notice by military commands around the globe.[7]

The U.S. State Department State Embedded Team. The U.S. State Department detailed two of its members to the Al Anbar region, and both made significant and long lasting contributions to the military and political situations in Iraq. Mr. Keith Kidd was assigned as a State Embedded Team (SET) chief in Ramadi, and Mr. Kael Weston was the SET chief assigned at Camp Fallujah. These two men bore much of the brunt of coordinating key leader engagement up the diplomatic chain, through the embassy in Baghdad, and all the way to Washington, D.C. In addition, their role in facilitating dialog and "connecting the dots" between military and diplomatic leaders was extremely valuable. There is no doubt that the $100 million initially committed to Fallujah restoration would not have been made available without the constant, high-level engagement fostered by Kael Weston.

Finally, the elections of January 30 were not only a high point for the MEF, but were also clear evidence of the value of committed and effective State Department staff within a military operational framework. Keith Kidd was instrumental in gaining the IECI's confidence in the MEF's election plan and the support of the provincial governor. Kael Weston lived at the Fallujah CMOC for weeks prior to the election and his dialog with key municipal and religious leaders gave significant impetus to the high voter turnout in the city. Just as a combatant commander needs a political advisor, operational commanders such as General Sattler should continue to fully integrate members of the SET into planning and operations.

The Inter-ministerial Working Group. The key mechanism for reconstruction in Fallujah was a dual-track interagency working group, operating at both the tactical and the strategic levels and linking issues in Fallujah with intergovernmental support through the MNF military headquarters and the U.S. and UK embassies in Baghdad. Its operation through twice weekly meetings ensured that the gap between local needs and national priorities was bridged for Fallujah. During November, MEF civil affairs officers effectively directed the affairs of the city while combat operations were the focus of effort, but by January, as the residents were beginning to return, Engineer Mahmoud had grown to be the key Iraqi figure in the city and the manager of daily activities.

The Baghdad meeting chaired by Deputy Minister of Industry and Minerals Mohammed Abdullah Mohammed ensured that the sometimes weak and traditionally vacillating IIG officials applied national resources where they were critically important and when they were available. Military representatives attended both these meetings and acted as a sort of connecting file at the local and national levels. Generals Kiszely, Farquhar, and Hejlik were critical linchpins in this effort, ensuring that the issues at all levels were coordinated and consensus was built as problems arose.

The one gap in coverage of this two meeting process was at the broader operational or provincial level. Like most nations, Iraq has a strong history of provincial government; however, they have rarely been very active because few national resources have been made freely available for provincial administrators to apply to situations such as Fallujah reconstruction. For the operation in Fallujah, the provincial government was in Ramadi, and the appointed Governor there was never very well integrated into the coordination process. He was in fact either dominated by his own self-interest and the needs of people in the provincial capital in Ramadi or was hamstrung by lack of support in Baghdad. This is an Iraqi governance shortfall that may pose significant problems as democracy takes root in the country.

Because operation Al Fajr was an Iraqi government-directed operation, the Iraqi government retained primary responsibility for the restoration of power, and supply of fuel, food, and potable water. By late December 1994, Fallujah was a city in significant distress and returning residents required immediate humanitarian assistance while the government began to difficult process of restoring essential services. A means for providing immediate humanitarian assistance had been planned for in advance by the CAG of the MEF, but military planners understood very well that they could in no way provide more than a temporary level of sustenance for nearly 100,000 people. With the construction engineering help of the U.S. Navy Seabees, three large parks in the city were used to store and dispense essential supplies (food, water, blankets, and health items) for a short period while the Iraqi government marshaled its resources. MNF maneuver battalions with Iraqi Security Forces support provided security in each site (lessons learned the previous year concerning food riots drove the MEF to use multiple protective measures, including wire, search machines, and security over watch). Luckily, and most likely a result of the strong security posture, no incidents occurred at any of the distribution sites.

The Role of Politics. There was some significant political pressure to resolve the Fallujah issue quickly. Prime Minister Allawi wanted to show the Sunnis that they would be cared for at least as well as the Shia populations in other areas of Iraq. The United Nations and the Iraqi Ministry of Migration had valid concerns about the residents who had been displaced prior to the fighting. Finally the Iraqi government had to allocate and distribute millions of dollars of reconstruction funds under very difficult circumstances. But even with these pressures, in 2005, it was the MNF who most frequently pushed for relief in Fallujah and it was the U.S. government who provided the first and the bulk of the funds that reached residents. Humanitarian pressures did bear on decision making, both during and after the battle. The displaced people did receive a great deal of aid, to include discounted fuel from the Iraqi government, for months. Luckily, most of this was planned in advance.

Still, operation Al Fajr required significant host nation leadership. The prime minister had to be personally involved on many occasions because of the sensitive nature of the fighting in the Sunni triangle[8] and the massive amount of funding required to rebuild and repair the city. Fundamental questions of emergency law and reestablishment of police capability also required a high level of governmental involvement, particularly as several of the ministers were reluctant to cooperate with each other. However, reconstruction of essential civic service sites, battle damage compensation, payments for damaged homes, and new economic development initiatives were apparent by March 2005. Funding the huge cost of restoring the city was a problem initially; however, Iraqi funding augmented by $100 million eventually began to flow into the city.

Coalition C2 Issues. None of this could have been accomplished without the development of effective host nation C2 structures. The value of having General Abdul-Qader and his deputy, Brigadier General Kassim, on site in Camp Fallujah during the fight was critical for the proper integration and motivation of the Iraqi forces within the 1st Marine Division. It was even more important during the immediate posthostilities phase, when General Abdul-Qader approved rules for Fallujah residents within the city and the timing of the resettlement plan.

Once the citizens began to return to their homes, having Engineer Mahmoud and his team available in the city not only helped immensely to restore the functioning of Fallujah public works, but also added much to the confidence and morale of the returned residents. By February, Mahmoud and his team were conducting town hall meetings in the center of the city (facilitated by civil affairs personnel) dealing with a multitude of problems but successfully meeting residents needs. None of this could have been done without the full involvement of Iraqis in and out of uniform. In a particularly xenophobic part of the world, local tribal, religious, and cultural influence was critical.

Resettlement and Reconstruction. After the most severe fighting was completed and the residents were returning to the city, the major civil military effort was designed to restore the city public works, food, water, and fuel distribution and traffic police to prior fighting levels.[9] Many thought the city of Fallujah could not be resettled without a return of the insurgents. Although it is certainly true that insurgents did flow back in the city, they did so in such reduced numbers and with so little resident tolerance for their activities that their capability within Fallujah remained insignificant through the early spring of 2005. The elections proved that Fallujahns wanted to be a functioning part of the future Iraq and it is difficult to conceive that they would have voted in such numbers without seeing a commitment to restoring their futures on the part of their government and the MNF.

Lack of tolerance for insurgent activity for the 3 months following the assault demonstrates that the local residents were no longer providing support. The return of a fully professional and effective police force in the city by midsummer of 2005 will signify the real victory of operation Al Fajr.

VOTING AS A MEASURE OF SUCCESS

Many people ask if the effort in Fallujah made a difference in the campaign against the insurgency or improved the lot of the Iraqi people. There can be no doubt that the tempo of the insurgency was slowed by the battle, that the price of weapons increased significantly, and that the number and types of attacks in the west of Iraq was reduced. Even more significant, however, was the symbolic effort of the returned Fallujah residents to vote in the national election in January 2005. In the immediate aftermath of resettlement, Iraq held its first national elections for a new transitional government; this was in effect a semiplebiscite for the Allawi government and a big indicator of popular sentiment in the city. In Fallujah, where little or no significant reconstruction had begun at the time of the election, nearly one-third of the residents stood in long lines to vote. Elsewhere in Al Anbar province, their mostly Sunni neighbors were severely intimidated and fewer than 18,000 people went to the polls, but in Fallujah a significant percentage felt safe enough to gain "the purple finger."[10] By voting in such numbers, the residents of Fallujah had bridged the past and committed to a new future.

THE ROAD AHEAD

Following from the killings of March 31, 2003, the year-long fight for Fallujah was a keystone in the overall campaign in Iraq because it eliminated a significant terrorist strong point that had symbolized insurgent power in the face of an MNF attack. The city had stood against the MNF in April 2003, and the Iraqi government had to cleanse it of its anti-Iraqi forces. As the first major battle in Iraq directed and controlled by the sovereign Iraqi government, it was a an effort with real strategic consequences. Because of its success, operation Al Fajr marked a turning point in the campaign and set a new tone for future operations in Iraq. It not only achieved its tactical objectives but also illustrated a way ahead for the entire MNF campaign in Iraq.

But what does the fight for Fallujah mean for the future of Iraq? The battle demonstrated that multinational forces and their Iraqi partners could work together to ensure the care and feeding of a local population during some of the most ferocious urban combat in modern history. It demonstrated the capability of the U.S. military to resettle and restore essential services in a medium-size city under extremely adverse circumstances. Operation Al Fajr also proved Iraqi battalions could perform well in high-intensity modern combat operations – this was important for those same Iraqi Security Forces are the best and most fundamental way for Iraq to defeat the insurgency that threatens its livelihood. Finally, the fight for Fallujah showed the world that the insurgency could not sustain itself in any sanctuary in Iraq and that it did not retain the support of the Iraqi people once they were free to make choices without insurgent intimidation.

The fight for Fallujah was not the first success in the MNF's Iraqi counterinsurgency campaign. Victories in Najaf and Samarra,[11] and even successes in sections of Baghdad like the former Sadr City, demonstrated that insurgents would be defeated if they engaged the coalition in conventional combat.[12] What made Fallujah different was the willingness of the Iraqi government to direct such a large-scale operation and to follow through on the resettlement and reconstruction. The fighting for Fallujah also set an important precedent for the Iraqi people. After operation Al Fajr, no Iraqis would permit the insurgents to dominate their city – no one was willing to suffer as had the people of Fallujah. Follow-on operations such as River Blitz, Matador, and New Market during 2005 built on the precedent set by the fight for Fallujah to ever more significantly sever the support that some Iraqis gave the insurgency. And, in every case, the Iraqi armed forces grew in capability and responsibility for maintaining the security of their nation.

The way ahead for Iraq requires a fully capable and apolitical police military that defends its borders and deters and defeats insurgents in Iraq. The Iraqi police can look back with pride as the primary security force in the country's successful January election, where no polling was stopped because of insurgent action. The Iraqi security capability grew significantly during the winter and spring of 2005 until large sections of Iraq were defended primarily by Iraqis. The unfortunate byproduct of the Iraqi military and security responsibility has been the deaths of a large number of Iraqi soldiers and police. But by their example they have become the new heroes for a new nation.

Along with a capable security apparatus, Iraq needs continued economic development. Although many improvements have been made in Iraq, the country overall remains extremely weak after over two decades of war and authoritarian rule. The only certain way to ensure that insurgents do not continue to disrupt life in Iraq is to improve the basic economic status of the people through a systematic development scheme that brings modern banking, investment, improved infrastructure, and increased trade to the country. Iraq has limited natural resources of great value, but its factories and state-run enterprises are grossly inefficient and bloated with an excess of workers and a lack of productivity.

Finally, to function effectively as a nation without dictatorial rule, Iraq needs to develop a capable government that responds to the needs of its people. The IIG was a solid step forward in that respect, as was the Transitional Iraqi Government of 2005, but the growth in the quality of provincial and municipal governance during the same period was much less reported and much more crucial for the future stability of the country. Iraq has a well-educated population and a strong culture to maximize its natural resources. It occupies a crucial position in the Middle East and should benefit from a great deal of regional trade. With a more efficient government that seeks to improve the livelihood of the Iraqi people and build a stronger economic base, Iraq can be a strong and prosperous regional state. Only then will the specter of terrorism be removed from the cradle of civilization and the Iraqi people gain the standard of living that they deserve.

A NEW BRIDGE

The old green bridge over the Euphrates was designed to bring trade and prosperity to Iraq from the west. It stood for years on the western edge of Fallujah as a landmark of Iraqi's willingness to open up to its neighbors. Although, with the death of the Blackwater contractors, it became the symbolic reason that the United States and its allies brought destruction to the city, the incident at the bridge was not the fault of the people of Fallujah. Openness not only invites progress and growth but also brings risk and possibly bad influences along with the good. At a Baghdad meeting in March 2005, a group of IIG government representatives discussed replacing the old bridge with a newer, more capable span. Some in the room hesitated to replace the old green bridge, wanting to keep its memory alive. For the good of all Iraqis, though, a new pathway to the west had to be created in Fallujah, so the group decided to allocate precious funds to the building of a new bridge across the Euphrates on the same site. Hopefully, this new bridge will do much more than ease movement to the west; ideally it will be a new venue linking the city to a better future.

Postscript

On June 24, 2005, a suicide bomber made his way inside the vehicle checkpoint on the east side of Fallujah on Highway 10. He waited until a Marine convoy approached his vehicle and then slammed his car into one of the 7-ton trucks bringing Marines into the city for security duty. Several Marines were killed and many more wounded in the first insurgent penetration in the city since the previous November. Two local residents were also killed in the blast, along with the bomber. The attack resulted in the single greatest number of female American casualties thus far in the war as the Marines loaded into the truck were part of the "females searching females" detachment created to better serve the female residents of Fallujah.

The attack was also noteworthy because it shattered an otherwise relatively calm period of rebuilding in the city. An insurgent group claiming responsibility for the bombing called on residents of the city "not to rebuild their houses and to save the money they have in banks . . . to start another battle with the infidel forces."[1] The war in Iraq was still taking a precious toll on Americans, but it was clear that the incentives offered by the insurgents had fallen to a new low. By advocating only more Iraqi suffering to continue attacks on Americans in a futile attempt to stop progress in the city, the insurgents appealed to no one; they had clearly lost the majority of their former support. In Fallujah, no one took the insurgent's bait – they had all seen the effects of war in the most personal way and they had also benefited from the policies of a new Iraq. Fallujahns had come to accept a new future.

This event certainly did not signal the loss of any part of Fallujah to the insurgents (quite the opposite in fact); however, it did testify to the fact that continued vigilance would be required as long as the Iraqi people could not yet control the territory inside their borders. By the summer of 2005, the Iraqi armed forces were rising in competence and taking on more and more of the missions in Al Anbar province, but they were still too few in number to give the Marines much of a break from their many responsibilities in the huge province.

Marine operations in Iraq had shifted north, toward the Syrian border, during the summer and fall, into towns like Haditha and Al Qaim. Ramadi remained restive and challenging throughout the year, but the population in the provincial capital shifted ever so slightly against the insurgency and some residents even began to actively support the MNF's efforts. The new provincial governor was well known to the Marines and had the right agenda for the people, so there was much hope.

The high costs of combat in and around Fallujah continued through the remainder of the year. On August 3, 2005, outside of Haditha, 14 Marines and their Iraqi interpreter were killed in a huge explosion that ripped their assault amphibian vehicle apart.[2] This attack was the deadliest roadside bombing of the war and also resulted in the largest number of reservists killed in a single day of the entire campaign. A second deadly explosion in the first days of December killed 10 Marines and wounded 11 others just outside Fallujah.[3] Terrorists and their insurgent supporters were much more restricted in their attacks, but when they did strike, they could be very effective.

Fortunately, improvements in responsible governance continued during 2005 as well. The new Iraqi constitution was endorsed by an overwhelming majority of the people and voter turnout in Sunni areas increased over the dismally small levels witnessed earlier in January. Voter turnout in Fallujah remained the highest in all of Al Anbar province. The national elections held in December demonstrated even more Sunni participation, and for many Sunni voters, a very real rejection of the insurgency.

In Najaf, where the MEF had fought so successfully in August 2004, continued economic development, reconstruction, and improvement in Iraqi Security Forces permitted the MNF to turn full control back to the Iraqi forces only 1 year later. The handover marked the first transfer of an entire city from U.S. to Iraqi military control. Although American logistics and advisors would remain to support the Iraqis, it was a moment to make all Najafis proud.[4]

Through 2005, the spirit of the Marines, Soldiers, and Sailors in Iraq remained high. Although many in Congress called for new exit strategies late in the year, the Pentagon continued to develop plans for future unit rotations into Iraq. The Iraqi Security Forces were improving each week and even began to conduct independent operations without direct U.S. assistance. In fact, multinational force operations in Tal Afar during September emulated many of the techniques proven effective during operation Al Fajr with an even larger percentage of Iraqi forces, and a similar level of success.

The operation in Tal Afar included months of preparation, an incentive for the residents in the affected area to leave their homes, and a significant political effort to smooth relations between the Sunni and Shia groups involved. The Iraqi

Security Forces were in the clear majority and led most of the operational actions, although the veteran 3rdACR, by then commanded by Colonel H. R. McMaster, contributed a great deal to the operation as well. As in Fallujah, a significant number of insurgents were killed when they stood their ground in the city. And, although some enemy fighters escaped, upwards of 150 of them were killed and 300 were captured.[5]

Conventional combat between the multinational forces and the insurgents was becoming increasingly rare in Iraq as the year passed. The enemy learned every time that defeat in conventional operations will not be followed by any rise in local support for the insurgency, and although the numbers of people attracted to martyrdom remained amazingly high, inspiring large numbers of fighters to engage in combat operations appeared over time to become increasingly more difficult for Zarqawi and his subordinates. Slowly but surely, the remaining enemy sanctuaries in Iraq were isolated and eliminated. In some cases, it was the local residents who put the pressure on the insurgents and pushed them on to more remote, yet still receptive, areas.[6]

The Iraqi Army made great strides during 2005. It not only grew in numbers of combat-ready units, but more importantly, its units also improved their cohesion and skill at arms and their commanders made great strides in combat leadership.[7] The Iraqi Army took responsibility for more and more areas of Iraq, and although it continued to take casualties, its recruitment numbers remained high. Iraqis began to see security force personnel, both soldiers and police, as protectors, not as the bullies they had once been under Saddam.

Support for the insurgents among the Iraqis themselves remains variable; they are extremely tired of such difficult wartime conditions, and even the Sunni residents in Iraq are beginning to blame the insurgents for their woes. Some Sunni tribes are now even fighting openly against the enemy in their hometowns. Still, many Iraqis see the presence of American forces in Iraq as very problematic and most are disappointed that reconstruction projects and a higher standard of living have not arrived quickly enough. Fuel and electricity remain in short supply. For many Iraqi people, the expectations they had when Saddam's regime fell have not been met.

During December 2005, the Iraqi Transitional Government's new constitution and another round of national elections testified to the continued development of democracy in the country. The Sunni minority still feels threatened by the rising power of the Shia majority in Iraq, but both sects are continuing the political dialog. There is no doubt that the central government of Iraq needs to be strengthened and its processes made more efficient, but those issues will only be solved with the passage of time.

A little over a year after the bodies of the Blackwater contractors were hung from the old green bridge, General Sattler met in Fallujah with General Abizaid, Ambassador James Jeffrey, and key U.S. congressional leaders, to show them the improvements made in the city. A week later, Deputy Secretary of State Robert Zoellick visited Fallujah to discuss the city's progress with members of the new city council. By June, one reporter described a Fallujah of "thriving markets, stores selling candy and ice-cream, and scores of children delighted to see Americans,"[8] what he didn't know was that potable water was still problematic and electricity would not be fully restored for months to come.

Each month essential services in the city were improved and unemployment was reduced, but the city remained wounded – perhaps because the amount of illegal economic activity in Fallujah was at an all-time low. Still, in December 2005, Fallujahns again went to the polls in huge numbers. They turned out in droves, demonstrating they would still give democracy and the new Iraq a chance. Later in the month, U.S. Secretary of Defense Donald Rumsfeld visited the city and its nearby Marine base. While there, he announced for the first time that President Bush had approved proposed troop reductions in Iraq for 2006.

Fallujah remains one of the safest cities in Iraq.

Notes

Chapter One. The Old Bridge

1. Blackwater, USA, was founded in 1997 to provide flexible training and security solutions. It consists of six separate business units: Blackwater Training Center (the largest private firearms and tactical training center in the United States), Blackwater Target Systems, Blackwater Security Consulting, Blackwater Aviation Worldwide Services, Blackwater Canine, and Raven Development Group. See http://www.blackwaterusa.com.

2. The three former Army Special Forces soldiers were Wesley Batalona, Michael Teague, and Jerry Zovko.

3. The Navy SEAL teams are composed of specially trained sailors who conduct reconnaissance and direct action missions as part of a naval campaign.

4. One of Blackwater's managers in Iraq, former U.S. Navy Captain Pat Toohey, believed the men had been set up by local Iraqi Civil Defense Corps members, who lured them into the city as part of the attack, "Marines Return Hostile Fire in Fallujah," Friday, April 9, 2004, found at http://www.foxnews.com/story/0,2933,116626,00.html.

5. Bing West. *No True Glory, A Frontline Account of the Battle for Fallujah.* Bantam Books, New York, 2005, 3.

6. Public Broadcasting Online Newshour, March 31, 2004, 12:30 p.m. EST edition, found at www.pbs.org/newshour/updates/iraq_3-31-04.html.

7. Please see http://www.answers.com/topic/fallujah.

8. Mike Tucker. *Among Warriors in Iraq.* Lyons Press, Guilford, Connecticut, 2005, 89.

9. See Jennifer Glass reporting for the BBC in "Town Vents Its Anger at US" at http://news.bbc.co.uk/go/pr/fr/-/2/hi/middle_east/2989923.stm and CNN's Karl Penhaul in "Two Killed in Second Clash in Fallujah" at www.cnn.com/2003/WORLD/meast/04/30/sprj.irq.fallujah/index.html.

10. Karl Penhaul, "Two Killed in Second Clash in Fallujah."

11. Even CNN's Penhaul was confused about the facts. See his "Karl Penhaul: Conflicting Stories from Fallujah" at www.cnn.com/2003/WORLD/meast/04/29/otsc.penhaul/index.html.

12. Charles J. Hanley, "Iraq Grenade Attack Hurts Seven United States Soldiers in Fallujah," at http://www.alor.org/Britain/OnTargetBritain%20Liberation%20of%20Iraq%20Part%202%20April2003.htm.

13. One of the insurmountable problems facing the 3rdACR in Iraq was the sheer size of its area of operations. No unit the size of an armored cavalry regiment could possibly control the whole of Al Anbar province.

14. This was the 2nd Brigade of the 3rd Infantry Division, commanded by Colonel David Perkins. This brigade had previously dominated the very heavy fighting in early April around the Baghdad International Airport.

15. The 3rdACR continued operations in Al Anbar province from its regimental headquarters in Al Asad air base until relieved by elements of the 7th Marine Regiment in March 2004.

16. The 3rdACR was commanded by Colonel David A. Teeples during its service in Iraq.

17. The 3rdID had more soldiers overall and many more vehicles than did the mixed bag of light infantry assigned to the 82nd Airborne's Brigade, but the paratroopers and light fighters provided by the 82nd were more numerous on the ground.

18. Hamza Hendawi, "American Soldiers Involved in Shooting of Iraqi Police Had Arrived in City a Day Earlier," Associated Press, September 18, 2003, at http://www.sfgate.com/cgi-bin/article.cgi?file=/news/archive/2003/09/18/international0548EDT0488.DTL.

19. This incident resulted in the greatest U.S. loss of life since the end of major combat operations in the late spring and set off a period of tension that eventually caused the U.S. units to withdraw again from Fallujah.

20. Please see http://www.cbc.ca/news/background/iraq/fallujah.html.

21. Michael J. Carden, 82nd Airborne Public Affairs, Operation Salm, at http://www.bragg.army.mil/afvc-c/Stories/Salm.htm.

22. Edward Wong, "U.S. Uncovers Vast Hide-Out of Iraqi Rebels," *New York Times*, June 5, 2005, 1.

23. These former members of the Ba'ath Party were also referred to as "Saddamists" by some officials, including President George Bush, who mentioned the residual strength of this group in his November 2005 speech to the nation on the nature of the war.

24. The 1st Marine Expeditionary Force was composed on one Marine Division, one Marine Aircraft Wing, one Marine Force Service Support Group, and additional attachments, including a brigade of U.S. Army soldiers. Later other units would augment the MEF; however, the 1st Marine Division remained the primary ground combat unit of the MEF.

25. This is not to say the Army units that had served in the region were lacking in aggression – they certainly were highly trained and superbly professional in their actions, but they were operating in the Fallujah area without any operational pause from the initial convention combat operations of the first phase of the war and had not been able to formulate a distinct concept of operations for counterinsurgency action.

26. The approach of "No Better Friend ... No Worse Enemy" was a long-standing construct of the Corps initially put into practice in the Shia south of Iraq following the first phase of the war. It did represent a set of techniques that were different from the U.S. Army's approach. General Mattis made the concept part of his commander's guidance – issued to

all of his Marines. See Mackubin Owens, "No Better Friend . . . No Worse Enemy," *National Review Online*, July 2003, at http://www.nationalreview.com/owens/owens073103.asp.

27. Because the initial assault to Baghdad was a very narrow penetration, significant restructuring was required to effectively control the entire country. It was during this period of repositioning forces that the initial leverage over the enemy was lost and opportunities for opponents of the coalition to begin insurgent activities commenced.

28. U.S. Marine Corps, *Small Wars Manual*. Pavilion Press, Philadelphia, 2004.

29. For a working bibliography of small wars readings, see http://www.smallwars.quantico.usmc.mil/reading.asp.

30. Conway turned over command of the MEF to Lieutenant General John Sattler in September 2004 and became the J3, Director of Operations, on the Joint Staff in Washington, D.C.

31. Mattis was promoted to Lieutenant General and assumed command of the Marine Corps Combat Development Command in the fall of 2004. He was followed in command of the division by Major General Richard Natonski, the former commander of Task Force Tarawa.

32. Dunford was promoted to Brigadier General while in Iraq. Following his service in Iraq, he was assigned as the Marine Corps Director of Operations.

33. The Blackwater contractors were not the only Americans to die that day near Fallujah. Five soldiers assigned to the MEF also died on March 31, in Habbaniyah, Iraq, when an improvised explosive device hit their armored personnel carrier. Killed were First Lieutenant Doyle M. Hufstedler of Abilene, Texas; Specialist Sean R. Mitchell of Youngsville, Pennsylvania; Specialist Michael G. Karr, Jr., of San Antonio, Texas; Private First Class Cleston C. Raney of Rupert, Idaho; and Private Brandon L. Davis of Cumberland, Maryland.

34. Operation Vigilant Resolve was directed on short notice, to be executed in less than 5 days, with the goal of capturing or killing the insurgents responsible for the killing of the American contractors. It was also designed to reestablish law and order and prevent Fallujah from acting as a sanctuary for the anti-Iraqi forces. Vigilant Resolve was essentially a two-battalion attack, although four Iraqi battalions had been requested in support and two additional Marine battalions joined the fight at a later time.

35. There was no doubt that the horrific nature of the attack required a response. CNN noted, "Paul Bremer, the U.S. civilian administrator in Iraq, promised that the deaths of the contractors would 'not go unpunished.'" "Marines, Iraqis Join Forces to Shut Down Fallujah," Cable News Network, April 5, 2004, at www.cnn.com/2004/WORLD/meast/04/05/iraq.main.

Chapter Two. Showing Resolve

1. The Marines did employ Civic Action Program (CAP) techniques in Iraq, integrating Marine units to live, eat, and sleep with local Iraqi Security Force units. In fact, at least one CAP unit was employed by the 1st Marines near Fallujah in the city of Naser Wa-Salem throughout the spring and summer of 2004.

2. The local security forces were frequently attacked by insurgents. In February, during a daytime raid on a police station, insurgents had attacked and killed 25 local policemen. Tony Perry and Edmund Sanders, "The Marines Roll into Fallujah," *Los Angeles Times*, April 5, 2004.

3. After months in the area and with more than $7 million in aid devoted to improving the quality of life in and around Fallujah, the leaders of the 82nd Airborne thought the city was progressing well.

4. Camp Fallujah, not to be confused with the city itself, was a former Iraqi army training center designed for the use of an Iranian unit loyal to Saddam Hussein. It was a well-designed and organized military camp, located on the main highway less than 5 miles from the city.

5. PFC Sandoval told his parents he was worried about going into Fallujah following the relief of the 82nd Airborne. "He asked his mom to pray for him; told her they were going into a real bad city," Steve Walters said. "He didn't like the name of that town from the start." Lucas Wall, "Iraqi Battle Claims Local Marine," *Houston Chronicle*, March 28, 2004, A37.

6. Interview with Colonel John Toolan, Quantico, Virginia, July 25, 2005. The surgeon, Army Major Mark D. Taylor of Stockton, California, died on March 20, along with Army Specialist Matthew J. Sandri of Shamokin, Pennsylvania.

7. The soldier was killed when his vehicle was hit by an IED rigged to the top of the underpass and then exploded by someone observing the vehicle. His name was not released.

8. The five soldiers were killed when an IED destroyed their vehicle in Habbaniyah, outside of Fallujah. Killed in the blast were Private Brandon L. Davis; Private First Class Cleston C. Raney; Specialist Michael G. Karr, Jr.; Specialist Sean R. Mitchell; and First Lieutenant Doyle M. Hufstedler.

9. Four members of the MEF were killed during early April in Al Anbar province prior to the main attack: Private First Class Dustin M. Sekula, Private First Class Geoffrey S. Morris, Lance Corporal Aric J. Barr, and Corporal Tyler R. Fey.

10. A Regimental Combat Team is formed by reinforcing the traditional infantry battalions of the regiment with additional ground mobility and firepower assets.

11. The coalition forces also wanted to occupy a downtown photo shop and capture its owner, who was implicated in the murders of the Blackwater team.

12. Once it became clear that the Iraqi forces were not willing to fight, 3rd Battalion, 4th Marines later joined the fight in the northeast along with 2nd Battalion, 2nd Marines in the southwest.

13. Ideally, the Marines wanted to completely surround the city, but given the local geography and few available forces, they could only control key points of access.

14. Bret Baier, Liza Porteus, and The Associated Press, "U.S. Forces Launch Major Fallujah Operation," found at http://www.foxnews.com/printer_friendly_story/0,3566,116144,00.html.

15. "U.S. and Iraqi Forces Encircle Fallujah," April 5, 2004, found at http://abclocal.go.com/kabc/news/print_040504_nw_iraq.html.

16. Lance Corporal Shane Lee Goldman, Corporal Jesse L. Thiry, Private First Class Christopher Ramos, and Lance Corporal Matthew K. Serio, all from 1/5, lost their lives on Monday, April 5, in Fallujah.

17. Pamela Constable, "Troops Gaining Grip in Sections of Fallujah," *The Washington Post*, April 7, 2004, 1. "Of the 250k-300 thousand population, it appeared that during April 2004 the insurgency totaled around 20 thousand. Some Iraqi police were reinforcing the insurgents and ICDC-giving them ammo, and Red Crescent Ambulances dropped off ammo and weapons and then picked-up bodies. The typical insurgent came out and fired at the Marines roughly half a dozen times each day, exposing himself for only a couple of seconds. There seemed to be one to two dozen groups of 'Hard Core,' or 'Minute Men,' each with

approximately two dozen members armed with IEDs, MGs, lots of RPGs, mortars, and some anti-aircraft weapons." www.globalsecurity.org/military/ops/oif-vigilant-resolve.htm

18. Constable, "Troops Gaining Grip in Sections of Fallujah."

19. Ibid.

20. April 6 was relatively quiet in Fallujah, resulting in no combat deaths; however, in the provincial capital of Ramadi, perhaps as a result of the fighting in Fallujah, Private First Class Christopher D. Mabry, Petty Officer Third Class Fernando A. Mendez-Aceves, Private First Class Benjamin R. Carman, Lance Corporal Marcus M. Cherry, Lance Corporal Anthony P. Roberts, Lance Corporal Kyle D. Crowley, Staff Sergeant Allan K. Walker, Lance Corporal Travis J. Layfield, Private First Class Ryan M. Jerabek, and Private First Class Christopher R. Cobb all lost their lives on that date.

21. Brent Baier, Steve Centanni, and The Associated Press, "At Least 12 Marines Killed as Iraq Fighting Rages," found at http://www.foxnews.com/printer_friendly_story/0,3566,116262,00.html.

22. Interview with Colonel John Toolan, July 25, Quantico, Virginia.

23. Brent Baier, Steve Centanni, and The Associated Press, "At Least 12 Marines Killed as Iraq Fighting Rages," found at http://www.foxnews.com/printer_friendly_story/0,3566,116262,00.html.

24. Ibid.

25. Pamela Constable, "Marines, Insurgents Battle for Sunni City," *The Washington Post*, April 8, 2004, A10.

26. Captain Brent L. Morel was killed in Fallujah. Elsewhere, in Ramadi, Second Lieutenant John Thomas "J.T." Wroblewski lost his life the same day.

27. Constable, "Marines, Insurgents Battle for Sunni City."

28. Robert D. Kaplan, "The Real Story of Fallujah," *Wall Street Journal*, May 27, 2004, 20.

29. Ibid.

30. The 3rd Battalion, 4th Marines was moved into the outskirts of the northeastern part of Fallujah and 2nd Battalion, 2nd Marines took up positions along the southern edge of the city, known as Queens.

31. Lance Corporal Michael B. Wafford, First Lieutenant Joshua M. Palmer, and Staff Sergeant William M. Harrell were all killed in Fallujah.

32. Most rooftops in Fallujah include a wall approximately 4 feet high. Marines learned to sand-bag the rooftop to build them up for sniper teams and mortar positions. Sniper use was heavy, especially to serve as forward observers and to cover the long axis of the roads. Snipers became even more valuable once Marine units assumed static positions. The typical Marine sniper had over 30 kills. The Marines had limited laser designation ability for mortars because there were no laser designators at the platoon level. Psychological operations (PSYOPs) teams were used to attract insurgents and position them for snipers. Marine platoons in the fight were organized with almost company strength.

33. Lieutenant General Ricardo Sanchez, "Coalition Provisional Authority Briefing," Baghdad, Thursday, April 8, 2004, found at: www.defenselink.com.

34. The Marines were initially not opposed to the cease-fires. They never intended for operation Vigilant Resolve to be such a high-intensity attack or for it to last beyond the week, plus their real intent was always to protect the Iraqi residents and that was becoming ever more difficult. Additionally, their supply lines were under attack in the province because most of their maneuver forces had been moved into Fallujah.

35. Private First Class Eric A. Ayon of Arleta, California, died April 9 from hostile fire in Al Anbar province, Iraq; he was assigned to 2nd Battalion, 4th Marine Regiment. Lance Corporal Chance R. Phelps of Clifton, Colorado, also died April 9 from hostile fire. He was assigned to 3rd Battalion, 11th Marine Regiment.

36. Numir El-Higazi, "U.S. Claims Fallujah Offensive Suspended," *The Palestine Chronicle*, April 9, 2004, found at www.Islamonline.net.

37. Karl Vick, "Rallying around an Insurgent City," *The Washington Post*, April 9, 2004, A01.

38. Kaplan, "The Real Story of Fallujah."

39. Concerns ranged from the international zone in Baghdad, all the way to the White House, which contacted the MEF staff directly on several occasions to stay abreast of the situation in the city.

40. Lance Corporal John T. Sims, Jr., of Alexander City, Alabama, died April 10 from hostile fire in Al Anbar province, Iraq. He was assigned to 2nd Battalion, 4th Marine Regiment. Private First Class George D. Torres of Long Beach, California, died April 11 as a result of enemy fire in Fallujah. He was assigned to 1st Battalion, 5th Marine Regiment. First Lieutenant Oscar Jimenez of San Diego, California, Corporal Daniel R. Amaya of Odessa, Texas, and Lance Corporal Torrey L. Gray of Patoka, Illinois, also all died April 11 as a result of enemy fire in Al Anbar province, Iraq. They were assigned to the 3rd Battalion, 4th Marine Regiment.

41. Corporal Kevin T. Kolm of Hicksville, New York, died April 13 from hostile fire in the initial action. He was assigned to 3rd Assault Amphibian Battalion. Lance Corporal Ronnie Garcia and Corporal Bruno J. Romera were both awarded Bronze Star medals for valor for their actions that day. For the details of this action, see Ross W. Simpson, "Fallujah: A Four-Letter Word," *Leatherneck*, March 2005, Vol. 88, Issue 3, p. 14. Lance Corporal Brad S. Shuder of El Dorado, California, and Lance Corporal Robert P. Zurheide, Jr., of Tucson, Arizona, were both killed in Fallujah on April 12; they were assigned to the 2nd Battalion, 1st Marine Regiment.

42. Still, Private Noah L. Boye of Grand Island, Nebraska, and 1/5 also died April 13 from hostile fire in Fallujah.

43. The Marine demands were always focused on the turn-in of heavy weapons, the apprehension of the Blackwater murderers, the identification of terrorist leaders, and the deescalation of the fighting. The insurgents wanted a number of things but seemed most focused on the withdrawal of snipers and tanks from the city.

44. Lieutenant General Conway was the key decision maker on the coalition side for the negotiations, although Colonel John Coleman and several Iraqi representatives from the Iraqi Governing Council played strong roles.

45. Lance Corporal Austin of Sunray, Texas, died April 26 because of hostile fire in Fallujah. On July 22, 2005, he was posthumously awarded the Silver Star for his actions during the firefight in the streets of Fallujah. See Tony Perry, "Marine Who 'Wouldn't Quit Fighting' Is Honored," *Los Angeles Times*, July 22, 2005.

46. Corporal Scott M. Vincent of Bokoshe, Oklahoma, and Corporal Joshua S. Wilfong of Walker, West Virginia, were the last two Marines to die in Fallujah in the month of April; both lost their lives on April 30.

47. John F. Sattler and Daniel H. Wilson, "Operation AL FAJR: The Battle of Fallujah–Part II," *Marine Corps Gazette*, July 2005, 12.

48. The Mahdi Militia was the military arm of the followers of Muqtada Al Sadr, a young Shia religious leader. They effectively took control of the central part of the holy

city of Najaf and began to conduct Sharia courts and kill accused violators of religious law. This began only days after the arrival in theater of the 11th Marine Expeditionary Unit, commanded by Colonel Tony Haslem.

49. Kaplan, "The Real Story of Fallujah."

Chapter Three. The Lion of Najaf

1. The Mahdi Militia was the military arm of the followers of Muqtada al-Sadr, a young Shia religious leader. They effectively took control of the central part of the holy city of Najaf and began to conduct Sharia courts and kill accused violators of religious law. This began only days after the arrival in theater of the 11th Marine Expeditionary Unit, commanded by Colonel Tony Haslem.

2. Muqtada al-Sadr was not a true cleric, having not received a holy degree, but he was born in 1974, the youngest son of Muhammad Sadiq Sadr – a senior Shia cleric who was assassinated in 1999. In June 2003, he had created the Mahdi Militia, in defiance of the coalition with the stated goal of protecting the Shia religious authorities in the holy city of Najaf. He was, however, not popular with the locals and his militia was composed mostly of outsiders. He began fighting against the coalition in April 2004, but that outbreak was ended by the mediation of Grand Ayatollah Ali Sistani. U.S. forces counterattacked his militia in Najaf after another outbreak in May.

3. It is highly likely that Berg was actually murdered in Fallujah.

4. One author, Thomas Hayden, has proposed that the insurgency in Iraq actually started following the April battle in Fallujah. In his article, "Counterinsurgency in Iraq Started with Fallujah," *Marine Corps Gazette*, July 2005, 28–29, Hayden demonstrates that vacillation and inconsistency build insurgent power and engender in an insurgency even greater confidence.

5. During May, Captain John E. Tipton, Petty Officer Second Class Scott R. McHugh, Petty Officer Second Class Robert B. Jenkins, Petty Officer Third Class Ronald A. Ginther, Petty Officer Second Class Trace W. Dossett, Petty Officer Second Class Michael C. Anderson, Gunnery Sergeant Ronald E. Baum, Corporal Jeffrey G. Green, Corporal Dustin H. Schrage, Specialist Kyle A. Brinlee, Lance Corporal Jeremiah E. Savage, Private First Class Brandon C. Sturdy, Private First Class Brian K. Cutter, Specialist Mark J. Kasecky, Specialist Carl F. Curran, Lance Corporal Bob W. Roberts, Private First Class Michael M. Carey, Corporal Rudy Salas, Lance Corporal Andrew J. Zabierek, Specialist Jeremy L. Ridlen, Staff Sergeant Jorge A. Molina Bautista, Army Privates First Class Richard H. Rosas and James P. Lambert, Corporal Dominique J. Nicolas, Corporal Matthew C. Henderson, Lance Corporal Kyle W. Codner, Lance Corporal Rafael Reynosa-Suarez, Lance Corporal Benjamin R. Gonzalez, Private First Class Cody S. Calavan, and Lance Corporal Dustin L. Sides all died in Al Anbar province.

6. Eleven servicemen, Private First Class Markus J. Johnson; Corporal Bum R. Lee; Lance Corporal Todd J. Bolding; Lance Corporal Jeremy L. Bohlman; Private First Class Sean Horn; Staff Sergeant Marvin Best; Corporal Tommy L. Parker, Jr.; Lance Corporal Deshon E. Otey; Lance Corporal Juan Lopez; Lance Corporal Pedro Contreras; and Lance Corporal Manuel A. Ceniceros died in Al Anbar province in June 2004. In July, operations in the province cost the lives of the following: Lance Corporal Timothy R. Creager; Sergeant Kenneth Conde, Jr.; Army Second Lieutenant Brian D. Smith; Lance Corporal James B. Huston, Jr.; Lance Corporal John J. Vangyzen IV; Lance Corporal Michael S. Torres; Corporal Dallas L. Kerns; Private First Class Rodricka A. Youmans; Corporal Jeffrey D. Lawrence; Lance

Corporal Justin T. Hunt; Lance Corporal Scott E. Dougherty; Army Sergeant Michael C. Barkey; Staff Sergeant Trevor Spink; Private First Class Christopher J. Reed; Sergent Krisna Nachampassak; Corporal Terry Holmes; Lance Corporal Bryan P. Kelly; Corporal Todd J. Godwin; Staff Sergeant Michael J. Clark; Lance Corporal Mark E. Engel; Lance Corporal Vincent M. Sullivan; Gunnery Sergeant Shawn A. Lane; and Lieutenant Colonel David S. Greene. During August, operations in Al Anbar outside of Najaf cost the lives of Corporal Dean P. Pratt; Sergeant Juan Calderon, Jr.; Captain Gregory A. Ratzlaff; Lance Corporal Joseph L. Nice; Gunnery Sergeant Elia P. Fontecchio; Lance Corporal Jonathan W. Collins; Lance Corporal Nicholas B. Morrison; Lance Corporal Kane M. Funke; Army Sergeant Daniel Michael Shepherd; Private First Class Geoffrey Perez; Private First Class Fernando B. Hannon; Lance Corporal Caleb J. Powers; Sergeant Harvey E. Parkerson III; Sergeant Richard M. Lord; Lance Corporal Dustin R. Fitzgerald; Corporal Brad P. McCormick; Private First Class Nachez Washalanta; Gunnery Sergeant Edward T. Reeder; Lance Corporal Seth Huston; Army Private First Class Kevin A. Cuming; Sergeant Jason Cook; Corporal Nicanor Alvarez; Corporal Christopher Belchik; Army Staff Sergeant Donald N. Davis; Lance Corporal Jacob R. Lugo; Corporal Barton R. Humlhanz; Specialist Omead H. Razani; Private First Class Luis A. Perez; Lance Corporal Nickalous N. Aldrich; and Sergeant Edgar E. Lopez.

7. Ambassador Lakhdar Brahimi was appointed Special Adviser to the United Nations (UN) Secretary-General on January 1, 2004. Brahimi was formerly the UN Special Representative of the Secretary-General for Afghanistan and head of the UN Assistance Mission in Afghanistan. He had previously served as the Secretary-General's Special Envoy for Afghanistan from July 1997 to October 1999. Between his Afghanistan assignments, Mr. Brahimi served as Under-Secretary-General for Special Assignments in Support of the Secretary-General's Preventive and Peacemaking efforts. In this capacity, he chaired an independent panel established by Secretary-General Annan to review UN peace operations. Prior to his first Afghanistan appointment, Mr. Brahimi served as Special Representative for Haiti (from 1994 to 1996) and Special Representative for South Africa (from December 1993 to June 1994). In the latter position, he led the United Nations Observer Mission until the 1994 democratic elections that resulted in Nelson Mandela taking the presidency of postapartheid South Africa. Thus, he was a very experienced and well-respected mediator for Iraqi government development.

8. Dr. Iyad Allawi was the cofounder of the London-based Iraqi National Accord (INA), an opposition group supported by the CIA that staged an unsuccessful coup d'etat against Saddam Hussein in 1996. A secular Shiite, he was a Ba'athist who served in the Iraqi intelligence services until falling out with the regime and leaving Iraq in 1971 to study medicine in London. On returning to Iraq, he became a member of the IGC and chair of its security committee. From the Council on Foreign Relations at http://www.cfr.org/background/background_iraq_ministers.php.

9. As a part of the ceremony, L. Paul Bremer read the following: "As recognized in U.N. Security Council resolution 1546, the Coalition Provisional Authority will cease to exist on June 28th, at which point the occupation will end and the Iraqi interim government will assume and exercise full sovereign authority on behalf of the Iraqi people. I welcome Iraq's steps to take its rightful place of equality and honor among the free nations of the world."

10. Allawi was a Ba'ath Party member for 10 years (1961–1971) before going into exile in Beirut and London. After a 1978 assassination attempt, he became even more committed to the cause. In 1990, he formed the INA, his CIA and British intelligence-backed opposition movement, which included many other former Ba'athists who had opposed Saddam

Hussein. Before Saddam was overthrown, the INA operated from Amman, Jordan, but he moved it to Baghdad in April 2003. According to council members, Allawi was chosen as prime minister because he was most capable of dealing with Iraq's security; he had been in charge of security matters in the governing council. He proved to be a very capable administrator and a firm and decisive leader. See "Allawi Takes on the Job from Hell," *The Economist*, May 31, 2004.

11. Ambassador Negroponte was a graduate of Yale University and served as Ambassador to Honduras from 1981 to 1985. He was also Assistant Secretary of State for Oceans and International Environmental and Scientific Affairs (1985–1987) and Deputy Assistant to the President for National Security Affairs (1987–1989) before being named Ambassador to Mexico, where he served from 1989 to 1993 and Ambassador to the Philippines from 1993 to 1996. Prior to his arrival in Iraq, he had served as the U.S. Ambassador to the United Nations from 2001 to 2004.

12. General Casey assumed command of Multinational Force Iraq (MNF-I) on July 1 from Lieutenant General Ricardo Sanchez, who had commanded Combined Joint Task Force 7 (CJTF-7) during and after the initial phase of combat operations in Iraq. When General Casey assumed command of MNF-I, Lieutenant General Thomas Metz, General Sanchez's deputy commander, assumed command of Multinational Corps-Iraq (MNC-I), which was charged with the operational prosecution of the war in the country under the strategic guidance of General Casey. Generals Metz and Casey both worked directly for General John Abizaid, the commander of U.S. Central Command in Tampa, Florida.

13. After General Casey assumed command in Iraq the coalition transitioned to the Multinational Force-Iraq. The terms *multinational forces* and *MNF*, will be used from this point forward to describe all coalition forces and activities in Iraq.

14. Sheik Ghazi Ajil al-Yawar was a Sunni and an important sheik in the Shammar tribe, one of Iraq's largest. He was the immediate past president of the Iraqi Governing Council – its presidency rotated on a monthly basis -- and won the support of the majority of its members for this post. He won the job after Adnan Pachachi, a former foreign minister, reportedly refused an offer from Brahimi. Born in Mosul, Yawar studied engineering at Georgetown University in Washington, D.C., and spent 15 years in exile in Saudi Arabia. From the Council on Foreign Relations at http://www.cfr.org/background/background_iraq_ministers.php.

15. http://www.globalsecurity.org/military/world/iraq/najaf.htm.

16. The Sunni attacks in Baghdad, Samarra, Ramadi, and Fallujah during the same week made early April a time of the most serious challenge to coalition control of Iraq.

17. The Najaf region was initially secured by American forces of the MEF, which departed Iraq in November 2003. The 1st Armored Division assumed control of the entire south central area of Iraq [Multinational Division Central-South (MND-CS)] following the departure of the MEF. Later, the Spanish contingent of the coalition was assigned to the area under the overall control of the Polish Division, which assumed the responsibility for MND-CS. An exclusion zone was set up, comprising the old city of Najaf, the cemetery, and the town of Kufa, to minimize friction and the appearance of troops in the holy areas of the city.

18. I MEF and 11th MEU staffs, "Battle for An Najaf, August 2004," *Marine Corps Gazette*, December 2004, 10.

19. Grand Ayatollah Ali al-Sistani, who lives in Najaf, is the most respected of the Shiite imams in Iraq. His position was initially contested by other clerics, including Mohammad Sadeq al-Sadr, Moqtada al-Sadr's father, but his role as successor to his teacher Abdul-Qassem Khoei, made him the favorite of most Shia. The assassination of Sadr by Saddam

Hussein made him the most influential Shia cleric in the country. In his role as Ayatollah, Sistani oversees sums amounting to millions of dollars, which he distributes in various ways, including payment for the religious education of would-be scholars across the Muslim world. See http://www.sistani.org/html/eng/.

20. On June 17, a small battalion task force relieved the 2ndACR after the truce. This second unit passed on very few of the pertinent factors of fighting in the area to the Marines who would follow them – another shortfall in transitioning critical information between units over the course of a relief in place.

21. "This is a revolution against the occupation force until we get independence and democracy," al-Sadr's spokesman, Ahmed Shaybani, said in a telephone interview with Jackie Spinner of *The Washington Post*; see her "Cleric's Attack Tests Iraqi Leaders, Rebel Cleric Declares 'Revolution' against U.S. Forces in Iraq," August 6, 2004.

22. The 11th MEU had been assigned to the area on short notice, as the CENTCOM theater reserve, working directly for MNC-I (General Metz), after the Spanish contingent was withdrawn from the coalition. The Spanish government pulled its forces out following the intimidation of the Madrid bombings of March 11, 2004.

23. The local police were holding over 100 Mahdi Militiamen. I MEF and 11th MEU staffs, "Battle for An Najaf, August 2004," *Marine Corps Gazette*, December 2004, 12.

24. "A large number of aggressors later confirmed to be members of the radical Shiite cleric Muqtada al-Sadr's Muqtada Militia, attacked the city of Najaf's main police station at 1 A.M. and were quickly repelled by the Iraqi police. Later, at 3 A.M., they attacked again, this time with heavy machine guns, rocket propelled grenades, mortars and small arms. Iraqi National Guardsmen from the 405th Battalion, 50th Iraqi Brigade, were notified and arrived on the scene and helped the Iraqi Police successfully defended the station from the Anti-Iraqi Forces." Chago Zapata, "11th MEU Battles anti-Iraqi Forces in An Najaf," *Marine Corps News*, August 11, 2004. See also Spinner, "Cleric's Attack Tests Iraqi Leaders, Rebel Cleric Declares 'Revolution' against U.S. Forces in Iraq," *The Washington Post*, August 6, 2004.

25. I MEF and 11th MEU staffs, "Battle for An Najaf, August 2004," *Marine Corps Gazette*, December 2004, 11.

26. Private First Class Raymond J. Faulstich, Jr., of the 7th Transportation Group, from Leonardtown, Maryland; Sergeant Yadir G. Reynoso, of BLT 1/4 and Wapato, Washington; and Sergeant Moses D. Rocha, of BLT 1/4 and Roswell, New Mexico, all died as a result of injuries received from hostile action in Najaf on August 5, 2004.

27. I MEF and 11th MEU staffs, "Battle for An Najaf, August 2004," *Marine Corps Gazette*, December 2004, 10.

28. The military term *chop* is peculiar to naval forces and is based on the acronym for "change of operational control." It signifies that a unit and responsibility for that unit has been shifted from one commander to another and that the receiving commander has full authority to organize and employ the unit as needed.

29. This made good sense for a variety of reasons. Najaf bordered the MEF area of operations, the MEF by that time had good situational awareness of Iraq (whereas the MEU had only just arrived in the country), and a MEU is not normally designed to control the operations of multiple, subordinate coalition commands in such a large area. At nearly the same time, the 24th MEU, commanded by Colonel Ron Johnson, was also assigned to combat operations in Iraq, southwest of Baghdad.

30. On May 27, 2004, the 11th MEU had sailed a month early aboard the *USS Belleau Wood* Expeditionary Strike Group, in response to a request from the U.S. Central Command

for additional forces in Iraq. Comprising BLT 1/4, HMM-166, and MSSG-11, the MEU assumed responsibility for the southern Iraqi provinces of Najaf and Qadisiyah on July 31.

31. Corporal Roberto Abad, Los Angeles, California, and Lance Corporal Larry L. Wells, Mount Hermon, Louisiana, both died of injuries received from hostile action in Najaf on August 6, 2004.

32. The fighting in Najaf was close, vicious, and costly; by this time the MEF estimated that coalition forces had killed over 450 of the enemy. Staff Sergeant John R. Howard, Covington, Virginia, and Lance Corporal Tavon L. Hubbard, Reston, Virginia, were both killed in a helicopter crash on August 11.

33. During this fight, Army Special Forces Captain Michael Yury Tarlavsky from Passaic, New Jersey, was killed in action in Najaf.

34. Second Lieutenant James Michael Goins, Bonner Springs, Kansas; Private First Class Brandon R. Sapp, Lake Worth, Florida; and Specialist Mark Anthony Zapata, Edinburg, Texas were all killed in action on August 15.

35. Sergeant Harvey E. Parkerson III, of Yuba City, California, was killed during this action in Najaf.

36. Lance Corporal Alexander S. Arredondo, from Randolph, Massachusetts, died on August 25 as a result of enemy fire.

37. Private First Class Nicholas M. Skinner, of Alpha Company BLT 1/4 and Davenport, Iowa, died as the last combat casualty of the August fighting in Najaf on August 26.

38. The day following the cessation of hostilities in Najaf, Private First Class Luis A. Perez from Theresa, New York, was killed when his vehicle hit a roadside bomb outside of Fallujah.

39. John F. Sattler and Daniel H. Wilson, "Operation AL FAJR: the Battle of Fallujah–Part II," *Marine Corps Gazette*, July 2005, 12.

Chapter Four. Shaping Operations Prior to the Assault

1. The AC-130 gunship and its internally mounted 105-millimeter cannon was one of the most frequently used and most effective systems delivering lethal fires into Fallujah.

2. Strikes against known, positively identified terrorist leaders, such as Zarqawi, were the only exception to this rule. The mathematical estimates of collateral damage were known as "bugsplats" because that term describes the likely damage to the target and any other objects nearby.

3. MEF staffers came to call the hospital director "Dr. Bob" because his wildly inaccurate and negative reporting of the facts reminded them of the former Iraqi Minister of Information, who had been given the nickname "Baghdad Bob." Still, the negative information passed at the hospital was of such a level that the MEF staff always ensured that full documentation of their actions was available to counter any claims of excessive damage.

4. On September 3, the 7th Marines lost Lance Corporal Nicholas Perez of Austin, Texas; Major Alan Rowe of Hagerman, Idaho; Lance Corporal Nicholas Wilt of Tampa, Florida; and 1st Lieutenant Ronald Winchester of Rockville Center, New York. Lance Corporal Michael J. Allred of Hyde Park, Utah; Private First Class David P. Burridge of Lafayette, Louisiana; Lance Corporal Derek L. Gardner of San Juan Capistrano, California; Lance Corporal Quinn A. Keith of Page, Arizona; Lance Corporal Joseph C. McCarthy of Concho, California; Corporal Mick R. Nygardbekowsky of Concord, California; and Lance Corporal Lamont N. Wilson of Lawton, Oklahoma were all killed just outside Fallujah on September 6.

Lance Corporal Gardner was from Headquarters Battalion, 1st Marine Division, the others were members of 2nd Battalion, 1st Marines.

5. Private First Class Sparks, of Monroeville, Ohio, was assigned to the 1st Battalion, 503rd Infantry Regiment.

6. First Lieutenant Alexander E. Wetherbee of Fairfax, Virgina, was assigned to 3rd Assault Amphibian Battalion; Private First Class Jason T. Poindexter of San Angelo, Texas, was assigned to 2nd Battalion, 5th Marine Regiment.

7. Thirty-four Marines and soldiers assigned to the MEF died as a result of hostile fire in September 2004 of a total of 80 deaths that month.

8. Lieutenant Colonel Kevin M. Shea was from Washington, D.C. Colonel Nicholson was medevaced from the theater to recuperate but was back in Iraq by the following spring as the division operations officer.

9. Marine fatalities in the Fallujah area during the last 2 weeks of the month included the following: Lance Corporal Mathew D. Puckett of Mason, Texas; Corporal Adrian V. Soltau of Milwaukee, Wisconsin; and Corporal Jaygee Meluat of Tamuning, Guam, who all died September 13. They were assigned to 3rd Assault Amphibian Battalion. Lance Corporal Dominic C. Brown of Austin, Texas, and Lance Corporal Michael J. Halal of Glendale, Arizona, also both died September 13 due to a non-combat-related incident; such incidents included vehicle accidents, falls, and drowning, all a constant threat in such a very dangerous environment. They were assigned to Headquarters Battalion, 1st Marine Division. On September 15, Lance Corporal Drew M. Uhles of DuQuoin, Illinois, died in combat in western Al Anbar and Lance Corporal Gregory C. Howman of Charlotte, North Carolina, and 2nd Battalion, 5th Marine Regiment was killed near Fallujah. First Lieutenant Andrew K. Stern, of Germantown, Tennessee, and 1st Tank Battalion; Corporal Steven A. Rintamaki of Lynnwood, Washington, and 3/1; Corporal Christopher S. Ebert of Mooresboro, North Carolina, and 2/1; Sergeant Timothy Folmar of Sonora, Texas, and 2/5; and Sergeant Benjamin K. Smith of Carterville, Illinois, and 1st Tank Battalion all died near the end of the month in the Fallujah area of operations.

10. Specialist Jessica L. Cawvey of Normal, Illinois, was killed October 6 in Fallujah, when an improvised explosive device detonated near her convoy vehicle. She was a member of the Army National Guard 1544th Transportation Company, from Paris, Illinois. Private First Class Andrew Halverson of Grant, Wisconsin, died October 9 near Fallujah; he was assigned to 2nd Battalion, 5th Marine Regiment. In nearby north Babil Province, Lance Corporal Daniel R. Wyatt of Calendonia, Wisconsin, died on October 12. Lance Corporal Wyatt was assigned to the Marine Corps Reserve's 2nd Battalion, 24th Marine Regiment, in Chicago, Illinois. Second Lieutenant Paul M. Felsberg of West Palm Beach, Florida, and Lance Corporal Victor A. Gonzalez of Watsonville, California, both died on October 13 as result of enemy action; they were assigned to 2nd Battalion, 5th Marine Regiment. Three Soldiers died in Ramadi as the tempo of operations increased in the whole region. Staff Sergeant Omer T. Hawkins II of Cherry Fork, Ohio, and Private First Class Mark A. Barbret of Shelby Township, Michigan, both from the 44th Engineer Battalion, and Specialist Bradley S. Beard, of Chapel Hill, North Carolina, and the 2nd Battalion, 17th Field Artillery Regiment, died October 14. Sergeant Douglas E. Bascom of Colorado Springs, Colorado, and 2/5, died October 20. Corporal Brian Oliveira of Raynham, Massachusetts died October 25 from injuries received from enemy action; he was assigned to 3/1. Private First Class Stephen P. Downing II of Burkesville, Kentucky, died October 28 in Ramadi from small arms fire while conducting combat operations shaping the Fallujah fight. Private First Class Downing was assigned to the 2nd Battalion, 17th Field Artillery. The following day, Sergeant Maurice

Keith Fortune, of Forestville, Maryland, and the 2nd Battalion, 17th Field Artillery was killed in Ramadi when a vehicle-borne IED detonated near his vehicle.

11. John F. Sattler and Daniel H. Wilson, "Operation AL FAJR: the Battle of Fallujah–Part II," *Marine Corps Gazette*, July 2005, 18.

12. The Corps Order stated, "MNC-I Forces, in partnership with Iraqi Security Forces, conducts full spectrum counter insurgency operations to destroy AIF operating in Fallujah in order to deny the use of Fallujah as a safe-haven from which AIF project terrorist activity against the Iraqi people, IIG and Coalition Forces."

13. On November 7, the MEF released its FRAGO 427 addressing DC operations to establish control measures and temporarily provide emergency food, water, shelter, and medical care to mitigate noncombatant/DC interference with military operations.

14. The Marines from 1/3 killed in this attack included Lance Corporal Jeremy D. Bow of Lemoore, California; Lance Corporal Michael P. Scarborough of Washington, Georgia; Lance Corporal Travis A. Fox of Cowpens, South Carolina; Corporal Christopher J. Lapka of Peoria, Arizona; Lance Corporal John T. Byrd II of Fairview, West Virginia; Sergeant Kelley L. Courtney of Macon, Georgia, Private First Class Andrew G. Riedel of Northglenn, Colorado; and Private First Class John Lukac of Las Vegas, Nevada. The next day, First Lieutenant Matthew D. Lynch of Jericho, New York, died from an IED attack in Fallujah. Lieutenant Lynch was assigned to 2/5.

15. It was impossible to completely surround the city because it was bordered by the Euphrates River. Some insurgents undoubtedly escaped by the river at night.

Chapter Five. Assault Operations

1. Corporal Jeremiah A. Baro of Fresno, California, and Lance Corporal Jared P. Hubbard of Clovis, California, both died November 4 from injuries received as a result of enemy action; they were assigned to 2nd Battalion, 5th Marine Regiment. Three members of the famed British Blackwatch regiment, Sergeant Stuart Gray, Private Paul Lowe, and Private Scott McArdle, died while manning a vehicle checkpoint, east of the Euphrates River, near Fallujah on November 5. Lance Corporal Sean M. Langley of Lexington, Kentucky, died November 7 from injuries received as a result of enemy action outside of Fallujah; he was assigned to 2nd Battalion, 5th Marine Regiment. Also on that day, Corporal Joshua D. Palmer of Blandinsville, Illinois, and Lance Corporal Jeffrey Lam of Queens, New York, died early November 8 as a result of a nonhostile vehicle incident in the Euphrates River west of Fallujah; both men was assigned to the Marine Corps Reserve's 6th Engineer Support Battalion, 4th Force Service Support Group, headquartered in Portland, Oregon.

2. The media reported the appointment after the attack had started; see http://www.abc.net.au/news/newsitems/200411/s1240087.htm.

3. Given their recent experience under Saddam, the Iraqis felt that written authority was very important. Lacking such a document bothered General Abdul-Qader for days.

4. General Abdul-Qader was completely dependent on the MEF staff for everything from communications to food, yet he frequently demonstrated his independence of mind in briefings with the commander of the MNF, General George Casey, the U.S. Ambassador, John Negroponte, and even his own Minister of Defense.

5. For example, the "no weapons" policy he directed in Fallujah was an exception to the policy everywhere in Iraq and would certainly have been opposed had it been announced by a U.S. commander.

6. The rules established by General Abdul-Qader for Fallujah residents were harsh, but well founded, and surprisingly none of the residents disputed them.

7. Lieutenant Colonel Dave Bellon of 1st Marines wrote in an email home, "Honest to God, I don't think I saw a single Marine even distracted by the enemy fire. Their squad leaders, and platoon commanders had them prepared and they were executing their assigned tasks." Viewed at *The Greenside*, http://www.thegreenside.com/story.asp?ContentID=11151.

8. Several members of the hospital staff had given frequent interviews indicating large numbers of civilian casualties during past actions in the city. They were so frequently interviewed, and so very critical of the coalition, that Marines referred to them collectively as "Dr. Bob," a reference to "Baghdad Bob," the Iraqi Minister of Information during OIF I.

9. That patient was evacuated to another hospital in Ramadi.

10. There was some concern that the prime minister might waiver in his convictions at the last minute and decide to pursue more negotiations (he had already been receiving Sunni spokesmen from the city for weeks), but with the 36th Commando attack it was clear that Allawi would not waiver.

11. See http://www.thegreenside.com/story.asp?ContentID=11151.

12. Ibid.

13. Jackie Spinner and Karl Vick, "U.S. Forces Launch Attack on Fallujah," *The Washington Post*, November 8, 2004.

14. A few reporters actually took up the insurgent offer to cover their side. Film and photos exist of the first day's fighting from the insurgent viewpoint. How these reporters escaped the fate of the insurgents and got out of the city remains unknown.

15. Marines often found thick wads of crisp, new $100 bills in these insurgents' pockets.

16. No Marines or Soldiers died in combat in Fallujah on November 8. Elsewhere in Al Anbar province, five members of the coalition lost their lives in the shaping actions designed to isolate the city. They were Corporal Nathaniel T. Hammond of Tulsa, Oklahoma; Lance Corporal Shane K. O'Donnell of DeForest, Wisconsin; Lance Corporal Branden P. Ramey of Boone, Illinois; Corporal Robert P. Warns II of Waukesha, Wisconsin (all three of 2nd Battalion, 24th Marines); Staff Sergeant David G. Ries of Clark, Washington; and Private Pita Tukutukuwaqa of the United Kingdom's Blackwatch Regiment.

17. Kevin Sites, "Street by Street," November 10, 2004, found at www.kevinsites.net/2004_11_07_archive.html.

18. Ibid.

19. Ten Marines and Soldiers died in the fighting in the city on November 9. They were Command Sergeant Major Steven W. Faulkenburg of Huntingburg, Indiana (he was assigned to 2nd Battalion, 2nd Infantry Regiment.); Sergeant Lonny D. Wells of Vandergrift, Pennsylvania, and 1st Battalion, 8th Marine Regiment; Lance Corporal Juan E. Segura of Homestead, Florida; Sergeant William C. James of Huntington Beach, California; Lance Corporal Nicholas D. Larson of Wheaton, Illinois; Lance Corporal Nathan R. Wood of Kirkland, Washington; Lance Corporal Abraham Simpson of Chino, California (all four of these Marines were assigned to 3rd Battalion, 1st Marine Regiment); Staff Sergeant Russell L. Slay of Humble, Texas (he was assigned to 2nd Assault Amphibian Battalion); Sergeant David M. Caruso of Naperville, Illinois (he was assigned to 2nd Force Reconnaissance Company); and Staff Sergeant Todd R. Cornell of West Bend, Wisconsin. Sergeant Cornell was assigned to the Army Reserve's 1st Battalion, 339th Infantry Regiment, Fraser, Michigan.

20. Embassy of the United States, Baghdad, Iraq, "Press Release, Iraqi, U.S. General Describe Campaign to Liberate Fallujah," November 10, 2004; see http://iraq.usembassy.gov/iraq/041111_Iraqi_u.s._generals.html.

21. First Lieutenant Dan T. Malcom, Jr., of Brinson, Georgia, died November 10 as a result of enemy action in Fallujah. He was assigned to 1st Battalion, 8th Marine Regiment. Petty Officer Third Class Julian Woods of Jacksonville, Florida; Lance Corporal Erick J. Hodges of Bay Point, California (he was assigned to 3rd Battalion, 5th Marine Regiment); Lance Corporal Aaron C. Pickering of Marion, Illinois (he was assigned to 1st Battalion, 3rd Marine Regiment); Staff Sergeant Gene Ramirez of San Antonio, Texas (he was assigned to 3rd Battalion, 5th Marine Regiment); Corporal Romulo J. Jimenez II of Bellington, West Virgina (he was assigned to 1st Battalion, 8th Marine Regiment); and Lance Corporal Wesley J. Canning of Friendswood, Texas (he was assigned to 2nd Assault Amphibian Battalion) were also killed in the city that day. In Ramadi, Private First Class Dennis J. Miller, Jr., of La Salle, Michigan, died when his unit came under enemy attack and a rocket-propelled grenade struck his M1A1 Abrams tank. Miller was assigned to the 2nd Battalion, 72nd Armor Regiment, 2nd Infantry Division.

22. General Abdul-Qader was quoted saying, "We have found hostage slaughterhouses in Fallujah that were used by these people and the black clothing that they used to wear to identify themselves, hundreds of CDs and whole records with names of hostages." The Associated Press, "Iraq Troops Find 'Hostage Slaughterhouses,'" *USA Today*, November 10, 2004. For additional coverage of insurgent atrocities, see Mathew McAllester, "Hostage 'Slaughterhouses' Found in Fallujah," *The Age*, November 12, 2004, found at www.theage.com.us/articles/2004/11/11/1100131133071.html; Cable News Network, "Troops Find Hostage 'Slaughterhouses' in Falluja," November 11, 2004, found at http://www.cnn.com/2004/WORLD/meast/11/10/iraq.main/; and James Hider, "US Forces Hunt down Guerrillas in Fallujah's Shooting Gallery," *TimesOnLine*, November 13, 2004, found at http://www.timesonline.co.uk/article/0,,737-1356086,00.html.

23. At the time, there were two prominent females missing in Iraq, Margaret Hassan and Teresa Borcz. A video was later released showing a woman thought to be Hassan being executed in Iraq; Borcz was later freed. See News24, "Mutilated Blonde Corpse Found," November 14, 2004, at www.news24.com/News24/World/Iraq/0,,2-10-1460_1620777,00.html.

24. Free Press News Service, "Insurgent Leaders Likely Fled Fallujah," *The Detroit Free Press*, November 11, 2004. Found at www.freep.com.

25. Lance Corporal Justin D. Reppuhn of Hemlock, Michigan, died November 11 as a result of enemy action in the fight for Fallujah (he was assigned to 3rd Light Armored Reconnaissance Battalion). Also killed on November 11 were Corporal Theodore A. Bowling of Casselberry, Florida, and 3rd Battalion, 1st Marine Regiment; Staff Sergeant Theodore S. Holder II of Littleton, Colorado (he was assigned to 1st Battalion, 3rd Marine Regiment); Second Lieutenant James P. Blecksmith of San Marino, California (Blecksmith was assigned to 3rd Battalion, 5th Marine Regiment, 1st Marine Division); and Lance Corporal Kyle W. Burns of Laramie, Wyoming (he was assigned to 1st Light Armored Reconnaissance Battalion). Just outside Fallujah, Staff Sergeant Sean P. Huey of Fredericktown, Pennsylvania, died in Habbaniyah, Iraq, when a vehicle-borne improvised explosive device detonated near his Humvee. Sergeant Huey was assigned to the 1st Battalion, 506th Infantry Regiment, 2nd Infantry Division.

26. Al Jazeera, "Fighting in Falluja Rages amid Confusion," November 11, 2004, found at http://english.aljazeera.net/NR/exeres/554FAF3A-B267-427A-B9EC-54881BDE0A2E.htm.

27. "Mosques Bombed in Falluja Fighting" can be found at http://english.aljazeera.net/NR/exeres/6E722418-6B50-4D2A-93E1-77C9A8FC6DAC.htm and "Falluja Facing Humanitarian Crisis" at http://english.aljazeera.net/NR/exeres/CC347D0D-663E-4BE6-A2C9-BB128D2997D9.htm.

28. Sergeant Morgan W. Strader of Crossville, Indiana, died November 12 as result of enemy action in Fallujah. Strader was assigned to 3rd Battalion, 1st Marine Regiment. Corporal Nathan R. Anderson of Howard, Ohio (he was assigned to 1st Battalion, 8th Marine Regiment); Lance Corporal David M. Branning of Cockeysville, Maryland; Lance Corporal Brian A. Medina of Woodbridge, Virgina (both were assigned to 1st Battalion, 3rd Marine Regiment); First Lieutenant Edward D. Iwan of Albion, Nebraska; and Sergeant James C. Matteson of Celoron, New York, were killed when a rocket-propelled grenade struck their Bradley fighting vehicle. They were assigned to the Army's 2nd Battalion, 2nd Infantry Regiment, 1st Infantry Division, Vilseck, Germany. Sergeant Jonathan B. Shields of Atlanta, Georgia, also died on November 12 when he was accidentally struck by a tank. Shields was assigned to the Army's 3rd Battalion, 8th Cavalry Regiment (Armor), 1st Cavalry Division, Fort Hood, Texas. Lance Corporal Nicholas H. Anderson of Las Vegas, Nevada, and Corporal Jarrod L. Maher of Imogene, Iowa, both lost their lives as a result of non-combat incidents near Abu Ghraib.

29. See CBS News, "22 GIs Killed in Fallujah Fighting," November 12, 2004, found at www.cbsnews.com/stories/2004/11/13/iraq.

30. See The Associated Press, "U.S. Clears Marine in Mosque Shooting," *The International Herald Tribune*, May 6, 2005, found at http://www.iht.com/articles/2005/05/06/news/abuse.php and "Marine Involved in Mosque Shooting Will Not Face Court Martial," *Henderson Hall News*, May 13, 2005, found at www.dcmilitary.com/marines/hendersonhall/10_19/national_news/34870.html.

31. Eight warriors died on November 13 supporting the fighting in Fallujah: Captain Sean P. Sims of El Paso, Texas, and TF 2-2; Lance Corporal Victor R. Lu of Los Angeles, California, and 3/5; Lance Corporal Justin D. McLeese of Covington, Louisiana, and 3/1; Lance Corporal Benjamin S. Bryan of Lumberton, North Carolina, and 3/1; Specialist Jose A. Velez of Lubbock, Texas, and TF 2-7; Sergeant Byron W. Norwood of Pflugerville, Texas, and 3/1; Lance Corporal Justin M. Ellsworth of Mount Pleasant, Michigan, and the 1st FSSG; and Corporal Kevin J. Dempsey of Monroe, Connecticut, and 2nd Recon Battalion.

32. Four Marines lost their lives in Fallujah on November 14. They were Lance Corporal George J. Payton of Culver City, California, and 3/5; Corporal Nicholas L. Ziolkowski of Towson, Maryland, and 1/8; and Corporals Dale A. Burger, Jr., of Bel Air, Maryland, and Andres H. Perez of Santa Cruz, California, both of 3/1.

33. See New24, "No Stone Unturned in Fallujah," November 14, 2004, at www.news24.com/News24/World/Iraq/0,,2-10-1460_1620938,00.html.

34. Because of a bombing strike on the one essential water pumping station in the city, a large area of central Fallujah was covered by over 6 inches of Euphrates River water for weeks.

35. Lieutenant Colonel Leonard Defrancisci's Civil Affairs Detachment 4-4 had been assisting local Iraqis with enemy burials in Fallujah, but as the numbers of enemy dead rose some other method of properly handling the corpses had to be found.

36. James Hider, "US Forces Hunt down Guerillas in Fallujah's Shooting Gallery," *TimesOnLine*, November 13, 2004, found at http://www.timesonline.co.uk/article/0,,7374-1356086,00.html.

37. This important accomplishment in Fallujah cost the lives of Lance Corporal Jeramy A. Ailes of Gilroy, California; Lance Corporal Travis R. Desiato of Bedford, Massachusetts; Sergeant Rafael Peralta of San Diego, California; Corporal Marc T. Ryan of Gloucester, New Jersey; Lance Corporal James E. Swain of Kokomo, Indiana; Lance Corporal Bradley L. Parker of Marion, West Virginia, and 1/8; Lance Corporal Shane E. Kielion of La Vista, Nebraska, and 3/5; Lance Corporal Antoine D. Smith of Orlando, Florida, and 3/5; and Lance Corporal William L. Miller of Pearland, Texas, and 1/8. Also killed that day, in Ramadi, were Captain Patrick Marc M. Rapicault of St. Augustine, Florida, and Corporal Lance M. Thompson of Upland, Indiana, both of 2/5.

38. I Marine Expeditionary Force, "Marines Reopen Fallujah Bridge," *Marine Corps News*, story 20041112015126, found at www.usmc.mil/marinelink/mcn2000.nsf.

Chapter Six. Clearing and Searching

1. CBS News, "U.S. Takes Fallujah," found at www.cbsnews.com/stories/2004/11/15/iraq.html.

2. Oliver North, "Hero in Fallujah: Marine Laid Himself on Top of Grenade to Save Rest of Squad," *Human Events Online*, December 16, 2004, found at www.humaneventsonline.com.

3. CBS News, "GIs May Have Found Zarqawi Base," found at www.cbsnews.com/stories/2004/11/19/iraq.html.

4. Sergeant Christopher T. Heflin of Paducah, Kentucky, and 3/1, and Lance Corporal Louis W. Qualls of Temple, Texas, and 2nd Battalion, 14th Marine Regiment, 4th Marine Division, both lost their lives in Fallujah on November 16. Lance Corporal Michael W. Hanks of Gregory, Michigan, and 3/1 died November 17. On November 18, Lance Corporal Luis A. Figueroa of Los Angeles, California, and 3/1 lost his life in the city. Also on that day, Army Sergeant Joseph M. Nolan of Philadelphia, Pennsylvania, died in Fallujah when an improvised explosive device detonated near his up-armored Humvee. Nolan was assigned to the 312th Military Intelligence Battalion, 1st Cavalry Division, Fort Hood, Texas. During the following 2 days, Lance Corporal Dimitrios Gavriel of New York, New York, and 1/8; Lance Corporal Phillip G. West of American Canyon, California, and 3/1; Corporal Bradley T. Arms of Charlottesville, Virginia, and the 4th Combat Engineer Battalion; Lance Corporal Demarkus D. Brown, of Martinsville, Virginia, and 1/8; Corporal Michael A. Downey of Phoenix, Arizona, and 1/3; Corporal Joseph J. Heredia of Santa Maria, California, and 3/5; and Lance Corporal Joseph T. Welke of Rapid City, South Dakota, and 3/1 all died. Downey died at National Naval Medical Center, Bethesda, Maryland, from wounds received as a result of enemy action on November 11. Heredia died November 20 at Landstuhl Regional Medical Center, Germany, from wounds received as a result of enemy action on November 10. Welke died November 20 at Landstuhl Regional Medical Center, Germany, from wounds received as a result of enemy action on November 19.

5. This first group did include the Deputy Minister of Industry, Mr. Mohamed Abdullah Mohamed, and the man who would eventually make the new Fallujah possible, Mr. Basil Mahmoud. It was a strange and strained meeting that succeeded because everyone was committed to the same goal – although at the time, no one knew how they would work together to accomplish such a task.

6. CBS News, "Troops Find Massive Arms Caches," November 25, 2004, found at www.cbsnews.com/stories/2004/11/26/iraq.html.

7. From November 20 to November 30, ten Marines and two Soldiers lost their lives as a result of the continued fighting in Fallujah. They were Corporal Michael R. Cohen of Jacobus, Pennsylvania, and 1/3; Sergeant Benjamin C. Edinger of 2nd Force Reconnaissance Company and Green Bay, Wisconsin (he died November 23 at Bethesda from injuries received November 14); Corporal Kirk J. Bosselmann of Napa, California, and 1/8; Lance Corporal Bradley M. Faircloth of Mobile, Alabama, and 1/8; Lance Corporal Jeffery S. Holmes of White River Junction, Vermont; and Lance Corporal David B. Houck of Winston-Salem, North Carolina, and 1/8; Lance Corporal Joshua E. Lucero of Tucson, Arizona, and 2nd Combat Engineer Battalion; and Sergeant Nicholas S. Nolte of Falls City, Nebraska, and 2nd Low Altitude Air Defense Battalion (who died November 24 at Bethesda from injuries received November 9). Corporal Gentian Marku of Warren, Michigan, and 1/8 died November 25, and Lance Corporal Blake A. Magaoay of Pearl City, Hawaii, and 1st Light Armored Reconnaissance Battalion died November 29. When an improvised explosive device detonated near their military vehicle, Army Sergeants Pablo A. Calderon, of Brooklyn, New York, and Jose Guereca, Jr., of Missouri City, Texas, were both killed in action. They were assigned to 1st Battalion, 5th Cavalry Regiment, 1st Cavalry Division, Fort Hood, Texas.

8. Two Marines died in Al Anbar province on December 3 guarding the border crossing into Iraq. They were Corporal Binh N. Le of Alexandria, Virginia, and Corporal Matthew A. Wyatt of Millstadt, Illinois. Both Marines died from injuries because of a suicide car bomb. They were assigned to 5th Battalion, 10th Marine Regiment.

9. Three soldiers assigned to I MEF died December 5 in Habbaniyah, Iraq, when an improvised explosive device detonated near their vehicle. They were assigned to the 1st Battalion, 506th Infantry Regiment. Killed were Staff Sergeant Marvin L. Trost III of Goshen, Indiana; Specialist Edwin W. Roodhouse of San Jose, California; and Staff Sergeant Kyle A. Eggers of Euless, Texas. Two days later, another soldier from the same battalion died in a similar IED attack. He was Sergeant First Class Todd C. Gibbs of Angelina, Texas, who died in Khalidiyah, Iraq, when an improvised explosive device detonated while his unit was on a dismounted patrol. On December 8, Sergeant Arthur C. Williams IV of Edgewater, Florida, and the 44th Engineer Battalion, died in Ramadi when his unit was conducting a dismounted patrol and was attacked by small arms fire.

10. See CBS News, "Fortress Fallujah Awaits Returnees," December 9, 2004, found at www.cbsnews.com/stories/2004/12/09/iraq.html.

11. 1st Marine Division After Action presentation, "Operation Al Fajr, the Battle for Fallujah," undated.

12. For a summary of the speech, see http://www.windsofchange.net/archives/006101.php#iraqi. For interpretation of bin Laden's message, see also the Middle East Media Research Institute web site: http://memri.org/bin/articles.cgi?Page=archives&Area=sd&ID=SP83704.

13. This was one of several references to the lack of equipment on the part of the insurgents in comparison with the American forces, who did fight with protective helmets and flack jackets.

Chapter Seven. Civil-Military Operations: The Bridge to a New Fallujah

1. During the first week of the new year, three Marines lost their lives in combat in Al Anbar province. The first of these was Sergeant Thomas E. Houser of Council Bluffs,

Iowa, who died January 3; he was assigned to 2nd Force Reconnaissance Company. Sergeant Zachariah S. Davis of Twentynine Palms, California, died January 6 as result of hostile action in Al Anbar province, Iraq. He was assigned to 3rd Light Armored Reconnaissance Battalion. Also on January 6, Lance Corporal Julio C. Cisneros Alvarez of Pharr, Texas, died; he was assigned to 1st Battalion, 7th Marine Regiment.

2. During the second week of the year, the action in Al Anbar province had shifted well away from Fallujah as the Division began to execute a series of operations targeting the northern "ratlines" leading into the country. Three Marines and one Soldier were killed during these efforts. They were Corporal Joseph E. Fite of Round Rock, Texas, who died January 9. He was assigned to the Marine Forces Reserve's 1st Battalion, 23rd Marine Regiment. Specialist Michael J. Smith of Media, Pennsylvania, died January 11 in Ramadi, when his military vehicle was hit by a rocket-propelled grenade. Smith was assigned to 1st Battalion, 503rd Infantry. Lance Corporal Matthew W. Holloway of Fulton, Texas, and Lance Corporal Juan R. Rodriguez Velasco of El Cenizo, Texas, both died January 13 from combat injuries; both were also assigned to Marine Forces Reserve's 1st Battalion, 23rd Marine Regiment.

3. On April 14, 1995, acting under Chapter VII of the UN Charter, the Security Council adopted resolution 986, establishing the Oil for Food program, providing Iraq with another opportunity to sell oil to finance the purchase of humanitarian goods and various mandated UN activities concerning Iraq. From these funds, every Iraqi family eventually received a monthly allocation of food and household essentials such as soap and cooking oil. These supplies were disbursed by the Ministry of Trade in Iraq through local food stores, using an Oil for Food Program identification card that included the residential information for the family. See: http://www.un.org/Depts/oip/background/index.html.

4. Staff Sergeant Thomas E. Vitagliano of New Haven, Connecticut; Private First Class George R. Geer of Cortez, Colorado; and Private First Class Jesus Fonseca of Marietta, Georgia, all died January 17 in Ramadi, when a vehicle-borne improvised explosive device detonated near their position. They were assigned to the 1st Battalion, 503rd Infantry Regiment, 2nd Infantry Division.

5. See Edward Wong, "Insurgent Leader in Iraq Vows to Wage Protracted Holy War," *New York Times International*, January 20, 2005. For additional information on the statement released by Zarqawi, see http://www.cbsnews.com/stories/2005/01/21/iraq/main668296.shtml, and http://www.foxnews.com/story/0,2933,144928,00.html.

6. There was a Jordanian field hospital that had been established east of Fallujah on Highway 10 in the aftermath of the first battle for the city, but no Jordanian forces participated in the November assault.

7. For additional background, see www.ieciraq.org. The Commission was formed in line with the U.N. Security Council Resolutions No. 1483 and No. 1511 that stressed upon the rights of the Iraqi People to choose in full freedom its political future and in line with the Iraqi State Administrative Law for the Transitional Period (TAL), which stipulates that the Iraqi People should choose its government by way of free and trustworthy elections.

8. In the period preceding the election, five Marines and one Soldier died conducting operations in Al Anbar province. Sergeant Jesse W. Strong of Irasburg, Vermont; Corporal Jonathan W. Bowling of Patrick, Virginia; Lance Corporal Karl R. Linn of Chesterfield, Virginia; and Corporal Christopher L. Weaver of Fredericksburg, Virginia, were all killed on January 26 in Haditha, Iraq. They were all assigned to the Marine Corps Reserve's 4th Combat Engineer Battalion. Specialist James H. Miller IV of Cincinnati, Ohio, died January 30 in Ramadi from an improvised explosive device detonation near his vehicle. Miller was assigned to the 1st Battalion, 503d Infantry Regiment.

9. Those killed in this accident included Captain Paul C. Alaniz of Corpus Christi, Texas; Lance Corporal Jonathan E. Etterling of Wheelersburg, Ohio; Captain Lyle L. Gordon of Midlothian, Texas; Lance Corporal Brian C. Hopper of Wynne, Arkansas; Lance Corporal Saeed Jafarkhani-Torshizi, Jr., of Fort Worth, Texas; Corporal Sean P. Kelly of Gloucester, New Jersey; Staff Sergeant Dexter S. Kimble of Houston, Texas; Lance Corporal Allan Klein of Clinton Township, Michigan; Corporal James L. Moore of Roseburg, Oregon; Lance Corporal Mourad Ragimov of San Diego, California; Lance Corporal Rhonald D. Rairdan of San Antonio, Texas; Lance Corporal Hector Ramos of Aurora, Illinois; Lance Corporal Darrell J. Schumann of Hampton, Virginia; 1st Lieutenant Dustin M. Shumney of Vallejo, California; Corporal Matthew R. Smith of West Valley, Utah; Lance Corporal Joseph B. Spence of Scotts Valley, California; Petty Officer Third Class John D. House of Ventura, California; Staff Sergeant Brian D. Bland of Weston, Wyoming; Sergeant Michael W. Finke, Jr., of Huron, Ohio; 1st Lieutenant Travis J. Fuller of Granville, Massachusetts; Corporal Timothy M. Gibson of Hillsborough, New Hampshire; Corporal Richard A. Gilbert, Jr., of Montgomery, Ohio; Corporal Kyle J. Grimes of Northampton, Pennsylvania; Lance Corporal Tony L. Hernandez of Canyon Lake, Texas; Corporal Nathaniel K. Moore of Champaign, Illinois; Lance Corporal Gael Saintvil of Orange, Florida; Corporal Nathan A. Schubert of Cherokee, Iowa; Corporal Timothy A. Knight of Brooklyn, Ohio; and, Lance Corporal Michael L. Starr, Jr., of Baltimore, Maryland. All these men died when their CH-53E helicopter crashed near Ar Rutbah. Alaniz, Gordon, and Kimble were assigned to Marine Heavy Helicopter Squadron 361, Marine Aircraft Group 16, 3rd Marine Aircraft Wing. The others were assigned to 1st Battalion, 3rd Marine Regiment.

10. Lance Corporal Nazario Serrano of Irving, Texas, died on Election Day in Al Anbar province; he was assigned to the Combat Service Support Battalion 1, Combat Service Support Group 11, 1st Force Service Support Group. Also killed that day was Army Specialist James H. Miller IV of Cincinnati, Ohio, who died in Ramadi from injuries from an IED that detonated near his vehicle. Specialist Miller was assigned to the 1st Battalion, 503d Infantry Regiment, 2nd Infantry Division.

Chapter Eight. A New Dawn: Lessons in Modern Warfare

1. The second worst month was the previous April, the month of the first battle in Fallujah; see http://icasualties.org/oif/USchart.aspx.

2. Kaplan, "The Real Story of Fallujah." *Wall Street Journal*, May 27, 2004, 20.

3. In Iraq, the modern U.S. military's consistent effort to minimize casualties to U.S. forces caused by U.S. or other coalition units [blue (friendly) force injuries on other blue forces] was expanded to cover host nation Iraqi security forces as well. Thus, the terms *green on blue* and *blue on green* came into vogue as well.

4. The formal Department of Defense definition is "the activities of a commander that establish, maintain, influence, or exploit relations between military forces, governmental and nongovernmental civilian organizations and authorities, and the civilian populace in a friendly, neutral, or hostile operational area to facilitate military operations, to consolidate and achieve operational US objectives. Civil-military operations may include performance by military forces of activities and functions normally the responsibility of the local, regional, or national government. These activities may occur prior to, during, or subsequent to other military actions. They may also occur, if directed, in the absence of other military operations. Civil-military operations may be performed by designated civil affairs, by other military

forces, or by a combination of civil affairs and other forces." Department of Defense Dictionary, *Joint Pub 0-2.*

5. There were problems, particularly initially. Theft, inappropriate weapons firing, and heavy-handedness by Iraqi soldiers were a frequent source of complaints by the residents in the early weeks. There were also complaints that ambulances were not given sufficient freedom of movement and that the entry control points caused long lines and delays in entering the city. Overall, however, the performance of the forces in Fallujah was roundly applauded.

6. It was obvious to most military serving in and around Fallujah that the ICRC was sympathetic to, if not supporting, the insurgency in Iraq. There were a few ICRC convoys that toured Fallujah, but the entire ICRC aid effort in the city provided nothing of real value to the population.

7. Of course, resources and understanding are not sufficient. A cadre of officers that really understand the cultural and religious intricacies of the local area and have negotions and public works skills needs to be continually developed within the civil affairs communities of both the Army and Marine Corps to make the CMOC tool work.

8. Sunni minority interests were always important, and the prime minister understood well the fine line he needed to walk to gain inclusion and yet to resist a negative reaction from other parties.

9. Fallujah sits on the banks of the Euphrates River, but much of the city is under the water level. Fallujah flooded significantly during the fighting (because of broken water mains and pumps), and immediate action was required to get 10 large pump stations back up in operation to keep the water off the streets.

10. Every Iraqi who voted had his/her right index finger marked with blue dye. Insurgents had claimed all such fingers would be cut off. It took commitment and bravery to gain the purple finger.

11. "3,000 Americans and 2,000 Iraqis launched a major offensive against insurgents in the city of Samarra on October 1, 2004. Troops of the 202nd Iraqi National Guard Battalion, 7th Iraqi Army Battalion, and 1st Infantry Division were part of the attacking force. . . . U.S officials estimated that there were anywhere from 500 to 1,000 insurgents entrenched in the city. . . . on October 4, 2004 coalition forces were able to claim victory. That same day the U.S military announced that the operation resulted in about 125 rebels killed and 88 were being detained. Operations in Samarra then shifted to civil-military operations designed at repairing parts of the city's infrastructure and improving basic services." Overview found at http://www.globalsecurity.org/military/ops/oif-baton-rouge.htm.

12. For an assessment of the success in Sadr City, see Jacon Silverberg, "Iraq's Sadr City Under Control," *The Washington Times*, August 13, 2005, 13.

Postscript

1. Andy Mosher, "Blast Kills at Least 2 Marines, Injures 13," *Washington Post*, June 25, 2005, A16. Lance Corporal Holly A. Charette from Cranston, Rhode Island, and Corporal Ramona M. Valdez of Bronx, New York (both from Headquarters Battalion, 2nd Marine Division); Lance Corporal Veashna Muy of Los Angeles, California and Corporal Chad W. Powell, of West Monroe, Louisiana (both from 8th Marine Regiment); Petty Officer 1st Class Regina R. Clark of Centralia, Washington; and Naval Construction Regiment Detachment 30, Port Hueneme, California, all died June 23 from wounds sustained when a suicide,

vehicle-borne IED struck their vehicle in Fallujah. The following day, Corporal Carlos Pineda, from Los Angeles, California, died from wounds sustained from enemy small-arms fire while conducting combat operations in Fallujah. He was also assigned to 8th Marines.

2. Ellen Kickmeyer, "14 Marines Die in Huge Explosion in Western Iraq," *The Washington Post*, August 4, 2005, A01. Lance Corporal Michael J. Cifuentes of Fairfield, Ohio; Lance Corporal Grant B. Fraser of Anchorage, Alaska; Lance Corporal Aaron H. Reed of Chillicothe, Ohio; Lance Corporal Edward A. Schroeder II of Columbus, Ohio; Lance Corporal Kevin G. Waruinge of Tampa, Florida; Lance Corporal William B. Wightman of Sabina, Ohio; Lance Corporal Timothy M. Bell Jr. of West Chesterfield, Ohio; Lance Corporal Eric J. Bernholtz of Grove City, Ohio; Lance Corporal Nicholas William B. Bloem of Belgrade, Montana; Sergeant Bradley J. Harper of Dresden, Ohio; Sergeant Justin F. Hoffman of Delaware, Ohio; Corporal David Kenneth J. Kreuter of Cincinnati, Ohio; Corporal David S. Stewart of Bogalusa, Louisiana; and Lance Corporal Christopher J. Dyer of Cincinnati, Ohio, were killed in the attack. All of these Marines died when the amphibious assault vehicle in which they were riding was hit by an IED while conducting combat operations south of Haditha, Iraq. They were all members of the 3rd Battalion, 25th Marine Regiment, 4th Marine Division, Cleveland Ohio.

3. Jonathan Finer and Hasan Shammari, "10 Marines Killed in Fallujah Blast," *The Washington Post*, December 3, 2005, A01. Staff Sergeant Daniel J. Clay of Pensacola, Florida; Lance Corporal John M. Holmason of Surprise, Arizona; Lance Corporal David A. Huhn of Portland, Michigan; Lance Corporal Adam W. Kaiser of Naperville, Illinois; Lance Corporal Robert A. Martinez of Splendora, Texas; Corporal Anthony T. McElveen of Little Falls, Minnesota; Lance Corporal Scott T. Modeen of Hennepin, Minnesota; Lance Corporal Andrew G. Patten of Byron, Illinois; Sergeant Andy A. Stevens of Tomah, Wisconsin; and Lance Corporal Craig N. Watson of Union City, Michigan, were all killed near an abandoned flour factory being used as a patrol base when the IED detonated. All 10 were assigned to the 2nd Battalion, 7th Marine Regiment.

4. Saad Sarhan and Omar Fekeiki, "U.S. Forces Give Iraqis Full Control of Najaf," *The Washington Post*, September 7, 2005, 20.

5. On Tal Afar, see Richrad A. Oppel, Jr., "Under Pressure, Rebels Abandon an Iraqi Stronghold," *New York Times*, September 12, 2005, A6; also Kathleen T. Rehm, "Commander Describes Routing Foreign Fighters from Tal Afar," American Forces Information Service, September 16, 2005.

6. Several authors and thinkers have espoused an "oilspot" strategy designed to relentlessly reduce the freedom of movement of the insurgent groups and then eliminate the areas that remain open to them, one after another, until no "spots" remain as sanctuaries. Some of this has already occurred. See Andrew F. Krepinevich, "How to Win in Iraq," *Foreign Affairs*, September/October 2005, 87–104.

7. This judgment made by General Robert H. Scales in his "The Emerging Iraqi Army," *The Washington Times*, October 14, 2005, 23, was echoed by many other experienced military officers who visited Iraqi units in 2005.

8. Micheal Fumento, "Fallujah Rises from the Ashes," *The Washington Times*, June 6, 2005, 20.

Glossary

AAV	Amphibious Assault Vehicle
Abdul-Qater, Mohammed	Iraqi General, Military Governor of Al Anbar province
Abizaid, John	General, U.S. Army, Commander, U.S. Central Command
Abrams	M1A2 main battle tank of the United States
AC-130	Dual-engine gunship aircraft
ACOG	Advanced Combat Optical Gunsite
ACR	Armored Cavalry Regiment
A-day	For operation Al Fajr, the day of the main attack, November 8
AH-1	Small attack helicopter used by Marines
AIF	Anti-Iraqi Forces
AK-47	Semi-automatic rifle
Al Anbar	Westernmost province of Iraq
Al Fajr	Name of the November assault on Fallujah, meaning "new dawn" in Arabic
Al Jazeera	Arabic language television network
Al Qaeda	Terrorist organization inspired by Osama bin Laden
Al Qaim	City in northwestern Iraq, on the Syrian border
Allawi, Iyad	Prime Minister of Iraq in 2004
Andalus	First district of Fallujah to be resettled

AO	Area of Operations
AV-8B	Jet attack aircraft used by the Marines
Ba'ath Party	Ruling party of Iraq under Saddam Hussein
BATS	Biometric Automated Toolset System
BCT	Brigade Combat Team
BIAP	Baghdad International Airport
Biometric ID Card	Identification card based on computer-generated data from retina scan and finger prints
BLT	Battalion Landing Team
Blue on Blue	Friendly fire
Bradley	Armored fighting vehicle of the U.S. Army
Brahimi Lakhdar	Special Representative of the United Nations Secretary General in Iraq
Bravo Surgical	Navy Medical Company in Camp Fallujah
Bremer, L. Paul	U.S. Administrator in Iraq
C2	Command and Control
CA	Civil Affairs
CACOM	Civil Affairs Command
Camp Blue Diamond	Base of operations for the 1st Marine Division, inside the city of Ramadi
Camp Fallujah	Base of operations for the MEF, located only a few miles east of the city of Fallujah
CAP	Civic Action Program
CAS	Close Air Support
Casey, George	General, U.S. Army, Commander, Multinational Force-Iraq
CAV	Cavalry
CENTCOM	U.S. Central Command
CG	Commanding General
CH-47	Troop-carrying helicopter
CJTF	Combined Joint Task Force
CMO	Civil–military operations
CMOC	Civil–Military Operations Center
Conway, James	Marine general, commander of I MEF 2002–2004
CP	Command Post
CPA	Coalition Provisional Authority
DCG	Deputy Commanding General
D-day	The day major operations commence, for Al Fajr, November 7, 2004

de-Ba'athification	Exclusion of members of the Ba'ath Party from any form of government service in the new Iraq
DET	Detachment
Dunford, Joseph	Marine general, assistant division commander, 1st Marine Division
ECP	Entry Control Point
EST	Election Support Team
Fallujah	Predominantly Sunni city just west of Baghdad
Fallujah Brigade	Iraqi organization developed to monitor Fallujah
Fallujahn	Resident of Fallujah
Farquhar, Andrew	British General, deputy commander, MNC-I
F-15	Fighter used by the U.S. Air Force
F/A-18	Fighter/Attack aircraft used by the Navy and Marines
FLT	Fallujah Liaison Team
FOB	Forward Operating Base
FRAGO	Fragmentary Order
FRE	Former Regime Elements
FSSG	Force Service Support Group
G1	General Staff, Personnel
G3	General Staff, Operations
G5	General Staff, Plans
GBU	Guided Bomb Unit
GPS	Global Positioning System
HA	Humanitarian assistance
Habbaniyah	Town between Fallujah and Ramadi
Haditha	City in Al Anbar, site of a hydroelectric dam
Hadid, Omar	Insurgent leader in Fallujah
Haslem, Anthony	Colonel commanding 11th MEU
Hejlik, Dennis	Marine general, the deputy commander of MEF
H-hour	Time of Attack
HMMWV	High Mobility Multipurpose Wheeled Vehicle (Humvee/Hummer)
HVT	High Value Target
ICDC	Iraqi Civil Defense Corps
ICRS	Iraqi Red Crescent Society
ICTF	Iraqi Counterterrorism Task Force
ID	Infantry Division
IECI	Independent Electoral Commission in Iraq

IED	Improvised explosive device
IIF	Iraqi Intervention Force
IIG	Interim Iraqi Government
III Corps	U.S. Army Corps, normally stationed in Fort Hood, Texas, but assigned to manage operations in Iraq during OIF II
IN	Infantry
ING	Iraqi National Guard
IO	Information Operations
Iron Mountain	Build-up of military supplies
ISR	Intelligence, Surveillance and Reconnaissance
Janabi, Abdullah	Insurgent leader in Fallujah
JDAM	Joint Direct Attack Munition
Jihadist	Someone who advocates war and anti-modern acts in order to bring about a more pure Muslim world order
Jolan	District in northwest Fallujah
JTF	Joint Task Force
Karbala	City south of Baghdad
Karma	Town east of Fallujah
KIA	Killed in Action
Kizseley, Sir John	British General, deputy commander of MNF-I
Kufa	Prominent mosque in Najaf
Kut	City in south-central Iraq
Latif, Mohammed	Commander of the Fallujah Brigade
LNO	Liaison Officer
Mahdi Militia	Armed followers of Muqtada al-Sadr
MarDiv	Marine Division
Mattis, James	Marine general, commanding general, 1st Marine Division, 2002–2004
MAW	Marine Air Wing
MECH	Mechanized
MEF	Marine Expeditionary Force
MEG	MEF Engineer Group
Metz, Thomas	Commanding General III Corps and Multinational Corps-Iraq
MEU	Marine Expeditionary Unit
MNC-I	Multinational Corps-Iraq
MNF	Multinational Force
MNF-I	Multinational Force-Iraq

MNSTC-I	Multinational Security Transition Command-Iraq
Mosul	Predominantly Kurdish city in northern Iraq
MOUT	Military Operations in Urban Terrain
MP	Military Police
MSC	Major Subordinate Command
MST	Municipal Support Team
Muqtada al-Sadr	Leader of a Shia rebellion and the Mahdi Militia
Najaf	One of the holy cities of Iraq, southwest of Baghdad
Najafis	Inhabitants of Najaf
Natonski, Richard	Marine general, commanding general, 1st Marine Division
NBC	Nuclear, Biological and Chemical
NCO	Non-Commissioned Officer
Negroponte, John	U.S. Ambassador to Iraq
NGO	Nongovernmental Organization (such as the Red Cross or Red Crescent)
Nonlethal	Tools designed to affect the enemy without causing casualties (including PSYOPs)
OIF	Operation Iraqi Freedom (OIF occurred from 2003–2004; OIF II began in 2004)
OPCON	Operational Control
OPORD	Operations Order
PA	Public Affairs
Phantom Fury	Original name for operation Al Fajr
POB	Public Order Battalion (Iraqi military police)
PSYOPs	Psychological Operations
Ramadi	Provincial capital of Al Anbar
RCT	Regimental Combat Team
RFA	Restricted Fire Area (a protective fire control measure)
ROE	Rules of Engagement
RPG	Rocket-Propelled Grenade
Sadr City	District of Baghdad, also known as Thowra
Saleh, Jasim	Commander of the Fallujah Brigade
Sanchez, Ricardo	U.S. general, commander of Combined Joint Task Force-7
Sattler, John	Marine general, commander of MEF
SET	Department of State Embedded Team
Sharia	Islamic law

Shiite	One of the principle Muslim subgroups, the majority of Iraqi are Shiite Muslims
Shupp, Michael	Marine colonel, commander of the 1st Marine Regiment
SOF	Special Operations Forces
SOP	Standard Operations Procedures
Sunni	One of the principle Muslim subgroups; most of the Iraqis who live in Fallujah and Al Anbar province are Sunni Muslims
TACON	Tactical Control
Tal Afar	Sunni city north of Baghdad
Taqaddum	Site of 1st FSSG's main logistics base
TCP	Traffic Control Point
TF	Task Force
Toolan, John	Marine colonel, commander of the 1st Marine Regiment, 2002–2004
TOW	Tube-launched Optically-tracked, Wire-guided Missile
Tucker, Craig	Marine colonel, commander of the 7th Marine Regiment
UAV	Unmanned Aerial Vehicle
UH	Utility Helicopter
UN	United Nations
U.S.	United States
USA	United States Army
USAF	United States Air Force
USMC	United States Marine Corps
USN	United States Navy
VBIED	Vehicle-borne, improvised explosive device
VCP	Vehicle Control Point
Vigilant Resolve	Name of the April assault on Fallujah
VTC	Video teleconference
WMD	Weapon of Mass Destruction
Yawar, Ghazi	Sunni president of Iraq in the IIG
Zarqawi, Abu Musab	Terrorist leader of al Qaeda in Iraq
Ziruffi, Adnan	Governor of Najaf province

Selected Bibliography

BOOKS

Beckett, Ian. *Modern Insurgencies and Counter-insurgencies: Guerrillas and Their Opponents since 1750.* New York: Rouledge, 2001.

Brisard, Jean-Charles. *Zarqawi, the New Face of Al-Qaeda.* New York: Other Press, 2005.

Cordesman, Anthony H. *The Iraq War: Strategy, Tactics, and Military Lessons.* Washington, D.C.: CSIS Press, 2003.

Crane, Conrad C., and W. Andrew Terrill. *Reconstructing Iraq: Insights, Challenges, and Missions for Military Forces in a Post-Conflict Scenario.* Carlisle Barracks: Strategic Studies Institute, 2003.

Dobbins, James, et al. *America's Role in Nation-Building: From Germany to Iraq.* Santa Monica: RAND, 2003.

Dodge, Toby. *Inventing Iraq: The Failure of Nation Building and a History Denied.* New York: Columbia University Press, 2003.

Franks, Tommy R. *American Soldier.* New York: Regan Books, 2004.

Gunaratna, Rohan. *Inside Al-Qaeda: Global Network of Terror.* New York: Columbia University Press, 2002.

Habeck, Mary. *Knowing the Enemy, Jihadist Ideology and the War on Terror.* New Haven, CT: Yale University Press, 2005.

Hoffman, Bruce. *Insurgency and Counterinsurgency in Iraq.* Santa Monica: RAND, 2004.

Ikenberry, G. John. *After Victory: Institutions, Strategic Restraint, and the Rebuilding of Order after Major Wars.* Princeton: Princeton University Press, 2001.

Jennings, Ray S. *The Road Ahead: Lessons in Nation Building from Japan, Germany, and Afghanistan for Postwar Iraq.* Washington, D.C.: United States Institute of Peace, 2003.

Kaplan, Robert D. *Imperial Grunts, the American Military on the Ground.* New York: Random, 2005.

Keegan, John. *The Iraq War*. New York: Alfred A. Knopf, 2004.

Kumar, Krishna, ed. *Postconflict Elections, Democratization, and International Assistance*. Boulder, CO: Rienner, 1998.

Lewis, Bernard. *What Went Wrong?* New York: Oxford University Press, 2002.

Murray, Williamson, and Robert H. Scales, Jr. *The Iraq War: A Military History*. Cambridge, MA: Belknap Press of Harvard University Press, 2003.

O'Neil, Bard E. *Insurgency and Terrorism: Inside Modern Revolutionary Warfare*. Washington, D.C.: Brassey's, 1990.

O'Neil, Bard E., and Edward C. Meyer. *Insurgency and Terrorism*. Dulles, VA: Potomac Books, 2001.

Packer, George. *The Assassin's Gate, America in Iraq*. New York: Farrar, Straus and Giroux, 2005.

Peters, Ralph. *Beyond Baghdad: Postmodern War and Peace*, with a foreword by Barry R. McCaffrey. Mechanicsburg, PA: Stackpole Books, 2003.

Phillips, David L. *Losing Iraq: Inside the Postwar Reconstruction Fiasco*. Boulder, CO: Westview Press, 2005.

Pugh, Michael, ed. *Regeneration of War-Torn Societies*. New York: St. Martin's Press, 2000.

Reynolds, Nicholas E. *Basrah, Baghdad, and Beyond: The U.S. Marine Corps in the Second Iraq War*. Annapolis, MD: Naval Institute Press, 2005.

Schultheis, Rob. *Waging Peace: A Special Operations Team's Battle to Rebuild Iraq*. New York: Gotham Books, 2005.

Shadid, Anthony. *Night Draws Near, Iraq's People in the Shadow of America's War*. New York: Henry Holt, 2005.

Tucker, Mike. *Among Warriors in Iraq*. Guilford, CT: Lyons Press, 2005.

U.S. Marine Corps. *Small Wars Manual*. Philadelphia, PA: Pavilion Press, 2004.

West, Bing. *No True Glory, a Frontline Account of the Battle for Fallujah*. New York: Bantam Dell, 2005.

Woodward, Bob. *Bush at War*. New York: Simon & Schuster, 2002.

Woodward, Bob. *Plan of Attack*. New York: Simon & Schuster, 2004.

ARTICLES AND PAPERS

Cassidy, Robert M. "Back to the Street without Joy: Counterinsurgency Lessons from Vietnam and Other Small Wars," *Parameters*, Summer 2004, 73–83.

Constable, Pamela. "Marines, Insurgents Battle for Sunni City," *The Washington Post*, April 8, 2004, A10.

Constable, Pamela. "Troops Gaining Grip in Sections of Fallujah," *The Washington Post*, April 7, 2004, 1.

Chiarelli, Peter W., and Patrick R. Michaelis. "Winning the Peace, The Requirement for Full Spectrum Operations," *Military Review*, July–August 2005, 1–13.

Hamre, John J., and Gordon R. Sullivan. "Toward Postconflict Reconstruction," *Washington Quarterly*, 25, 2002, 85–96.

Hayden, Thomas. "Counterinsurgency in Iraq Started with Fallujah," *Marine Corps Gazette*, July 2005, 28–29.

I MEF and 11th MEU staffs. "Battle for An Najaf, August 2004," *Marine Corps Gazette*, December 2004, 10–16.

Kaplan, Robert D. "The Real Story of Fallujah," *Wall Street Journal*, May 27, 2004, 20.

Krepinevich, Andrew F. Jr. "How to Win in Iraq," *Foreign Affairs*, September/October 2005, 87–104.

Manwaring, Max G. "Peace and Stability Lessons from Bosnia," *Parameters*, Winter 1998, 28–38.

Metz, Steven. "Insurgency and Counterinsurgency in Iraq," *The Washington Quarterly*, Winter 2003–2004, 25–36.

Perry, Tony. "Review Clears Marine Who Was Filmed Killing Iraqi Insurgent," *Los Angeles Times*, May 5, 2005, A32.

Perry, Tony. "For Marine Unit, Fallouja Is 'One Big Ordnance Dump,'" *Los Angeles Times*, January 9, 2005, A7.

Perry, Tony. "After Leveling City, U.S. Tries to Build Trust; In Fallouja, Marines," *Los Angeles Times*, January 7, 2005, A3.

Perry, Tony. "Falloujans Return to All They Lost," *Los Angeles Times*, January 5, 2005, A3.

Perry, Tony, and Edmund Sanders. "Marines Roll into Fallujah," *Los Angeles Times*, April 5, 2004, A1.

Sattler, John F., and Daniel H. Wilson, "Operation AL FAJR: the Battle of Fallujah–Part II," *Marine Corps Gazette*, July 2005, 12–24.

Simpson, Ross W. "Fallujah: A Four-Letter Word," *Leatherneck*, March 2005, Vol. 88, Issue 3, 14–18.

Spinner, Jackie. "Cleric's Attack Tests Iraqi Leaders, Rebel Cleric Declares 'Revolution' against U.S. Forces in Iraq," *The Washington Post*, August 6, 2004, A10.

Spinner, Jackie. "U.S. Feeling Pressure to Rebuild Fallujah Troops Have Little Time to Secure Residents' Faith," *The Washington Post*, February 20, 2005, A24.

Spinner, Jackie. "In a Calmer Fallujah, Marines Still Feel the Insurgents' Pulse," *The Washington Post*, February 16, 2005, A15.

Spinner, Jackie. "A Return to Fallujah to See What Remains Residents Pass Military Checkpoints before Reentering Devastated Iraqi City," *The Washington Post*, February 14, 2005, A09.

Spinner, Jackie. "More Fallujah Hostage Sites Found Troops Locate Cage Believed to Have Held British Engineer," *The Washington Post*, November 22, 2004, A14.

Spinner, Jackie. "Insurgent Base Discovered in Fallujah U.S. Troops Find Ammunition, Written Orders in House Used by Zarqawi's Network," *The Washington Post*, November 19, 2004, A18.

Spinner, Jackie. "Fallujah Residents Emerge, Find 'City of Mosques' in Ruins," *The Washington Post*, November 18, 2004, A01.

Spinner, Jackie. "Fallujah Battered and Mostly Quiet after the Battle," *The Washington Post*, November 16, 2004, A13.

Spinner, Jackie. "Fighting in Fallujah Nears End; U.S., Iraqi Forces Target Small Pockets of Insurgents, Commanders Claim Victory," *The Washington Post*, November 15, 2004, A16.

Spinner, Jackie. "In Fallujah, Marines Feel Shock of War 'We Knew When We Got to the South We Were Going to Get Pounded,'" *The Washington Post*, November 14, 2004, A31.

Spinner, Jackie, and Karl Vick. "U.S. Forces Launch Attack on Fallujah," *The Washington Post*, November 8, 2004, A01.

Spinner, Jackie, and Karl Vick. "Troops Battle for Last Parts of Fallujah; Senior Iraqi Officials Claim City Is Liberated," *The Washington Post*, November 14, 2004, A01.

Spinner, Jackie, and Karl Vick. "Troops in Southern Fallujah Encounter Fierce Resistance, Mosul Police Force Splinters under Wave of Rebel Attacks," *The Washington Post*, November 14, 2004, A22.

Spinner, Jackie, and Karl Vick. "U.S. Forces Meet Fierce Resistance in Fallujah; Push South Greeted 'Hornet's Nest,'" *The Washington Post*, November 13, 2004, A01.

Vick, Karl. "Rallying around an Insurgent City," *The Washington Post*, April 9, 2004, A01.

Vick, Karl, and Omar Fekeiki. "U.S. Forces Battle into Heart of Fallujah; Units Meet Scattered Resistance Attacks Continue Elsewhere," *The Washington Post*, November 10, 2004, A01.

Vick, Karl, and Omar Fekeiki. "Defense Minister Exhorts Iraqis: 'Liberate This City' Battle for Fallujah Will Test New Force as U.S. Military Partner," *The Washington Post*, November 8, 2004, A18.

Wong, Edward. "U.S. Uncovers Vast Hide-Out of Iraqi Rebels," *New York Times*, June 5, 2005, 1.

INTERVIEW

Colonel John Toolan, USMC, Quantico, Virginia, July 25, 2005.

Index

About the Author

JOHN R. BALLARD is currently assigned to the office of the Secretary of Defense in the Pentagon. He commanded the Marine Corps' 4th Civil Affairs Group in Iraq during operations Iraqi Freedom and Al Fajr. He is Professor of Joint Military Operations at the U.S. Naval War College.